ROBIN HOOD: MEDIEVAL AND POST-MEDIEVAL

Robin Hood
Medieval and Post-Medieval

Helen Phillips

EDITOR

FOUR COURTS PRESS

Published by
FOUR COURTS PRESS LTD
7 Malpas Street, Dublin 8, Ireland
e-mail: info@four-courts-press.ie
http://www.four-courts-press.ie
and in North America by
FOUR COURTS PRESS
c/o ISBS, 920 N.E. 58th Avenue, Suite 300, Portland, OR 97213.

ISBN 1–85182–931–8

Printed in England
by MPG Books, Bodmin, Cornwall

Contents

LIST OF ABBREVIATIONS   7

Introduction   9
Helen Phillips

Everybody's Robin Hood   21
Douglas Gray

Little John and the ballad of *Robin Hood and the Monk*   42
Derek Pearsall

The hermit and the outlaw: new evidence for Robin Hood's death?   51
Richard Firth Green

The literary Robin Hood: character and function in Fitts 1, 2 and 4
    of the *Gest of Robyn Hode*   60
Roy Pearcy

Merchant adventure in *Robin Hood and the Potter*   69
Thomas H. Ohlgren

'Oublïe ai chevalerie': Tristan, Malory, and the outlaw-knight   79
Timothy S. Jones

A grave tale   91
David Hepworth

Framing Robin Hood: temporality and textuality in
    Anthony Munday's Huntington plays   113
Liz Oakley-Brown

'Meere English flocks': Ben Jonson's *The Sad Shepherd* and the
    Robin Hood tradition   129
Stephen Knight

The noble peasant   145
Linda Troost

Robin Hood, the prioress of Kirklees and Charlotte Brontë   154
Helen Phillips

Contents

Robin Hood and the fairies: Alfred Noyes' *Sherwood* 167
Lois Potter

Robin Hood in the landscape: place-name evidence and mythology 181
Michael R. Evans

Appendix: written epitaphs of Robin Hood 188
David Hepworth

INDEX 191

Abbreviations

BL		London, British Library
Child		Francis James Child (ed.), *English and Scottish popular ballads*, 10 vols (Boston, 1869–92)
EETS	ES	Early English Text Society, Extra Series
	OS	Original Series
	SS	Supplementary Series
EPNS		English Place-Name Society
JEGP		*Journal of English and Germanic Philology*
Hahn		Thomas Hahn (ed.), *Robin Hood in popular culture: violence, transgression, and justice* (Cambridge, 2000)
Holt		J.C. Holt, *Robin Hood* 2nd. ed. (London, 1990)
Keen		Maurice Keen, *The outlaws of medieval legend*, rev. ed. (London and New York, 1977)
Knight, *A complete study*		*Robin Hood: a complete study of the English outlaw* (Oxford, 1994)
Wiles		David Wiles, *The early plays of Robin Hood* (Cambridge, 1981)
ME		Middle English
MED		*Middle English dictionary*, ed. H. Kurath, S.M. Kuhn, John Reidy et al. (Ann Arbor, 1952–2002)
RHASC		Stephen Knight (ed.), *Robin Hood: an anthology of scholarship and criticism* (Cambridge, 1999)
RHFM		*Robin Hood: the Forresters manuscript, British Library Additional MS 71158*, ed. Stephen Knight, with Hilton Keliher (Cambridge, 1998)
RHOOT		*Robin Hood and other outlaw tales*, ed. Stephen Knight and Thomas H. Ohlgren, TEAMS Middle English Texts Series (Kalamazoo, 1997)

RRH   *Rymes of Robyn Hood: an introduction to the*
                             British outlaw, ed. R.B. Dobson and J. Taylor
                             (Stroud, 1976)

Ritson   *Robin Hood, a collection of all the ancient poems,*
                             songs and ballads now extant relative to the cele-
                             brated English outlaw (to which are prefixed his-
                             torical anecdotes of his life), ed. Joseph Ritson, 2
                             vols (London, 1795).

Introduction: studying Robin Hood

HELEN PHILLIPS

An upsurge of scholarly interest in Robin Hood studies during the past decade has produced TV documentaries, several new editions, translations and academic studies, and Robin Hood has become a subject increasingly often studied in university courses. A series of biennial international conferences, starting in 1997, and the formation in 2000 of the International Association for Robin Hood Studies are further signs of growing intellectual investigation into the outlaw. Reasons for this are easy to find and they are very contemporary ones. The Robin Hood tradition matches well with characteristic aspects of academic inquiry today: Robin Hood studies are interdisciplinary; they are concerned with popular culture; they illuminate the history of national identity; they include the study of medievalism – the reception and reformulation of the medieval past by later periods. The tradition relates to other topics that are currently prominent across a range of academic fields: law and violence, class and politics, attitudes towards wilderness, gender and masculine identities, 'heritage', the relationship between high and low culture, and also the history of film and TV, performance and of oral or non-literary texts.

The tradition comprises a massive, diverse body of material, much of which remains under-researched, and it presents some puzzles to which answers are still lacking or matters of dispute. Advances continue to made in the field of texts. A recent major discovery was the Forresters Manuscript, a seventeenth-century collection discovered in 1993 and published in 1999, whose importance Gray stresses in his essay. Thomas Ohlgren's paper in the present volume includes research into the manuscript containing *Robin Hood and the Potter*, which he believes may be linked to the fifteenth-century Paston family, in whose household Robin Hood plays are known to have been performed.

Robin Hood had already become a national treasure and a subject for antiquarian study by the late sixteenth century, even while he was, as always, inspiring popular entertainment and being reinvented in boisterous or decorous new forms. Folkloric associations, though these have often been seen by post-Renaissance readers and scholars seen as evidence for primeval origins behind the medieval outlaw, may in fact stem in large part from a strong Early Modern antiquarian interest in English folklore (interest in figures like Robin Goodfellow, hobgoblins and fairies, as well as Robin Hood). This scholarly Renaissance interest in English folklore was related to post-Reformation England's reformulation of Robin Hood to take his place as part of a safe type of medieval heritage, one suitable for a newly Protestant nation

when Catholic festivals and the cults of local saints and shrines had been
banned. Some learned sixteenth-century authors, including Leland and Stow,
celebrated the English outlaw and the traditions associated with him; in contrast, others, including Latimer and the puritan Philip Stubbs, condemned
them. Enthusiasm for Robin Hood did not divide neatly or simply along sectarian lines. Approval for the old entertainments associated with Robin Hood
was expressed by both Catholics and Protestants – though for different aspects
of the tradition – while other adherents of both faiths disapproved, again for
different reasons. The time is ripe to re-examine folkloric aspects of Robin
Hood, a topic which has been avoided by serious studies in recent times,
undoubtedly because of excessive and unproven claims by earlier folklore
enthusiasts. Two themes that recur in the present volume of essays are those
of the many cultural roles played by folklore in the history of Robin Hood
and the manipulation of the tradition to suit a multiplicity of political and
ideological purposes. The latter is not just a feature observed in the past.
Douglas Gray points to the contemporary use of Robin Hood as a political
slogan, and journalists in the UK and Canada have recently hailed a 'Robin
Hood' budget and a 'Robin Hood' election manifesto. The debate about
whether Robin Hood was gay excited a lot of comment in the world-wide
media in 1999 and in the last twenty years, in particular, the tradition has
generated many interpretations informed by feminism.

The researches of antiquarians and local historians have sometimes themselves engendered popular celebrations and relics, and encouraged a sense of
local ownership of the hero: scholarship can create tradition. An example that
became newsworthy in January 2004 involves the long-established rivalry of
Nottinghamshire and Yorkshire, which is as fierce over claiming Robin Hood
as in matters of football. The *Sunday Times* front page carried a demand by a
Yorkshire MP that Nottinghamshire must take down its tourist-encouraging
'Robin Hood Country' road signs, having no right to him because, as the MP
had known since boyhood, Robin Hood came from Wakefield. This apparently
'traditional'—imbibed in childhood—belief derives from the researches of
Joseph Hunter, published in the early 1850s, and those of the Yorkshire local
historian J.D. Walker a century later, into the medieval Hood family of
Wakefield, and a particular Robert Hood who appears in royal household
records as a servant in the 1320s and may have come from Wakefield. David
Hepworth's paper in this volume includes a discussion of Hunter and Walker's
work and their influence, and provides other examples of the invention of tradition and the inter-relationships of scholarly research with local beliefs and
celebration. For a cultural historian, the part played by local identity and rivalry
(as well as the heritage industry and tourism – which, as both David Hepworth
and Michael Evans illustrate, goes back at least to Early Modern times) and
the economic and other backgrounds to these, is as central to the study of
Robin Hood as the history of morris dances or the long-bow.

The history of the Robin Hood studies is itself illuminating as cultural history. For example, the century of questing by historians, from the mid nineteenth to the mid twentieth century, for a 'real Robin Hood' testifies to a prevailing culture of individualism and of positivist and empirical thinking, as well as to the confidence and stimulus given to the pursuit of exact historical fact by the nineteenth-century establishment of institutions such as the Public Record Office (where Hunter was an archivist), local history societies, record offices and journals. At an earlier period, the attempts in the fifteenth and sixteenth centuries by Scottish and English chroniclers to contrive a specific historical dating and location for a previously dateless Robin Hood, who was celebrated in plays all over much of England and Scotland, reflected a new interest in constructing national history. This led to Anthony Munday's revolutionary recasting in 1598 of the merry thief as a major figure on the national stage of English royal history: as an aristocrat involved in affairs of state in a history play, *The Downfall of Robert Earl of Huntington*. Liz Oakley-Brown in this volume analyses the implications of Munday's use of that particular genre in the context of the Elizabethan concept of history.

Similarly, speculations by nineteenth-century scholars, beginning with Joseph Wright, that Robin might have originated as a Germanic god or wood-spirit were central ingredients in a set of assumptions about pre-Christian European myth and religion that would produce, a century and a half after Wright, to the influential 1980s TV series 'Robin of Sherwood' with its New Age, pagan and ecological mythology. Despite widespread popular interest in and acceptance of that kind of mythic and folkloric approach, both have gone out of academic fashion: modern anthropology and social history have produced caution and scepticism about many older assumptions about pagan religion and myth in early Britain. Michael Evans here assesses evidence for supernatural origins for Robin Hood, particularly in relation to place-names and other monuments in the landscape. He observes that, despite post-medieval enthusiasms for naming large landscape features after Robin and John, as if they were giants, the medieval Robin Hood material always presents his exploits as merely human. One might add that this contrasts with the medieval narratives about several other outlaws, includes ones based on historical figures such as Hereward and Fouke Fityz Waryn, who are occasionally depicted as defeating fantastic enemies like a giant or magical animal.

Before the current burgeoning of outlaw studies, there was an earlier period of intense interest in Robin Hood material, in the 1950s and early 1960s, most famously in the debates in *Past & Present*. Thomas Hahn has recently argued that those debates were the beginning of modern cultural studies.[1] In that post-war period discussion about the subject was mostly

---

[1] 'History, politics, populism: Robin Hood and the rise of cultural studies', lecture, 10 December 2003, Cardiff University.

between historians and concentrated on the dating, possible historical origins and political import of the early ballads. The most important names here are those of Rodney Hilton, James Holt and Maurice Keen.[2] The orthodoxies of literary criticism holding sway in universities at the time, New Criticism or Leavisism, were not well adapted either to appreciation of the ballad as a literary genre or to analysis of the non-literary and popular dimensions of this material. The pioneering critical studies of Bessinger, 1974, and Gray, 1984, stood somewhat in isolation.[3] A tradition that had often flourished in village games rather than urban theatres, or in Victorian boys' books, pantomimes (and as likely as not to be freely morphed there with Red Riding Hood or the Babes in the Wood), or films and comic books did not, however strong its hold on imaginations nationally and internationally, seem an entirely fit subject for scholarship as then conceived either in the Arts or History – except in as far as historians could uncover from archives the names of real medieval individuals with names like 'Robin Hood', and provide hypotheses, which themselves proved subject to debate, about how these individuals and their political contexts might have bearing on the Robin Hood ballads. There were some impressive discoveries in the course of these investigations and the discussion they generated greatly advanced the subject.[4] Yet the tradition remained on the margin of mainstream history and virtually out of sight, off the margins, of literary study – rather like the merry men themselves.

A distinguishing mark of the present renaissance of Robin Hood studies is a fruitful partnership between historians and critics, symptomatic of a revolution in the relationship of the two disciplines. The quest for a historical Robin Hood may have lapsed, at least temporarily, but there is clearly still a important object for historical study and that is the mass of material itself and its ever-changing cultural use and re-use. The individual study which, more than any other, prefigured this new approach was Douglas Gray's 1984 article 'The Robin Hood Poems'. In the present volume Gray surveys the field as it has developed since then, charts new discoveries and some quite major shifts in interpretation, discusses the evolving debates and offers both new material (especially from Scottish sources) and some judgements on the major questions, as they appear today.

2 Rodney Hilton, 'The origins of Robin Hood', *Past & Present* 14 (1958), 30–44; repr. RHASC; J.C. Holt, 'The origins and audience of the Ballads of Robin Hood', *Past & Present* 18 (1960), 89–110; repr. RHASC; Maurice Keen, 'Robin Hood – peasant or gentleman?' *Past & Present* 19 (1961), 7–15.   3 Jess B. Bessinger, Jr, 'The *Gest of Robin Hood* revisited', in *The learned and the lewed*, ed. L.D. Benson (Cambridge, Mass., 1974), pp 355–69; Douglas Gray, 'The Robin Hood poems', *Poetica* 18 (1984), 1–18; both repr. in *RHASC*.   4 See especially Holt; David Crook, 'Some further evidence concerning the dating of the origins of the legend of Robin Hood', *English Historical Review* 99 (1984), 530–4; repr. *RHASC;* John Bellamy, *Robin Hood: an historical enquiry* (Bloomington, 1985).

Perspectives on outlaws were influenced, from its first publication in 1969, by Hobsbawm's theory of the world-wide myth of the 'social bandit' and by growing interest in the study of the literature, history, and sociology of crime, law and suppression, which encompasses areas ranging from Australian or South American bandits to the history of crime fiction or the Newgate Calendar.[5] Recent years have also seen several studies of the outlaw theme in general in literature and of medieval British outlaws apart from Robin Hood, including Hereward and Fouke Fitz Warin, and Timothy Jones' examination in this volume of the 'outlaw' elements in the Tristan romances is part of this expanding vista.

By the late 1990s not only had the scope of Robin Hood research greatly widened, but a degree of consensus or at least agreement about its parameters – agreement about what sort of interdisciplinary study this was – had crystallized. This built especially on the work of the historians R.B. Dobson and J. Taylor, on the criticism and cultural analysis of Stephen Knight, on John Marshall's studies of Robin Hood drama, and the work of Kevin Harty and Jeffrey Richards on the cultural history of films.[6]

There is, however, an air of revisionism about the present collection of essays ('Had I read too much Christopher Hill in my youth? Was I stuck in my Hobsbawmian view of Robin Hood as a 'social bandit?' asks Douglas Gray at the start of his essay here). That revisionist move is articulated most explicitly by Derek Pearsall, challenging, among other things, the codifying and unifying effect of the whole concept of 'Robin Hood studies' and the widely-accepted assumptions about the 'good outlaw' as their subject-matter. The medieval ballad that Pearsall takes as his subject, *Robin Hood and the Monk,* shows, he contends, England's favourite outlaw acting like a brutal saga hero or as 'Dirty Harry not Philip Marlowe'. In his view the subsequent shaping of the tradition has metamorphosed the serious impulses towards social rebellion, which are for him still discernable in *Robin Hood and the Monk* (which he interprets, recalling Hilton's 1958 *Past and Present* argument, as a relic of the 1381 Rising), into a increasing conformity with the establishment. For Pearsall it is Robin Hood who carries this ignominious conformity, as his tradition evolves, while the Little John of the *Monk* is the proponent of an earlier and unassimilated, or pre-assimilation, state of the legend. Both Gray and Pearsall open up the striking multivalency of the powerful image of community offered by the greenwood, citing an array of

5 Eric Hobsbawm, *Bandits* (London, 1969, 2nd ed. 1985).   6 See the excellent collection edited by Thomas Hahn, *Robin Hood in popular culture: violence, transgression and justice* (Cambridge, 2000). We could add among more general studies of outlaws, Keen; Barbara Hanawalt, 'Ballads and bandits: fourteenth-century outlaws and the Robin Hood Poems', in Hanawalt (ed.), *Chaucer's England: literature in historical context* (Minneapolis, 1992), pp 154–75; Graham Seal, *The outlaw legend: a cultural tradition in Britain, America and Australia* (Cambridge, 1996).

extremely varied ideological parallels that include Malory's chivalric fellowship, through the apocalyptic 1381 *magna societas,* or Victor Turner's concept of 'communitas', involving a ritual levelling of ranks, to Colin
Richmond's hypothesis of 'a potentially anarchist streak' which typified fifteenth-century disillusion with collapsing feudalism and early capitalism.

The tension which Pearsall sees established already in the earliest extant
texts, between, on the one hand, a voice of serious medieval radicalism, a re-
thinking of bonds of 'fellowship', and an unsentimental approach to banditry,
and, on the other, a slide towards endowing the 'social outlaw' with a more
conventional morality and an aristocratic persona to match his righteous
worldview, was eventually to produce the extraordinary plays of Anthony
Munday. These plays elevated the hero's social status, as Earl of Huntington
(a feature which became entrenched in the story in centuries to come, losing
its normative power only with the appearance of some radically-inclined peasant Robins in the twentieth century), and also elevated the literary genres
through which his story is told. The outlaw becomes here a protagonist of a
Renaissance history play and a tragedy, moving amid conspiracies and high
matters of state, and ensnared by the sexual and political intrigues of princely
adversaries. In contrast, the far less dignified, though more physically aggressive, Robin of the short medieval ballads had been brought into peril by an
often almost-comic Sheriff of Nottingham or by his own propensity to rash-
ness, cockiness or quarrelling over betting debts. At the same time, as Oakley-
Brown shows, Munday creates a hero of unstable dual identity: the Robin
Hood of contemporary May games and a tragic twelfth-century lord involved
in political plots and saving the government. In a temporal *mise-en-abîme,* the
Downfall is located in three periods: the 1590s, the late fifteenth-century of
the poet Skelton and a freely imagined twelfth century, with the actors going
in and out of their fictional historical characters. Munday's cultivation of
instabilities like these parallels, she suggests, the unstable opposition between
fiction and history, as well as 'the textual politics of history itself', a topical
issue during a century that saw a determined production of printed and
widely influential national chronicles. Perhaps the dual persona of the hero
(and many other of the main characters) and the intricate play-within-a-play
structures of this text, as well as the high-level political intrigues, reflect
Munday's own role as a double agent in the conflicts between the Protestant
English government and its Catholic conspirators.

Past studies of early outlaw legends tended to identify the tradition primarily with the ballad and to identify the ballad itself as an isolated form, a
genre belonging to a literary and social 'folk' world. The ballad, until the
advent of the film, has certainly been the main and most characteristic genre
associated with the myth of the social outlaw (bandit ballads, composed soon
after an exploit, are still a popular genre in modern Brazil), but several essays
in this volume extend investigation into other genres whose links with the

tradition have hitherto been little studied. These other genres include the exemplum in the essays by Roy Pearcy and Richard Firth Green, and the Arthurian romance in Jones' essay, as well as the high Renaissance forms of the pastoral, tragedy and history play examined by Knight and Oakley-Brown, while Gray shows the existence of 'Robene Hude' as a shepherds' dance in mid sixteenth-century Scotland.

Two early ballads, *Robin Hood and the Monk* and *Robin Hood and the Potter*, are subject to critical reappraisal by Pearsall and Ohlgren. It is *A Gest of Robyn Hode* which, more than any other single text, comes under frequent scrutiny in this volume, as does the story of Robin's death at Kirklees, of which the *Gest* is the earliest extant witness, a topic which has hitherto been strangely neglected. The picture of the *Gest* emerging from recent criticism conveys a new recognition of it as an ambitious literary text of the era of Malory, Caxton, and Skelton as well as a major influence on authors handling Robin Hood material in the Early Modern period, a status undoubtedly owed partly to its substantial early sixteenth-century appearance in print.

As Hepworth's researches show, the relationship it has with a mysterious non-literary text, the alleged inscribed gravestone and the associated epitaphs at Kirklees, is both complex and important. Hepworth provides here the first comprehensive history of the Robin Hood grave, and an assessment of the traditions and scholarly speculations associated with it over the centuries. The issues are intriguing. Did the tale of Robin's murder, as found in the *Gest*, precede the presence of a gravestone with 'Robard Hude' on it, on a hillside above Kirklees Priory, or did the names and the stone follow from the story? Did the motif of Robin shooting an arrow, found in the ballad *Robin Hood's Death*, arise because of the present location of the grave a short distance from the Priory? Or was it moved here? A seventeenth-century sketch depicts the gravestone with its inscriptions but did the words really exist? Even if they did, were they a fake? And does any trace of this stone still exist? Hepworth observes that the stone's design suggests an early – thirteenth-century – date. While confirming that the earlier theories of Hunter and Walker about a Wakefield Robin Hood should be regarded sceptically, Hepworth raises a new possibility that there actually were connections between Kirklees and the Hood family's properties in Wakefield.

'Gest' in Middle English usually denotes a narrative with literary dignity and substance, a romance with claims to historical truth. The *Gest of Robyn Hode*, composed perhaps around 1450 and with its first, printed, extant texts dating from early in the sixteenth century, is considerably longer than the other extant medieval ballads (*Robin Hood and the Monk, Robin Hood and the Potter, Robin and Gandelyn*, and, probably also medieval in origin, *Robin Hood and Guy of Gisburne*, as well as some other ballads only recorded later, including *The Death of Robin Hood* and *Robin Hood and the Curtal Friar*). When we try to assess where the *Gest* stands critically and politically, it proves a multi-faceted, even ambivalent text. Critics have often judged its social and political affinities in monologic terms. The lengthy narrative, with its elaborate design in *fitts*, more like a romance or even a short epic than a ballad, its interlace plot, and its tragic knight and an outlaw-hero with moral and religious dignity, who observes Arthurian etiquette and commands a longbow troop of seven score retainers who kneel respectfully before him, has elicited a gamut of readings, some of them completely incompatible: a text for the gentry household for Holt; 'anti-authoritarian' for Gray; 'courtly' in its structures for Aers; and 'mercantile' for Ohlgren.[7] Coss, 1985, however, suggested it was paradoxically romance-like in form yet 'subversive' in attitude and Douglas Gray's essay for this volume discusses the ballad form and its overlap with other genres as well as the history of attempts to define the genre of the *Gest*. Far from producing a monologic text, its author emerges from current criticism as master of the convergence of discourses and genres, producing a smoothly sophisticated yet dialectic masterpiece. Roy Pearcy argues that the *Gest*'s 'debt' plot reflects in pure form neither the feudal social model of its *exemplum* analogue nor the bourgeois commercialism of the fabliau but incorporates the social model of both genres. He suggests that the *Gest* has mixed political affiliations and these arose from a disillusion among the yeoman class with 'the corrupt officialdom of a burgeoning profit-based economy', a commercialization which led both to a readiness to see true 'curtesye' in outlaw society and to texts where yeoman–outlaws paradoxically seem to uphold the conservative values of those who would normally be their masters

The *Gest* today begins indeed to look more like the start of the *post*medieval Robin Hood and less the candidate for the earliest and most classic of medieval Robin Hood ballads, as it sometimes seemed in the past. Knight shows the *Gest* was an important source for Ben Jonson's pastoral drama, *The Sad Shepherd*, composed around 1630. One might see Jonson himself in this as opening up a range of new possibilities for Robin Hood drama which led directly to the eighteenth-century operas which Linda Troost discusses (indeed, a play based on the *Sad Shepherd* was produced in 1783). A certain temporal complexity, a mixture of nostalgia with innovation, is now discernable in the *Gest*, and replaces a single reading, whether such a reading emphasizes its courtly or subversive aspects. It prefigures features regarded as typical of the post-medieval development of Robin Hood: Robin as a national icon; a dignified figure in English national destiny; the

---

7 See Holt, pp 109–46; Peter Coss, 'Aspects of cultural diffusion in medieval England: the early romances, local society and Robin Hood', *Past & Present* 108 (1985), 35–79, pp 68–75; repr. *RHASC*; Gray, 'Robin Hood poems'; David Aers, '*Vox Populi* and the literature of 1381', in David Wallace (ed.), *The Cambridge history of medieval English literature* (Cambridge, 1999), 432–53, p. 451; Thomas H. Ohlgren, 'The "Marchaunt" of Sherwood: mercantile ideology in *A Gest of Robyn Hode*', in Hahn, pp 175–90.

valued friend of royalty; a noble defender of the weak and defenceless, and the proto-Protestant scourge of corrupt Catholic ecclesiastics. In design, especially in its poignant and (again) potentially anti-Catholic account of the death, the *Gest* also prefigures the Early Modern taste for 'Lives' of the outlaw, a phenomenon that Hepworth discusses. Ending with 'he was a good outlawe, / And dyde pore men moch god', it contains our earliest extant hint of 'robbing the rich to help the poor', the encomium that was to surface in some versions of the epitaphs that made their appearance, starting *c.*1631, first on paper and eventually in stone at the Kirklees grave.

Richard Firth Green explores the *Gest* in conjunction with two hitherto neglected medieval texts: a Derbyshire chronicle and a poem with an exemplum-inspired plot. Taken together, these shed new light on the story of Robin Hood's death, and also on the *Gest*'s picture of his pious later years and his foundation of a chapel. Green first examines several versions of an exemplum about a penitent, one of which, the skilfully-written poem *The Hermit and the Outlaw*, depicts its protagonist specifically as an outlaw and robber who dies from bleeding. Green's other text, a story in the *Chronicle of Dale Abbey*, concerns an outlaw who, having received a message from God in a dream, bids farewell to his companions in crime and devotes the rest of his days contritely to amendment of life. The place of his dream indicates the future site for Dale Abbey, near Ilkeston and within the old Sherwood Forest. Green suggests these texts are evidence, mysterious but striking, for several motifs first found in the *Gest* and the ballad *Robin Hood's Death*. Since the chronicle is thirteenth century (while the poem is dated by scholars to before the mid fifteenth century) this research suggests that the unexpectedly pious and tragic Robin Hood motifs that appear at the end of the *Gest* could have been current, in some form, considerably before the *Gest*'s composition (usually dated now to around 1450) and before Langland's allusion to Robin Hood 'rymes' in the 1370s. Alternatively, linking an outlaw to the theme of penitence in both stories may be the result of clerics cashing in for didactic purposes on the general popularity of outlaws – not specifically Robin Hood – as heroes. If the stories are evidence that the foundation of a religious place was already associated with Robin, then the Dale Abbey chronicle is notable for making that a Sherwood foundation, whereas the *Gest* makes it the chapel of Mary Magdalene near Barnsdale in Yorkshire. We are back with the rival Sherwood – Yorkshire claims again. But at a medieval date, at a time when Robin Hood plays were still being performed in many parts of England and Scotland from Devon to Aberdeen, and yet there were developments like these two texts that were beginning to claim him as an illustrious figure associated with monuments in particular places.

Douglas Gray stresses the variety of medieval outlaws to be found across the range of medieval literature – from Cain to Mak the Sheepstealer and even Henryson's Country Mouse – and urges that modern scholarship needs to reject both too unitary an approach to the question of likely audiences for early texts and too doctrinaire a readiness to assimilate the May games and Robin Hood plays to concepts of misrule and Bakhtinian carnival (another aspect of 'revisionism' against a recent consensus). Thomas Ohlgren argues that *Robin Hood and the Potter* introduces verbal elements from the discourse of the courtly love tradition into the outlaw ballad and uses such a tone to create a satirical equation analogous to that in Chaucer's *Reeve's Tale*, in which sex is the payment for a wrong. Examining the manuscript and the *Potter*'s language, Ohlgren argues that it reworks the common tale of an outlaw's adventures while disguised as a potter to fit a more commercial, fifteenth-century context: adventure, he argues, has become 'merchant adventure'. The poem's language is that of the marketplace and business speculation: a form of risk-taking and gamble which replaces the risk-taking of conventional knightly romance and also Robin's simple habit of making bets.

This collection of essays considers relationships between medieval and post-medieval tradition and also what happens when a low-culture and popular, communal, entertainment like the medieval and Tudor figure of Robin Hood, of the may games, ballads and pageants, is transferred into the forms and modes of high culture, an experiment that we find intermittently throughout the post-medieval centuries of the Robin Hood tradition, which is always interesting and never achieved smoothly.

The bandit does not always go quietly into the mansions of high art. This becomes clear in Stephen Knight's account of Ben Jonson's extraordinary marriage of classical pastoral and native outlaw tradition in *The Sad Shepherd*, despite the many strengths of that achievement. That this play works in performance has been demonstrated more than once recently, including a production by John Marshall and an animated play-reading at the 2003 conference of the International Association for Robin Hood Studies. Yet Knight argues here that the encounter between native popular tradition and classical pastoral brought about the ultimate destruction of Jonson's enterprise, and further that a blindness to the power of the presence of non-classical native elements has led Jonson's scholarly editors into a state of denial about the contribution of English and popular inspirations for the play.

Linda Troost studies a hitherto disregarded outlaw opera by the eighteenth-century radical Thomas Holcroft, *The Noble Peasant*, 1784, showing how medieval English yeoman-outlaws (Adam Bell and his comrades from a ballad known in the medieval period) could be used to figure political discontents of the day within a climate of vigilant censorship of the theatre. This is an adaptation of the popular ballad to the urban entertainment of light opera for the metropolitan theatre and it was a box-office success. Helen Phillips also considers aspects of Robin Hood in the age of revolutions and their influence on Charlotte Brontë's political novel *Shirley*, together with newly-discovered sources for the novel. Lois Potter examines the personally intense vision of the pre-Reformation outlaw as a vehicle for humanitarian and Christian ideals in the era of World War One by the Georgian poet and playwright Alfred Noyes.

Noyes draws on the association that had developed since the late sixteenth century between fairies and Robin Hood. Fairies came to be of considerable interest to artists and writers in the late nineteenth and early twentieth century and Noyes, like Charlotte Brontë, used fairy tradition to explore serious ideas and especially the survival of human values in an era of harsh change. Other discussions of folkloric issues include Gray's demonstration of how far back in the tradition the taste goes for introducing Robin Hood among folkloric and fantastical figures and Knight points out that it was Ben Jonson who introduced the witch into the Robin Hood legend, a typical preoccupation of early seventeenth-century society rather than the medieval period, and an innovation that was to gain a permanent place in the tradition thereafter. In Brontë's *Shirley* the legend of the outlaw is interwoven with belief in rural fairies as an image of pre-industrial northern English landscape and society, but also linked to a more idiosyncratic form of mythology – that of Brontë's own brand of feminist myth-making.

Outlaw traditions have, it seems, finally demonstrated their place as a central part of medieval literary culture, not a marginal adjunct to it, of interest only to specialist enthusiasts. Early Robin Hood material cannot simply be subsumed under a unitary social definition – as texts about peasants, written by and for 'folk' and articulating a simple protest from the oppressed. No tradition that could catch, during the sixteenth-century, the royal imagination of Henry VIII, the national mythologizing labours of Tudor chroniclers or attract respectable funding from Scottish burghers and municipal authorities, could owe its attraction simply to that (though all these also suggest a neutralizing of a potential for subversiveness). Nor can the post-medieval British outlaw tradition – whether found in an opera, film or novel, in pastoral drama or adventure comic – be regarded as peripheral to the history of British culture. Robin Hood, as the essays collected here indicate, manifests, in Kevin Carpenter's phrase, 'many faces' in different political and historical contexts.[8] He frequently and, it seems, most characteristically, becomes the site of deeply contradictory forces: conformity versus subversion, deference and rebellion, and fellowship versus knightly, heroic individualism (as evidenced, as Pearsall shows, in his dangerously daring egotism in the *Monk*) and, as Gray demonstrates, expresses ideologies of both Right and Left. Perhaps the radical potential of this outlaw tradition is to be found as much and as deeply in its dialectic forces and counter-forces as in the enactment of the explicit rebellions, lawless acts or subversiveness that are its explicit subject matter.

8 Kevin Carpenter, *Die Vielen Gesichter des Edlen Räubers Robin Hood/ The many faces of the celebrated English Outlaw*, exhibition catalogue (Oldenburg, 1995).

Thanks are due for help with this volume to Irralie Doel, Stephen Knight and John Scattergood. I am also very grateful to the contributors and to Martin Fanning of Four Courts Press for their expertise and patience. The University of Liverpool Davenport Fund generously awarded a grant toward publication.

This book is dedicated to the memory of Julian Wasserman, a fine scholar and critic, and a much loved friend of many of the contributors to this collection.

Everybody's Robin Hood

DOUGLAS GRAY

The title of this paper suddenly flashed on me when I was looking at a BBC documentary which revealed that the right-wing Austrian politician Jörg Haider in the 1990s saw himself as a kind of Robin Hood – and used images of the outlaw hero in his political campaigns. My immediate reaction was one of startled and amused incredulity. But then I began to question this reaction. Had I read too much Christopher Hill in my youth? Was I stuck in my Hobsbawmian view of Robin Hood as a 'social bandit'? Was I guilty of concentrating on *one* possible significance of the legend (or legends) to the exclusion of other possibilities? After all, perhaps Haider saw himself, or chose to present himself as the defiant 'little' man standing up to the power of the Austrian political establishment, just as he seemed to see little Austria standing up to the tyrannical European bureaucrats of Brussels. As the medieval poets would say, I was in a 'study'. What followed was not a dream which might have brought illumination, but an invitation to address the third Robin Hood conference in London, Ontario.

To re-enter the greenwood after twenty years is a somewhat daunting task. Obviously one should not march determinedly over the same old track, yet must avoid getting lost in new mazes. My first impression is that though it is still full of mysteries the forest is now much better signposted than it once was, and in some areas we can now see much more clearly. But not in all – and for a variety of reasons. One old problem for instance that deserves to be mentioned at the beginning is that our surviving corpus of early ballads or poems (which is what I shall be concentrating on) is certainly far from complete. Furthermore, those that do survive are often written in a simple formulaic style which denies modern readers all kinds of information which they would wish to have. The poems generally eschew any elaborate formal descriptions – of people, for instance – so that we are not explicitly told what our heroes and villains actually looked like. Later illustrators and film makers have attempted to fill in this blank space. And later outlaws, it would seem at first sight, were better served, though even here there are uncertainties and ambiguities. We have a photograph of Billy the Kid, which is often said to show that he was left-handed. (We are never told whether Robin Hood was right-handed or not, though most modern readers seem to assume that he was.) Nevertheless that photograph of Billy is not exactly definitive. It seems to have been a tintype or ferrotype which produced a print that was 'laterally reversed' (as in a reflection in a mirror). So it may be, I'm told, that Billy was right-handed after all.[1] Even if we think we know something, things sometimes turn out to be more uncertain. This kind of 'double image' is, as we shall see, curiously appropriate for Robin Hood himself, but here I make it an excuse for putting up a small signpost of my own at the edge of the forest, with a simple moral text: 'We sometimes have to say quite firmly, "We do not know".' Notoriously the paucity and the nature of the early Robin Hood material has not prevented a great deal of speculation, which has been countered by a great deal of skepticism. This, in my view, has produced a rather healthy and effective dialectic.

My title has an obvious ambiguity: Robin Hood 'belongs to' everybody, and everybody sees himself or herself as Robin Hood, 'the hero that lives in you all'. Certainly, when we survey the tradition as a whole it is hard to avoid the conclusion that he can become all things to all men. J.C. Holt lamented this as 'adulteration'; Dobson and Taylor pose the question how in the modern world 'a myth now apparently drained of its radical and indeed emotional content should retain its remarkable appeal at the level of popular entertainment'. 'Can it really be', they ask, '– it seems hardly likely – that Robin Hood is so attractive in the late 1980s because he has ceased to raise any controversial issues at all?'[2] Some might argue that it is less a matter of adulteration or draining than of change, but I would simply note at this point that these remarks draw attention to one of those central paradoxes of this outlaw hero in his various manifestations that he both acts and is acted upon. This is obviously to be found in the stories of many heroes, but in the case of Robin Hood it has a curious intensity. Not only do the early tales show him often as a victim, but the developing tradition shows him to be an extremely adaptable not to say malleable figure. We seem to have managed to mould him into all kinds of forms, yet at the same time he has remained potentially active – elusive, restless, always ready to act.[3] This is there in the early poems with their stress on his deeds or 'gestes' rather than on his reflective qualities (if he had been more of an intellectual he might well have thought that 'im Anfang war die Tat'), and resonates through the later tradition. He does not like to be confined to prison – any kind of prison. He is transformed into a revolutionary social leveler in Joseph Ritson,[4] but he cannot be confined to that role. Nor is he simply the romantic, idealized figure used by the modern English heritage industry, still offering sometimes a model for the young male:

> The Robin Hood story, as everyone knows it, tells of one who is idealized by every English boy – gentle in his dealings with the poor

1 See Robert M. Utley, *Billy the Kid: a short and violent life* (Lincoln, Nebraska, 1989), fig. 1 and note. One of the westerns devoted to him is called *The lefthanded gun*.   2 Holt, pp 159–86; *RRH*, p. xv.   3 A point well made in Knight, *A complete study*, p. 261.   4 Ritson, pp x–xii.

and oppressed, he was ruthless with the rich, the upstart, the cruel, and with traitors to his beloved King Richard the Lionheart; loyal even when his King was abroad at the Crusade, or captive in the dungeons of an enemy abroad; never harming womenfolk under any circumstances, and insisting that his followers, too, show them equal consideration; and though despoiling the wealthy, giving their wealth to poor folk who were the victims of the unjust Forest Laws, or of ill-fortune.[5]

Dobson and Taylor use the word 'myth', as does Stephen Knight, and I think they are right to do so. (I was very cautious way back in suggesting that there was a 'mythical quality about him, a curiously deep appeal which goes beyond any single "significance"'[6] – I feel emboldened now.) I know that 'myth' can still be a slippery word. I will use it in the sense of a Story – of especial significance and longevity (and characteristically often illustrating or enacting cosmological, religious and cultural beliefs and patterns). This myth or story is larger than the many individual stories, legends, re-enactments that make it up. I would like to look again at the early literary material to see if there are any hints or premonitions there of the later 'adaptability' of the myth. But first, some reminiscences and recapitulations, and a glance at some of the new signposts.

By the early 1980s the legends of Robin Hood had excited considerable interest among British historians, and some lively controversy.[7] Dobson and Taylor's anthology of poems and plays had appeared in 1976, and proved itself to be an invaluable help to literary work. J.C. Holt's book came out in 1982. An important concern of these studies was the quest for an historical Robin Hood. This quest may now seem sometimes rather narrow and obsessive, but there is certainly no doubt that it provided much illuminating material on actual medieval outlaws and on their historical and social background. Dobson and Taylor's anthology in particular had a wider scope, offering texts of other poems, sometimes non-English ones, and an account of the reception of the Robin Hood legends which was the beginning of an enterprise that has since flourished greatly. In 1981 David Wiles had published his study of the early plays of Robin Hood,[8] but as far as the poems were concerned, literary scholars had shown very little interest. There had been some useful earlier studies of story material and motifs,[9] but it was the enthusiastic and

5 *Guide to the Robin Hood country* (Mansfield, Notts, 1973, 1977), p. 4.   6 Douglas Gray, 'The Robin Hood poems', *Poetica* 18 (1984) 1–39; reprinted in *RHASC*, p. 38.   7 See, for instance, the articles in *Past & Present* by R.H. Hilton (1958), J.C. Holt (1960), M. Keen (1961), and by J.R. Maddicott in *English Historical Review* (1978).   8 David Wiles, *The early plays of Robin Hood* (Cambridge, 1981).   9 For instance, Rudolf Kiessmann, *Untersuchungen über die Motive der Robin-Hood-Balladen* (Halle, 1895); W.H. Clawson, *The Gest of Robin Hood* (Toronto, 1909); Ingrid Benecke, *Der Gute Outlaw* (Tübingen,

distinguished Canadian Jess Bessinger who first discussed in detail the specifically literary qualities of the poems.[10] It is worth emphasizing how some of his ideas seem well ahead of his time. In 1966, for instance, calling the figure of the early Robin Hood as 'a remarkable composite' he remarks 'we are so far from agreement, and indeed of knowledge, about the outlaw's origins that we might better concentrate on the growth of his tradition'. One of several reasons for this neglect of the early poems (hesitatingly called 'ballads') was their sometimes distinctly 'non-literary' nature. Richard Green has lamented the way in which the traditional ballads have fallen out of favor with modern medievalists (a striking and shameful contrast with the beginning of the century, when a number of distinguished scholars were building on the foundations laid by F.J. Child – including the great W.P. Ker, who produced a number of wide-ranging essays and lectures on the European as well as the English and Scottish examples).[11] If the traditional ballad was coming to be ignored there was little hope for a Robin Hood poem, which might look like its odd or ugly sister ('probably not folk-song at all, but minstrelsy of a somewhat debased type').[12]

Since those days our understanding has been deepened by a number of literary studies, notably the excellent book by Stephen Knight (1994), a fine literary and socio-cultural study of the entire tradition, its reception, and its various significances (and which lobs one or two grenades into the lairs of historians – for instance by drawing attention to the existence of another Barnsdale outside Yorkshire, in Rutland, now the site of the Rutland Country Club – which would seem to be a suitable venue for the later Earl of Huntingdon!).[13] Richard Green has brought his knowledge of the law to provide an illuminating commentary on the ballads.[14] Thomas Ohlgren has looked again at the manuscript contexts of the earliest poems.[15] Much new and valuable material is to be found in the collections of essays edited by Thomas Hahn and Lois Potter.[16] The poems were made much more accessible in the collections of the continuing critical discussions of them edited by Knight.[17]

There have also been one or two significant discoveries. One was historical, by David Crook (1984)[18] – and, like other discoveries in the area of

1973).   10 Jess B. Bessinger, 'Robin Hood: folklore and historiography 1377–1500', *Tennessee Studies in Literature* (1966) 61–9, p. 61, and 'The Gest of Robin Hood revisited' in L.D. Benson (ed.), *The learned and the lewd* (Cambridge, Mass., 1974).   11 Richard Firth Green, 'The ballad and the Middle Ages' in Helen Cooper and Sally Mapstone (eds), *The long fifteenth century: essays for Douglas Gray* (Oxford, 1997), pp 163–5.   12 E.K. Chambers, *The medieval stage*, 2 vols (London, 1903), vol. 2, p. 178. 13 Knight, *A complete study*, pp 29ff. See also Helen Phillips, 'Forest, town and road: the significance of place names in some Robin Hood texts', in Hahn, pp 197–214.   14 Richard Firth Green, *A crisis of truth: literature and law in Ricardian England* (Philadelphia, 1998). 15 Thomas H. Ohlgren, 'Richard Call, the Pastons and the MS context,' *Nottingham Medieval Studies* 45 (2001), 210–33.   16 Hahn; Lois Potter (ed.), *Playing Robin Hood: the legend as performance in five centuries* (Newark, NJ, 1998).   17 *RHASC*.   18 David

Robin Hood studies, presented some new questions and problems as well as new information. (I am tempted to erect another signpost in the forest with an adaptation of the old proverb, 'Many men speak of Robin Hood that never bent his bow / The more we find out, the less we seem to know'.) This was a very significant discovery, that in a Berkshire document of 1262 William the son of Robert Le Fevere of Enborne, associated with larcenies and the harboring of thieves, had his name changed to William Robehod. As Crook said, 'whoever altered the name was aware of the Robin Hood legend in some form or other, probably associating specifically with the status of fugitive and criminal'. When this hit the popular news it became entertainingly entangled with 'heritage'. A newspaper report said that Bill Smith of Enborne was not upmarket enough for Berkshire's image, quoting its coordinator of tourism: 'we're unlikely to have much interest in a minor crook. He was an outlaw of dubious background.' His Nottinghamshire equivalent said, 'Robin Hood was not just a robber – he's more a hero to love, a champion of the underdog. People are uplifted and charmed by the legend'. Another Nottinghamshire official remarked, 'our Robin Hood is not from a dubious background and we're happy to be associated with him'.

In academia, the discovery caused considerable shockwaves. Crook thought that it reinforced Holt's argument for a thirteenth-century origin for the legend. Perhaps ... but a skeptic instantly thinks that 1262 does not allow much time for the exploits of Holt's northern Robin Hood *fugitivus* of 1228/1230 to have become so famous down in Berkshire. Crook rightly pointed out that the alteration was probably made by a royal clerk or the personal clerk of one of the eyre justices, who could have come from anywhere in England, or beyond. A northern clerk, perhaps? I wonder, even so. And I wonder about what was in the legend that is supposed to have been known. But that we certainly do not know. R.B. Dobson distinguished two possibilities: that as early as the second half of the thirteenth century Robin Hood had become a name with which to conjure, either because a flourishing outlaw tradition was already in being, or because his sobriquet 'Robin Hood' had emerged as a popular nickname or alias for an especially notorious thief. 'Could it be', he continued, 'that the time has finally come [...] when it is no longer profitable to search for a fourteenth-century Englishman whose name was Robert or Robin Hood at all?'[19] If the outlaw legend was flourishing by 1262 then the fourteenth-century Robin Hoods that have been sug-

Crook, 'Some further evidence concerning the dating of the origins of the legend of Robin Hood', *English Historical Review* 99 (1984), 530–4 (reprinted in *RHASC*). See also David Crook, 'The sheriff of Nottingham and Robin Hood: the genesis of the legend' in P.R. Coss and S.D. Lloyd (eds), *Thirteenth Century England*, vol. 2 (Woodbridge, 1988), pp 59–68; R.B. Dobson, 'Robin Hood: the genesis of a popular hero', in Hahn, pp 61–78; Henry Summerson, 'The criminal underworld of Medieval England', *Journal of Legal History* 17:3 (1996), 197–224. **19** *RRH*, p. xxii.

gested as originals have bitten the dust. For one who has always had doubts about the search for a real Robin Hood it was refreshing to find another historian, Colin Richmond, saying that Crook's discovery has made redundant much if not all of the discussion of a possible historical original: 'it has been a liberating discovery: the Robin Hood ballads have been released from their historical context (or cage). They are fictions purely [...] [and] do not owe anything to history in the direct way historians have yearned for them to do.'[20] And yet, we should not be too carried away. There is a real question over what the Berkshire clerk's alteration can mean or imply. If it implies a legend, it would be nice to know something of the form it took in 1262; if it is simply a nickname, then it is more uncertain. Even as a skeptic, I would hope that some day someone might find (probably not through a formal 'search') some clear and incontrovertible evidence.

I was about to add to the preceding sentence a phrase to the effect that I doubt whether they will, but strange things turn up in the forest. Dobson and Taylor said (1989) that 'the day has long since past when the student of English popular literature could hope for the discovery of a genuine Robin Hood "ballad", additional that is to the thirty-eight such poems and songs published in Francis James Child's *English and Scottish Popular Ballads* a century ago'.[21] However, another discovery, this time of a literary kind, produced some not quite 'genuinely new', but pretty new ballads. This was the discovery in 1993 of the Forresters MS, now well edited by Stephen Knight.[22] This provides some earlier, fuller and better texts for some of the Child Ballads (it has an impressive version of *Robin Hood's Death*). The collection, apparently put together by an intelligent and informed 'supervisor' for a Robin Hood Garland, is of major importance for the study of seventeenth-century balladry (where, as Knight remarks, it disturbs the 'settled state' suggested by Child's collection). It is equally important, however, for the study of the ways in which the ballads and the 'matter' of the legends were transmitted and transformed. The student of the earlier period finds some fascinating links with the past – in the lively survival of older motifs and story patterns – adventures and combats, and even the Barnsdale setting. There is a traditional 'feel' about much of the material: Maid Marian only appears in a list, and there is little sign of 'gentrification'.[23]

---

20 Colin Richmond, 'An outlaw and some peasants: the possible significance of Robin Hood', *Nottingham Medieval Studies* 37 (1993), 90–101 (reprinted in *RHASC*).   21 *RRH*, p. xiv.   22 *RHFM*. The MS was identified by A.R. Heath in 1993.   23 There have also been some similar discoveries. A Takamiya manuscript in Tokyo has a different and earlier version of the nonsense song of Ignorance (see *English Manuscript Studies* 1 (1989), 213–21, p. 218. The late fifteenth-century *Rous Roll*, a history of the earls of Warwick, mentions that about the time of Earl Guy (d. 1315) there lived 'the famous outlawe Robyn hode and lytyl John and there felawis. hit is marvel that no croniclar writis of hem': John Rous, *The Rous roll* (Stroud, 1980). This might suggest an intriguing possible link with

The games and plays of Robin Hood (which seem to have been very common in southern England and in Scotland) had been largely ignored by literary scholars before the publication of the study by David Wiles. There has been some inconclusive discussion of which came first, ballads or plays: Wiles says that 'Robin Hood games did not merely derive from ballads but often inspired the creation of ballads', Knight that the games in fact 'were a performance-based version of the same myth presented in the early ballads'.[24] It would seem that the large gaps in the records would prohibit the giving of a simple answer to what is probably an over-simple question. Later writers have developed and refined some of Wiles' ideas. It has been argued, for instance, that perhaps his emphasis on the element of 'misrule' in the games has led to a popular picture of them which owes a little too much to the overheated accounts of later Puritan moralists like Stubbes, of how the heathen company marches to the church, 'their pipes playing, their drummers thund'ring, their stumps dauncing, their bels jangling, their handkerchieves swinging about their heads like madmen, their hobbie horses & other monsters skirmishing among the rout [...]', etc. (Wiles 11).

There is some evidence for outbreaks of riotous behaviour and 'laddism' but the more sober parish records sometimes make the 'church-ales' sound rather more like modern English church fetes than Bacchanalian revelry. The collecting of money – fundraising –seems to have been very important. The parish game provided 'a structure for charitable giving in a convivial atmosphere' (into which Robin Hood and the Greenwood could easily be inserted). It is often not at all clear what form the entertainment took. It seems likely that some kind of procession or 'riding' was frequent – as in the Scottish *The Maner of the Crying of a Play*: 'addres yow furth with bow and flane / In lusty grene lufraye, / And follow furth on Robyn Hude'.[25] This may sometimes have been associated with or followed by the 'presiding' of Robin Hood or Little John (or Marian): sometimes with a dramatic performance (perhaps of pieces like the surviving prints of Robin Hood Plays),[26] some-

---

Child No. 149, a rather wildly inclusive ballad, which says that Robin Hood's mother was niece of Guy of Warwick. A more negative 'find' is that the fragment of a poem listed in *The index of Middle English verse* (834.5) turns out to be a couple of leaves from a printed version of *King Edward and the Shepherd*. I was once elated to find a reference to a Lancastrian ship (1416) called *Little John* (a ship called *Robin Hood* is found at Aberdeen in 1438), but in this case any link with the outlaw legend seems dubious – it may have simply been the smaller 'follower' to a larger vessel, the *Cog John;* see Susan Rose (ed.), *The navy of the Lancastrian kings, 1422–1427* (London, 1982), p. 37.   24 Wiles, *Early plays*, p. 2; Knight, *A complete study*, p. 113.   25 Previously sometimes attributed to Dunbar. Text in *Poems of William Dunbar*, ed. W. Mackay Mackenzie (London, 1932), no. 86.   26 See John Marshall, '"Goon in-to Bernysdale": The trail of the Paston Robin Hood play' in Catherine Batt (ed.), *Essays in honour of Peter Meredith, Leeds Studies in English*, New Series 29 (1988), 185–217; and John Marshall, 'Playing the game: reconstructing *Robin Hood and the Sheriff of Nottingham*' in Hahn, pp 161–74.

times perhaps with athletic games or combats.[27] The mid-sixteenth century Scottish *The Complaint of Scotland* includes among the shepherds' entertainments a tale of 'robene hude and litil ihone' and a dance called 'Robene hude' ('in ane ring, euyrie ald scheiphyrd led his vyfe be the hand & euyrie yong scheiphird led hyr quhome he luffit best'), so perhaps tale-telling and dances might also have been found.[28] The parish games involved dressing up, the collection of money and communal enjoyment. The records of Croscombe (expertly analyzed by John Marshall)[29] suggest that here Robin Hood was less a figure of 'misrule' than a champion of the ideals of communality and local identity. Marshall points out how elements found in the ballads – the greenwood and its hospitality (and its redistribution of wealth), its 'yeomanry', its ideals of independence and fellowship – were singularly appropriate to parish community celebrations:

> The relationship between myth and parish was [...] reciprocal: it is why it lasted so long. In the games or revels, Robin Hood acquired a presence in performance that sustained and energized the myth. And the parish elected a heroic representative who successfully embodied the values of fraternity and charity. In the event, at Croscombe and elsewhere, these explanations count for nothing without the sheer fun to be had from dressing up in Lincoln green and brandishing a bow and arrows with some friends.[30]

If the quest for the historical origin of Robin Hood is now perhaps 'on the backburner' (but not totally abandoned), what do we now make of the surviving material – the ballads, and their audiences, and their reception? After Crook, I think that we should be cautious in our attempts to find 'history' in the individual texts. I feel uneasy about trying to read off historical allusions or social references. These may be present, but can we be sure that we can isolate them successfully? (The variety of the suggestions for dating the poems might give some cause for caution.) These poems are not simple

27 The duty of Little John in Edinburgh in 1518 was 'to mak sportis and jocosities in the toun', Anna J. Mill, *Medieval plays in Scotland* (Edinburgh and London, 1927), p. 28. Combats are important both in the early ballads and in the surviving dramatic pieces. They continue in the 'mumming plays' recorded later: in one at Shipton-under-Wychwood a version of 'Bold Robin Hood and the Tanner' is followed by the killing and the resurrection of Little John, R.J.E. Tiddy, *The Mummers' play* (Oxford, 1923), pp 209 ff. In such plays apparently some of the 'jocosity' was found in 'the bragging of the combatants before they fight' (Tiddy, p. 84). And combats continue to excite in the films of the twentieth century.   28 Ed. J.A.H. Murray, EETS ES 17,18 (1872), pp 65–6.   29 John Marshall, '"Comyth in Robyn Hode": paying and playing the outlaw at Croscombe' in Sarah Carpenter, Pamela King, and Peter Meredith (eds), *Porci ante Margaritam: essays in honour of Meg Twycross, Leeds Studies in English*, New Series 32 (2001), 345–68.   30 Marshall, 'Comyth in Robyn Hode', p. 360.

collections of historical or sociological data, nor simple 'reflections' of the society in which they were produced. Literature may present a distorting mirror. 'History' may be distorted in literary development, or overlaid with different layers of legend (Theodoric and Ermanaric become contemporaries, Roland's Basque enemies become Saracens). We are also still confronted by the old problem of 'lost literature'. Our few surviving verse texts give us only some hints of the total Robin Hood tradition. It would seem likely that it was characterized by variety and that it was not a static one, with changes and layering occurring in a way that we can barely glimpse. We cannot realistically hope to produce a clear pattern of development in a way we might attempt to do in a later period where more material has survived. Perhaps we should train ourselves to say, 'in this text, as we have it ...'[31]

We also need to be cautious in trying to describe or define the audience, about which some rather dogmatic statements have been made (peasants, gentry, etc.). References to the popularity of the Robin Hood material would seem to suggest a wide audience ('all over Britain' says Major)[32] – perhaps rather, 'audiences' (for different types of material)? We need also to resist the temptation to restrict the tastes of any putative group. In Scotland, for instance, James IV had a court poet in Dunbar who was very responsive to popular literature and made a burlesque poem about 'Sir' Thomas Norny, probably a court fool, comparing his exploits to those of famous outlaws – Robin Hood, Guy of Gisborne, Adam Bell, etc. – whose names he clearly expects his audience to recognize. Down in England known members of various audiences of various kinds of Robin Hood material include Sir John Paston, Henry VIII, and the parishioners of Croscombe.

There has been much interest in craftsmen and members of guilds, as in Tardif's fascinating and influential article, arguing that 'the action of all the ballads is played out across a dichotomy of town and forest', and stressing the importance of mobile servingmen, craftsmen, fraternities. 'The economic organization of the forest band', he says, 'when it becomes explicit, is that of the master-craftsman's shop'.[33] Yes, perhaps, but... Could that be possibly true of other kinds of fictional 'bands' of heroes or adventurers? And I note that David Aers thinks that it is a replica of the court,[34]

---

31 The situation is in some ways analogous to that in the mystery cycles, where the texts that we have represent a kind of frozen moment in a process of change for which we have scraps of evidence.   32 John Major, *Historia Majoris Britanniae* (Paris, 1521), extract in *RHOOT*, pp 26–7.   33 Richard Tardif, 'The "Mistery" of Robin Hood: a new social context for the texts' in, Stephen Knight and S.J. Mukherjee (eds), *Word and worlds: studies in the social role of verbal culture* (Sydney, 1983), reprinted in Knight. See also Thomas H. Ohlgren, 'Edwardus redivivus in *A Gest of Robyn Hode*', *JEGP* 99 (2000), 1–28 (which boldly ends with the statement that the 'urban merchant classes' are 'the producers and consumers of the early poems and plays of Robin Hood').   34 In David Wallace (ed.), *The Cambridge history of medieval English literature* (Cambridge, 1999), p. 451

and that John Marshall suggests that it mirrors the parish. I begin to suspect that we have found another example of the adaptability characteristic
of the Robin Hood myth. And the distinctive 'isolation' of the technique,
where action takes place against a relatively plain, undetailed background
whether in forest or in town perhaps works against too much explicitness.
Where did Robin keep all that cloth in the forest? As for audiences, I am
sure that yeomen would enjoy the ballads, and I can envisage yeomen as
part of the several audiences, though not perhaps the exclusive audience. I
can easily imagine mixed audiences, and even some unmixed ones, like
members of a guild. In fact, given our knowledge of the taste of some
medieval monks, it might not be too far-fetched to think of a group of
monks quite enjoying them – monks with a sense of humour, and enough
intelligence to realize that bad monks were the butt of the satire and that
it was not a Wycliffite attack on monks in general.[35] Even sheriffs, perhaps
...? But I must resist the urge to speculate. There is no doubt that Robin
Hood tales had a wide and varied appeal, and this is perhaps a pointer to
the subsequent history of the myth.

Looking again at the early poems, it is perhaps more profitable to stress
their diversity, rather than the evident similarities and links between them
which have sometimes led to them being discussed almost as a single unit.
The surviving poems, from the earliest fragment where Robin Hood stands
in Sherwood with twenty-two arrows in his hand to those in the Percy Folio
MS which seem likely to preserve or go back to medieval versions, like *Guy
of Gisborne* or *Robin Hood's Death*, show a surprising variety. *Robin Hood's
Death* sounds like one of the 'tragedies' that the chronicler Bower mentions.
Both poems are powerful, alarming and violent.[36] *Robin Hood and the Monk*
is an excellent example of narrative with interesting alternations of mood,
and an excellent example of the way in which a generally plain style may
allow significant details to stand out (Nottingham's gates and St Mary's
church) or be emphasized by a kind of repetitive focusing:

> As they went talking be the way,
>   The munke and Litull John,
> John toke the munkis horse be the hede
>   Fful sone and anon.
> John toke the munkis horse be the hed,

35 Interestingly, one example of the topic that idle folk prefer to read various romances
rather than God's word is found with Robin Hood in the list in a text in a Wycliffite
context; see M. Deanesly, *The Lollard Bible* (Cambridge, repr. 1966), p. 274 – though the
author is probably not Purvey (Anne Hudson, 'John Purvey: a reconsideration of the evidence for his life and writings', *Viator* 12 (1981), 355–80).   36 See also now the fuller
version of the *Death*: RHFM, no. 17.

> Fforsothe as I yow say
> So did Much the litull page
> Ffor he shulde not scape away   183–90

Or, elsewhere, 'I have spyed the kynggis felon [...] I have spyed the false felon' (85, 87). The narrator increases the audience's excitement and involvement with an exclamation: 'Beside hym stode a gret-hedid munke / I pray to God woo he be!' (75–6).[37] This poem has a number of the characteristic themes found in much of the tradition – fellowship, the breaking of fellowship and its resolution – and also much 'beguiling', deception, and ambiguity.[38]

Robin Hood and the Potter belongs clearly to the category of 'comedies' mentioned by Bower, although some serious patterns of ideas are intertwined with the comedy. Robin's men are delighted by the knockabout combat (again endorsed by the narrator – it was a good sight to see). If *Robin Hood and the Monk* shows the hero's vulnerability when he leaves the forest alone, this 'road adventure'[39] reveals him as a rather incompetent tradesman and businessman; in general he is less than successful at anything other than archery and robbery. This (more or less controlled) comic treatment of the hero shows another aspect to him which is probably important in his development in the later tradition. He is a strong hero, but his strength can be matched: he is not of towering heroic stature – he is human, even vulnerable, and it is possible to smile and laugh at him as well as with him. Laughter is central in this tale, culminating in the loud laughing of the sheriff's wife and the good-humoured ending. There are some ironies, of a jovial kind, as in the lovely line of the sheriff – 'Potter, thou art a man!' (212).

There is general agreement that the *Gest of Robyn Hode* is a poem made from several ballads – 'it seems', said W.P. Ker, 'to be an attempt to make an epic poem by joining together a number of ballads'. He found it 'rather mechanical'[40] – it seems to me to be quite successful. Whether or not it should

---

37 Cf. *Gest* 1808. Unless otherwise indicated all quotations are from the texts in *RHOOT*. An 'exclamation' from the narrator is a tried and tested device, not surprisingly found in texts from all cultural 'levels' and in a variety of literary kinds – in epic from Virgil to the *Chanson de Roland* e.g. 3973–4, 'Guenes est mort cume fel recreant. / Hom ki traïst altre, non est dreiz qu'il s'en vant!' ('So Ganelon has died a felon's death. / A traitor should not live to vaunt his deeds!', trans. D.D.R. Owen), and from early ballads to later ones, like the exclamation against the traitor Jim Murphy in the Ozark ballad of 'Young Sam Bass': 'Oh what a scorchin' he will git / When Gabriel blows his horn!' 38 I am not convinced, for instance, that it is quite right to claim (as do Knight and Ohlgren, *RHOOT*, p. 32) a 'miracle of the Virgin' as a straightforward 'source' – Robin's rescue is actually due to Little John's trickery and courage. I continue to think that Robin's devotion to the Virgin is presented as both genuine and ambiguous. 39 Phillips, in Hahn, p. 204. Her remarks on this poem are especially illuminating. 40 W.P. Ker, *Medieval English literature*, Opus Books Series 43 (London, 1912; repr. 1969), p. 90. It might be compared to the Danish 'Long Ballad' of Marsk Stig, with more than 100 quatrains, which he discusses elsewhere; see R.W. Chambers (ed.), *Form and style in poetry* (London, 1928), pp

be described as an 'epic' in a strict sense may be debatable. Bessinger remarked that it contained features of ballad, romance (including an interlace pattern), and epic. Perhaps we might be content with the term 'popular epic.' Our understanding of the *Gest* has now benefited from much illuminating criticism. The careful topography allows places to serve as 'symbolic homes' (Robin in the forest, the abbot in his convent), or to stand out, as castle and dungeon, As in the other poems, it is both mysterious and precise: Helen Phillips, noting the threefold topography of forest, town and highroad, says 'the Robin Hood tradition [...] has topography, but is not necessarily located in a region – 'Robin Hood is everywhere and nowhere'.[41] Although its ambitious structure differentiates it from the other poems, the *Gest* uses many of their techniques – making the significant detail stand out against the simple background, for instance: the abbot 'cast his hede on his shulder, / And fast began to stare' (487–8); when the sheriff 'saw his vessell / For sorowe he myght nat ete' (764–5). And occasionally we catch a hint of a slightly more elaborate rhetorical emphasis – 'where we shall take, where we shall leve / [...] where we shall robbe, where we shall reve' (45–7) – which is appropriate for its more elaborate structure, dialogue, and dramatic scenes.

Its blending of 'game' and 'earnest' is also elaborate, and more subtle than critics sometimes allow. The similarities with King Arthur hinted at in the beginning seem to me to be a nice mixture of gentle parody and irony with seriousness. I do not believe in a determinedly and 'destructive' ironic reading, but think that the poet is rather sophisticated in the way he can combine different tones (or play with the ambiguous sense of a word like 'proud'). At the same time he can produce straightforward and touching little scenes of pathos, or demonstrations of pity and generosity of spirit – the good knight (139) 'had ruthe of this yoman' (553). I would therefore persist in my straightforward reading (though acknowledging that other readings are possible) of the scene in which Little John measures out the cloth for the poor knight (285–97). Little John's hyperbolic excess certainly has comic overtones – he characteristically and comically 'goes one better' than Robin. Yet I still think it is an instance of Robin's *largesse*, and that the scene is not particularly 'mercantile' – the remark, 'Ther is no marchaunt in mery Englond / So ryche' (283–4), suggests a fundamental *difference* as well as a comic comparison.[42]

Readers may also differ in their views of the ending of the *Gest*. It may be seen as abrupt and hasty, after the more relaxed long narrative that pre-

17ff; cf. p. 37, a reprint of his British Academy lecture, *Proceedings of the British Academy* 4. *Adam Bell*, though not as long as the *Gest*, is longer than other English ballads.   41 Phillips, in Hahn, p. 201. Again, her discussion of the *Gest* is very suggestive.   42 See Thomas H. Ohlgren, 'The "Marchaunt" of Sherwood: mercantile ideology in *A Gest of Robyn Hode*' in Hahn, pp 175–90. To say (187) that 'the scene dramatizes the friction between a master guildsman and his lesser tradesman' seems to me a little over-solemn for the context.

cedes it, as if the poet felt he was running out of time. Alternatively, it might be argued that it is a deliberately abrupt and stark ending, the culmination of a pattern of triumph and sorrow. The triumphant entry of the king and Robin to Nottingham is followed by the account of Robin's sojourn at court. From here on it seems that the rhythm of the narrative is played off against the (unusual) indications of 'real' time, 'twelve monethes and thre', when Robin is left with only two companions and little (if any) 'welthe', and, saddened by the sight of the young archers, longs to return to the greenwood, which the king allows him to do for seven nights. Weariness and sadness seem to be dispelled by the return, the finding of himself again as hunter and the reunion with his band (all in a few stanzas), but his remaining time in the greenwood, for twenty-two years, is simply recorded in a single stanza. We hear nothing more of a pilgrimage to his chapel of Mary Magdalen, and the old outlaw has ignored the king's time limit – but with a certain irony he is now 'beguiled' by the prioress. The remaining few stanzas briefly tell the story of treachery and murder in a detached style as if in a chronicle, but with an undertow of feeling which is allowed to surface in a single exclamation from the narrator, 'Full evyll mote they the!' (1808) and in the final prayer. The *Gest* now seems a less straightforward and more complex poem than it once did, and there is still much scope for the study of it and related poems as narratives.

In common with others I once made rather heavy weather of the Robin Hood poems as 'ballads,' partly because of the weight of discussion of the definition of the 'ballad' and also because of the discussion of the ballad's development provoked especially by David Fowler. I now feel less worried about generic overlaps and terminology. As with other forms, early terminology here is highly flexible: among the words used are 'ryme,' 'song,' 'talking,' 'tale,' 'gest'. Speaking of Dunbar's list in 'Sir Thomas Norny' of heroes and outlaws, Priscilla Bawcutt remarks, 'Dunbar ignores not only the geographical frontiers between England and Scotland, but other boundaries, drawn by modern scholars, between literary kinds, such as the ballad and the chivalric romance'.[43] Perhaps we should consider adopting 'a short verse narrative' as a working definition? ('Short' being a variable, as it is the comparable definition of a Middle English lyric as a 'short poem'.) We might profitably compare other types of short verse narrative in England and Scotland – in the thirteenth century 'Judas' and what Karl Reichl called 'geistliche Spielmannsdichtung';[44] even earlier, the lost songs of Hereward ('his deeds were celebrated by the country people, and women and girls sang of them in their dances');[45] and later, the poems of Minot, merry tales, miracles of

---

43 Priscilla Bawcutt, *Dunbar the makar* (Oxford, 1992), p. 27.   44 Karl Reichl, *Religiöse Dichtung in Englischen Mittelalter* (Munich, 1992).   45 Quoted by R.M. Wilson, *The lost literature of medieval England* (London, 1952), p. 124. (A translation of the *Gesta* by Michael Swanton is now to be found in *RHOOT*.)

the Virgin. Outside Britain, the Scandinavian ballads and rímur, German Spielmannsdichtung (as 'King Rother') would be relevant. The 'ballad' in the widest sense, and in the narrowest, would definitely not be static: there would be changes in style and technique, from period to period and from country to country. There would, for instance, be differences in the manner of performance: the older Scandinavian ballads were sung and danced, as were the later Greek songs of the Klephts, rebels against the Turks;[46] and apparently, some songs of Hereward the Wake, and the Scottish dance of Robin Hood. Peter Dronke (who questioned the notion of a specific period as the 'origin' of the fabliau) has attacked 'the prevailing view that ballad-poetry as such did not arise before a determined historical moment, a particular social situation' (usually in the late Middle Ages) and produced earlier evidence.[47] I would not wish us to return to the view of the 'timeless antiquity' of every ballad recorded in the eighteenth century, but narrative poems of this general type may well be much older than we have been taught to think. If 'short verse narratives' have been around for centuries, perhaps the best we can do, if there is any evidence, would be to try to fix the emergence of certain types, certain stories, certain styles. W.P. Ker once said, 'Ballad is an Idea, a poetical Form, which can take up any matter and does not leave the matter as it was before' – and warned us to be cautious about 'the people' (in Denmark he remarked, 'everyone, as far as poetry is concerned, belongs to the "folk"').[48] We should probably avoid the notion of a 'pure ballad', and be cautious about its supposed inevitable connection with a 'ballad society'.

To return briefly to our 'ballads' of Robin Hood. They use a simple formulaic style; they have a liking for direct speech (sometimes abruptly introduced), for dramatic, 'expressionist' scenes, for the singling out of an expressive detail, while generally, the background is often not filled in, and the action ('deeds' are extraordinarily important) continues in a curious isolation.[49] Similarly, the figures, though starkly differentiated, are not analyzed or given

---

46 Cf. Elizabeth Gaskell, discussing C. Fauriel's *Chants populaires de la Grèce moderne* in *Household Words*: 'Some of these songs are literally ballads in the old Provencal sense of the word: they are exclusively sung by the dancers as they dance. Indeed it is a characteristic of the Greek popular poetry that it is so frequently intended to be sung while the singers are dancing. The dancing is, in fact, with them, a pretty mimicry of the emotions and movements which the song describes [...] Of course, the dance is not a mere mimicry of that of the ballad sung; but the character of the dance depends on that of the song. If the latter relates to deeds of arms or feats of warriors, the movements are abrupt and decided [...]'.   47 Peter Dronke, 'Learned literature and popular ballad in the Early Middle Ages', *Studi Medievali* 3a Series 17 (1976), 1–40.   48 Chambers, *Form and Style*, p. 36; cf. pp 26–33.   49 This is another narrative technique that is commonly found outside the ballad tradition (e.g. in Henryson, Malory, and Spenser). Upton, noting an example in *The Faerie Queene*, II.2.ii, offers the note, 'this sudden transition of the poet to the speaker, without any notice or preparation, shows a kind of earnestness or passion; as the

much in the way of explicit characterization or even physical description. Such figures can be 'realized' in dramatic performance, as John Marshall has pointed out, and in terms of their later development they are wonderfully adaptable. Another characteristic element, found in some songs and carols rather than in the narrative ballads (though related to the knockabout comedy at Robin's expense in *Robin Hood and the Potter* and the mixture of realism and the fantasy in others) is that of nonsense or fantasy.[50] This element is seized upon by moralists and serious folk: that the formulaic phrase 'Robin Hood in Barnsdale stood' becomes a legal tag (= an unprovable assertion) might suggest that it was widely known or suspected.[51] Gavin Douglas in his *Palice of Honoure* mentions Robin and Gilbert with the White Hand alongside what sound like fantastic or 'eldrich' tales – 'how the Wran come out of Ailssay' and 'how Hay of Nauchtoun flew in Madin land'.[52] Some carols or parts of carols put Robin Hood material or references into the tradition of nonsense and *fatrasie*. Ignorance's song, in Rastell's *Interlude of the Four Elements* (1520), beginning 'Robyn Hode in Barnsdale stode / And lent hym tyl a mapyll thystyll', is correctly described by R.L. Greene as 'cheerfully incoherent'.[53] Another carol with the burden 'Newes, newes, newes, newes! / Ye never herd so many newes!' has the item 'Robyn is gone to Huntingdon / To bye oure gose a flayle'.[54] Yet another, a song against women, in one version is 'signed off' by 'He that made the songe ful good / Came of the north and the sothern blode, / And somewhat kyne to Robyn Hode'. 'The author knows the wisdom of anonymity in the case of a piece like this one', comments Greene, and points out that it seems to be a proverbial figure 'used to indicate what is unworthy of credence'.[55] These references perhaps give some hint of why the poet Skelton later came to be associated with Robin Hood material,[56] and perhaps the joyous and sometimes wild comedy they exemplify may have been of some importance for later developments.

Some contemporaries seem to have found Robin Hood's adventures and behaviour wild and fantastic; the Scottish chroniclers who mention him single out his central social feature: he is an outlaw. Sometimes they add a comment, sympathetic or explanatory. For Wyntoun he is a 'waithman', but (rather mysteriously) 'commendit gud'; for Bower, 'the famous murderer,' but 'certain praiseworthy things' are told about him; for Major a famous

rhetorician Longinus observes in his treatise of the Sublime [...]' (citing a Homeric example), *Spenser's 'Faerie Queene': a new edition with a glossary and notes explanatory and critical*, ed. John Upton (London, 1758). **50** Gray, 'The Robin Hood poems,' pp 4–5. **51** Green, 'The ballad and the Middle Ages,' p. 173. **52** Ed. Priscilla Bawcutt, *Scottish Text Society* Fourth Series, 3 (1967), p. 109. **53** Richard Leighton Greene, *The early English carols*, 2nd ed. (Oxford, 1979), p. 505. **54** Greene, No. 472. **55** Greene, No. 401 B; note on p. 453. It would probably be being too serious to suggest also an allusion to the mysterious ubiquity of the outlaw hero and to his traditional 'devotion' to women (see Major, or *Gest* 39–40) – or to the relative absence of them in the poems. **56** Skelton

robber, but one who only robbed the rich, and took life only when he was attacked or resisted. In a less detached or even-handed way, the poems often reveal a similar ambiguity. It is remarkable that none of them seem to know how Robin's outlawry came about.[57] The fact that in them he simply is there in his greenwood increases a sense of isolation and mystery. We have learnt a great deal about outlaws from historical and comparative studies. Perhaps a quick glance at some of the outlaws elsewhere in medieval English literature may indicate a further variety of attitude. They are a somewhat miscellaneous group (within a larger group of 'outcasts,' like werewolves, lepers, and exiles of various kinds). They range from the great rebels against God, like Lucifer or Cain, to more comic villains like Mak the sheepstealer, who claims to be a yeoman of the king and a messenger from a great lord, and demands 'reverence' from the shepherds. He would be associated with the 'gentlery men' (probably landowners' supervisors and bailiffs: men 'that ar lord-fest', wear livery, and behave outrageously) that the shepherds had earlier complained about. He is also a sinister figure, 'a man that walkis on the moor': the third shepherd remarks 'me thought he was lapped in a wolfskin'. His attempt at thieving receives a comic symbolic punishment.[58] Henryson's fable of the Two Mice has a gentler allusion (with another interesting ambiguity) – the country mouse who is eventually to spurn the dangerous delights of the town presided over by her sister, a 'gild-brother', is said at the beginning to live 'solitary', 'under busk and breir', 'for comonly sic pykeris luffis not lycht'. Henryson's foxes offer more sinister examples of solitary outcasts.[59] Dunbar, who knew outlaw ballads, is more hostile: he has his 'feigned

knew how to use 'nonsense' in a clever way, of course. He became the 'Skelton' of the *Merry Tales* and in Gabriel Harvey's phrase a 'mad brayned knave'. Drayton lists 'Ellen of Rumming' together with Robin Hood, other merry tales and Bevis (*Skelton: the critical heritage*, ed. A.S.G. Edwards (London, 1981), p. 65. He is also associated with an older merry England, e.g. by Humphrey King ('Let vs talke of Robin Hoode, / And little John in merry Shirewood, / Of poet Skelton with his pen, / And many other merry men [...]'), Edwards, p. 68.   57 Among the chroniclers Bower associates him with are the 'disinherited' followers of Simon de Montfort. Perhaps if there was no explanatory tale in the early tradition, the impetus to provide an historical context for him was increased. 'Disinherited' followers might also suggest an early step towards 'gentrification'. It is interesting though that the early rumbustiousness and physical strength continues to survive in places (e.g. the Forresters MS) – as does that of heroes brought up away from courts, like Gamelyn (from whose story is ultimately derived the wrestling in *As You Like It*) or Havelok. See also Richard Wilson, '"Like the Old Robin Hood": *As You Like It* and the Enclosure Riots', *Shakespeare Quarterly* 43 (1992), 1–19.   58 See *The Towneley Plays*, ed. Martin Stevens and A.C. Cawley, 2 vols, EETS SS (1994), pp 13–14. *The Towneley Plays* contain two other references to 'wolfshead', the cry for the pursuit of an outlaw, and the sounding of 'outhorne' (21/202 and 30/812 – in Last Judgement, Tutivillus commands 'of these cursed forsworne... Blaw wolfys-hed and outehorne').   59 *The poems of Robert Henryson*, ed. Denton Fox (Oxford, 1981), pp 9–19. The feast provided by the burgess mouse is not only a contrast to rural poverty, but has something of friar', a Turk from Tartary, enter Lombardy and live there as a renegade 'full lang in waithman weid', and in his Flyting against Kennedy describes his adversary as 'ane gallow breid' [one destined for the gallows] in Galloway, a highland reiver – 'I saw thair in to thy wathemanis weid' – living in a leper-lodge in the glen, and spending his time stealing.[60] This blending or alternation of 'earnest' and 'game' may well echo the attitudes of contemporary life: besides the hostility Richard Green has pointed out evidence for sympathy for actual medieval outlaws.[61]

The Robin Hood of the medieval poems is treated with something of the same ambiguity. He is a mysterious figure, but some things about him are clear. He is a yeoman (unlike the better connected outlaws and outcasts, such as El Cid or Marsk Stig). He has a number of the characteristics of later 'social bandits', the noble outlaws of fiction – their isolation and 'invisibility,' their dependence on loyalty. Like some of them he excites sympathy and admiration, but also fear encapsulated in the proverb 'Good even, good Robin Hood', alluding, as Ritson so precisely put it, to 'civility extorted by fear'. Skelton understood this well, and memorably used it of the overbearing behavior of Wolsey in *Why Come Ye Not to Court*, clapping his rod on the table ('no man dare speke a worde, / For he hath all the sayenge / Without any renayenge'), and declaring 'How saye ye, my lordes? / Is nat my reason good?' – and at this point the voice of the narrator interjects, 'Good evyn, good Robyn Hode'.[62]

The tradition suggests definite ambiguity, and, we might suspect some genuine puzzlement like that expressed in a song about Ned Kelly:

> Some say he's a hero and gave to the poor,
> While others 'a killer' they say.
> To me it just proves the old saying is true,
> The saying that crime doesn't pay.

> Yet when I look round at some people I know,
> And the prices of things that we buy,

the exhilarating wickedness of stolen feasts (with a touch perhaps of the land of Cockaigne). One of the foxes once has a twinge of conscience (29). **60** *William Dunbar: Selected Poems*, ed. Priscilla Bawcutt (London, 1999), pp 59, 271. **61** See, for instance, Green, 'Medieval literature and law' in Wallace, *Cambridge history*, 425–6. Perhaps some shared the rather cynical view of Chaucer's Maniciple that as the 'sentence' told to Alexander had it, there is no difference between a 'titlelees tiraunt' and ' an oulawe or a theef erraunt'. The tyrant has greater power for destruction, and is therefore called 'a capitayn', whereas the outlaw has only a 'smal meynee' and cannot do as much damage, so that 'men clepen hym an outlawe or a theef' (*Canterbury Tales* IX, 223–234). Cf. Barbara Hanawalt, 'Ballads and bandits: fourteenth-century outlaws and the Robin Hood poems' in Hanawalt (ed.), *Chaucer's England: literature in historical context* (Minneapolis, 1992, repr in *RHASC*). **62** John Skelton, *The complete English poems* ed. John Scattergood (London, 1983), p. 283.

> I just think to myself, well, perhaps, after all,
> Old Ned wasn't such a bad guy.[63]

The *Gest* states firmly that Robin was 'a good outlawe' – though some of the stories hint at more violent, darker undertones. The world of the greenwood seems to embody true justice, where the world outside is often manifestly unjust. Its positive qualities include 'trouthe' and the bonds of fellowship (though there are sometimes acts of aggressive individuality, like Robin's quarrel with Little John). This 'fellowship' is similar in its intensity to that celebrated in other kinds of medieval literature – as in Malory, though that chivalric fellowship is based on social and kin bonds of a different kind. Here it is a band of outcasts who have created a separate realm. I continue to think that it has something in common with Victor Turner's 'communitas', involving the throwing off or forgetting of the usual social relationships, and of status and hierarchy, adopting a 'natural' and 'simple' mode of dress (note the ritual 'levelling' of knight, sheriff, and monk).[64] In the greenwood ballads the bonds of Robin's fellowship seem much more important than those of kin (indeed in the *Gest* it is the wicked prioress 'that nye was of hys kynne').[65] 'Communitas' is opposed to structure, preferring an unmediated relationship between person and person; the greenwood band is a kind of 'order' or fraternity.[66] When at the beginning of the *Gest* Little John asks Robin ('maistar') what kind of life they should lead, the reply (or 'lesson') that he receives is both serious and playful. This element of playfulness may be one reason why (as John Marshall pointed out) the 'communitas' of the outlaw band could be easily adapted to the celebration of the communality of the parish, and robbery transformed into a game (for which there are clear hints in the poems) – the game of collecting donations. 'Communitas' is often thought of as a timeless condition, and this too is to be found in the fictional world of the greenwood. Perhaps this contributed to the longevity of the myth, and perhaps also intensifies the melancholy felt at the end of the *Gest* when real time enters the golden world.

---

63 Charles Osborne, *Ned Kelly* (Melbourne, 1930), 204. Major's remark, 'The robberies of this man I condem, but of all robbers he was the humanest and the chief' makes a similar point, with slightly greater ethical conviction.   64 See Gray, 'The Robin Hood poems', pp 37–8.   65 In the ballad tradition treachery by a member of one's own kin is especially reprehensible. In *Adam Bell* William of Cloudesley is a wedded man, but the idea of family seems peripheral in the early Robin Hood poems.   66 In *Dramas: fields and metaphors* (Ithaca, 1974), p. 274, Victor Turner remarks that where structure 'defines differences and constrains', communitas is at the opposite pole with the egalitarian 'sentiment for humanity [...] the desire for a total, unmediated relationship which nevertheless does not submerge one in the other but safeguards their uniqueness in the very act of realizing their commonness'. This is similar to the egalitarian sense of liberty and freedom in a revolutionary situation described by George Orwell at the beginning of *Homage to Catalonia*.

Robin may seem to embody true justice, and there is certainly a strong streak of idealism in the poems, but as so often, these qualities are made ambiguous by the juxtaposition of scenes of straight 'beguiling' (especially when Little John is in control), which seem to lurch into the amoral world of the fabliau. It is hard to resist the thought that some of the poets delight in playing on the borders of right and wrong. The elusiveness of the outlaw hero, and his refusal to be pinned down to a single significance continues to be a constant source of frustration and fascination.

There is clear evidence even in the earliest material for the potential adaptability of the hero.[67] He has some of the characteristics of what has been called the 'universal folk hero'.[68] In the early ballads Robin does not live in a world filled with magic like that of some romances, but there is something mysterious about his forest —a place of wonder even if it does not have dragons or giants, just as there is something distinctly mythical about him. The forest lies at the edge of the ordinary world, and its creatures and inhabitants share its wildness. Its liminality can be a source of danger, fear and joy.[69]

[67] Robin Hood never seems to have quite become a 'sleeping deliverer' like Arthur, Prince Marko, Emilio Zapata and others – partly, as one scholar said to me, because he never really died, and also, perhaps, because in the stories about him the scope of his power and his generosity is more limited: he is in his greenwood, a 'liminal' character on the edge of society. Nor was he ever, like the outlaws Zapata and Villa, given the status of a popular saint (his chances of achieving this faded after the Reformation), although the very widespread practice of naming places after him might suggest a kind of secular 'cult' – and it is recorded (Holt, 42) that in the nineteenth century railway workers building a line took fragments from the 'grave-slab' at Kirklees as a cure for toothache. Robin Hood is devoted to the Virgin Mary (although some ambiguity lurks here) and more mysteriously to Mary Magdalene, another solitary 'liminal' figure, who lived in the wilderness and was fed by angels. Did he build the chapel (which we never see him visit as a pilgrim) as an act of penitence, or simply as a devout recognition of affinity? ll. 1757 ff. have a general (probably largely formulaic) similarity to the lyric 'Maiden in the Moor lay', apparently a dance-song which has – without any solid evidence – been associated with Mary Magdalene.   [68] Orrin Klapp, 'The folk hero', *Journal of American Folklore* 62 (1949), 17–25: as historical personages (if Robin Hood is one) become legendary, 'they are made into folk heroes by the interweaving and selection of mythical themes appropriate to the character as popularly conceived' – feats, contest, test, deeds of generosity, martyrdom (by treachery), etc. As Robert Weimann, *Shakespeare and the popular tradition in the theatre* (Baltimore, 1978), p. 28, remarks, 'the assumption that Robin Hood is in part a mythical figure need not necessarily contradict the historical approach if it is understood not as a theory of his origin but as an indication of the popular reception of the figure'.   [69] Gray, 'The Robin Hood poems', p. 37; Phillips in Hahn; Corrine Saunders, *The forest in medieval romance* (Cambridge, 1993). Cf. the reference in *Sir Gawain and the Green Knight* (701) to the wilderness of Wirral –'wonde þer bot lyte / þat auþer God oþer gome with goud hert louied'. Wirral was made into a forest by Ranulph le Meschin, fourth earl of Chester (d. 1129), one of the possible contenders for the hero of the 'rymes', and was a haunt of criminals; see Henry L. Savage, 'A note on *Sir Gawain and the Green Knight* 700–2', *Modern Language Notes* 46 (1931), 455–7. Another example of a banished lover is found in the poem 'I must go walke the woed so wyld', Rossell Hope Robbins

Arguments over the nature of the radical 'protest' (and indeed its existence) in the earlier tradition continue. Two contributions have been especially interesting and suggestive. Colin Richmond has stressed the remarkable independence of Robin, a truly 'free man', a 'yeoman' of a radical kind.[70] He has rejected service to a lord, service in a household, altogether – he serves only the king at special request, and only for a time. All this is contrary to the social mores of a world in which everybody served someone else. He is a man of purposeful toughness. It is, Richmond argues, only in the England of 1350–1500 that an English yeoman would embody the dreams of Englishmen. He directs our attention to the relatively unsuccessful and the 'downwardly mobile': 'yeomanliness' represents an alternative allegiance to 'failing feudalism and fledgling capitalism' – 'too few took it up'. Local government and the common law are not depicted as 'corrupt' because 'corruptly' administered. Government and law are unjust per se. The Sheriff of Nottingham is not an evil man – he is bad because he is a sheriff. As far as the Sheriff is concerned, I think that this is probably going beyond the texts, but Richmond may well be right in detecting a potentially anarchist streak in the early tradition.

The remarks of Richard Green are in some ways complementary. In *Adam Bell* and the *Gest* 'the folklaw world of oath, borrow and wed is contrasted with the untrustworthy machinery of the king's law'. The Peasants' Revolt also has some characteristics of resistance to the king's law (shown particularly in local cohesiveness and ritual parody – as in the smashing up of Archbishop Sudbury's Lambeth manor with cries of 'A revel!' 'A revel!'). In the poems we may see the clash of two legal orders, and a consequent hostility to the representative of the king's law. The gleeful brutality of the outlaw poems is not just resistance to central authority, but a last ditch appeal to older legal strategies. This is a very significant observation. It seems likely that the poems tapped a widespread dissatisfaction and a yearning for a better, juster (and probably older) world.[71]

Sympathy for Robin and the outlaws continues through the tradition, especially if injustice can be seen to be there. W.F. Prideaux in 1886 notes

---

(ed.), *Secular lyrics of the XIVth and XVth centuries* (Oxford, 1952), no. 20.   **70** Richmond, see note 21 above. Robin is a truly 'free man' (368).   **71** Green, 'The ballad in the Middle Ages', especially chapter 5, pp 198, 203. The eating of the victuals and drinking of the wine of Sir Robert Hales make us think of Little John's actions in the sheriff's house in the *Gest* (685 ff.) In the greenwood feasts produce moments of recognition, and are a celebration of fellowship (See also D.C. Fowler and Barbara Hanawalt, in *RHASC*, pp 68 ff. 283–4). It should be emphasized that nostalgia, here for the old law, is by no means necessarily 'escapism' (see also Wilson, '"Like the old Robin Hood"'). Perhaps A.L. Lloyd (*Folk song in England*, London, 1967), p. 137 is right when he remarks of the medieval outlaw that 'a certain nostalgia for the older social order and an idyllic notion of the free life of the greenwood gives him a romantic rather primitive air that brings him near the epic hero'.

the 'sturdy commonsense of the English character', which 'in a lower form [...] tends to a sympathy with criminals of a bold and manly type'.[72] Earlier Ritson saw Robin Hood as 'a man who in a barbarous age, and under a complicated tyranny, deployed a spirit of freedom and independence, which has endeared him to the common people, whose cause he maintained (for all opposition to tyranny is the cause of the people)'. Naturally enough, such sympathy is likely to be more acutely felt by those who are themselves poor and oppressed. In some Ozark songs about murderers and outlaws, sometimes endowed with courage and generosity, the hillmen (says Vance Rudolph) generally against the power of the 'Guv'ment' showed a 'weakness for the light-hearted rascality of bank-robbers and the like'.[73] It is not surprising that the Robin Hood myth, though almost infinitely adaptable retains some potential for 'protest' however vague or attenuated. As far as the early poems are concerned, much would depend on particular circumstances of the place or the manner of performance. They perhaps present a kind of 'generalized protest' similar to the very general satires on the abuses or wickedness of the age which could be rapidly and powerfully adapted to, or 'realized' in a particular context.[74]

So here I am deep in the greenwood, but still lacking complete enlightenment. No vision, no mystic stag, not even a glamorous bandit queen. I still continue to muse on whether I was right to be surprised by Jörg Haider as Robin Hood. Of course not, says one voice, echoing the wise words of Stephen Knight: 'Over time there have been many Robin Hoods, and an increasing number of Maid Marians; the authority against which they make resistance seems to have had as many forms as there are periods and contexts for the elements of the tradition: the meaning of the myth is never stable, and may be quite contradictory even in one period'. But another voice keeps reminding me of the medieval outlaw as a radical and challenging figure, and I hear the louder voices of his medieval followers, 'We are Robynhodesmen War War War!'[75] I suspect that in the end it was the particular circumstances of Haider's 'performance' that got me going. But my visit has convinced me that the greenwood is a genuinely 'merry' place in which academic 'boundaries' have little importance and where searchers – even if they cannot quite hunt down the elusive hero – can still find some of his strange and rich treasures.

---

72 'Who was Robin Hood?' *Notes and Queries*, 7th Series, II (1886), 421–4; repr. in *RHASC.* 73 *Ozark folksongs*, ed. Vance Rudolph (Columbia, Missouri, 1948), vol. 2, chapter 4. 74 See Gray, 'The Robin Hood poems', and *Robert Henryson* (Leiden, 1979), pp 241–2. 75 Richmond, 'An outlaw and some peasants', p. 376 – and some later ones: see Wilson, '"Like the old Robin Hood"'.

Little John and the ballad of
Robin Hood and the Monk

DEREK PEARSALL

There is good reason always to question the categories that are customarily employed in the organization of our view of the past. The shape that the past assumes in our minds is sometimes not much more than the product of those categories of thinking. The most obvious example is periodization, the organization of the past into periods ('the Middle Ages', the 'early modern' period) which acquire a spectral reality far beyond their original utilitarian function as labels. One cannot manage without periodization of some kind, and the only solution is to keep arguing with the practice that is current while making grudging use of it. But it is the same with other categories, including those that are used to organize discussion of genres, topics, themes – and of characters like Arthur and Robin Hood. A 'Robin Hood' conference, for example, will tend to perpetuate the notion that there is a single aspect of symbolic culture toward which we can all address ourselves. A particular danger of this is that elements in a tradition will be missed because of the distorting effects of a prevailing mode of perception, as with the Ptolemaic universe. So it is with the ballad of *Robin Hood and the Monk*. Little John, who is much the most important person in the ballad, indeed its hero, is not even mentioned in the title.[1] The poem has been swept into one of the bins into which history gets sorted, given a misleading title, and deprived of its special identity.

Most discussions of Robin Hood try to organize the body of surviving early writing into some form of coherent cultural narrative.[2] Robin Hood began his 'real life', it is most generally agreed, as a local bandit and high-

---

1 The title traditionally given to the poem is 'A little Jest of Robin Hood and the Monk' (see *Index of Middle English Verse*, no. 1534). In the unique manuscript (Cambridge University Library MS Ff.5.48) the poem has no title (I am grateful to my friend Tony Edwards for checking the manuscript for me). The standard edition of the ballad is that of Child, vol. 3 (1888), pp 97–101. The text printed in *RRH*, pp 115–22, is closer to the manuscript, and is used in this paper. 2 The most influential accounts of the Robin Hood tradition have been those of R.H. Hilton, 'The origins of Robin Hood,' *Past & Present*, 14 (1958), 30–44; J.C. Holt, 'The origins and audience of the ballads of Robin Hood,' *Past & Present* 18 (1960), 89–110; Dobson and Taylor, *RRH* introduction; Douglas Gray, 'The Robin Hood poems' *Poetica* 18 (1984) 1–39; and most recently and importantly, Stephen Knight, *A complete study*. The wording of the account that follows is taken from my own summary of received opinion in the headnote to the edition of the ballad in *Chaucer to Spenser: an anthology of writings in English, 1375–1575* (Oxford, 1999), p. 413.

way robber in South Yorkshire, one of the kind that won popularity because of their opposition to increasingly centralized bureaucratic control. Some time in the fifteenth century his career began to ripen under the influence of models from chivalric romance, and he became the outlaw-hero of a so-called 'yeoman' culture, loyal to the king and the knightly class but an enemy of predatory civil and clerical officials. In subsequent centuries the image was further polished: he became not just a mirror-image of knighthood, but a knight himself, temporarily exiled; always now chivalrous to women, he was equipped with a lady-friend, and became a staunch upholder of the true king Richard against the upstart John.

So the story goes. But the ballad of *Robin Hood and the Monk* does not fit into this cultural narrative. Its hero is not Robin Hood but Little John. Robin Hood is not presented at all in a favourable light: in fact the values commonly ascribed to Robin Hood, including the value he attaches to the outlaw band, are represented here by Little John, not by Robin Hood, with the addition of an element of violence, not gratuitous but certainly cruel and abhorrent, which survives from an older stratum of story-telling. The ballad seems to belong to another world than the one into which Robin Hood became incorporated, and needs to be understood as an anomaly in the record.

Robin Hood and the Monk has some claim to be the earliest surviving Robin Hood ballad; it is the longest, apart from *The Gest of Robin Hood,* which is a doubtful rival as a ballad; and it is certainly the best. 'Too much could not be said in praise of this ballad, but nothing need be said', was the opinion of Francis James Child, expressed with a taciturnity worthy of the ballad-form itself.[3] I shall follow his example and not speak at length in praise of the ballad – some idea of its quality will come through in the quotations – except to say that it has to perfection that hauntingly empty and belated quality of the traditional ballad, in which no-one in the story seems to know exactly what is going on, but meanwhile everyone seems to know more than the reader. The abrupt handling of the narrative, often carried forward through unconnected scraps of dialogue, means that little is explained, and the reader, like the viewer in some modern art-films, has the sense of having arrived on the scene when only the residues and traces of the narrative are still present.

The story begins on a May morning in Whitsuntide. The description of the woodland scene, with the sun slanting through the full leaves of early summer, the birds singing, and the deer 'drawing to the dale', though conventional enough, is alive with delight. Little John is vigorously open to the joy of the season:

> 'This is a mery mornyng,' seid Litull John,
> 'Be hym that dyed on tre;

3 Child, vol. 3, p. 95.

> A more mery man then I am one
> Lyves not in Christiante.   (stanza 4)[4]

He calls on his master to share with him in his pleasure, but Robin Hood
has other things on his mind. He is sorrowful, he says, that he has not taken
communion for a fortnight and more, and he announces his intention of going
to Nottingham so that he can go to church and 'see his Saviour'. Such a
quixotic and dangerous act in the service of some impractical ideal is readily recognized as a romanticized version of a heroic formula. It appears in
suitably homely form in the wonderful ballad of 'Adam Bell, Clim of the
Clough, and William of Cloudesly', where the outlawed William of Cloudesly
goes to visit his wife and children, and takes a meal with them even though
he knows the house is being watched.[5] In Robin Hood's case, it has to do
with religious devotion, in particular devotion to the Virgin Mary – '"Today
wil I to Notyngham", seid Robyn, / "With the myght of mylde Marye"'
(stanza 7) – to which Robin Hood attached himself as his story underwent
its process of social elevation (contrast Little John's brisk acknowledgement
of his Saviour).

Robin Hood refuses the sensible suggestion of Much the Miller's son
that he should take a band of twelve outlaws with him for protection – this
again is part of the older heroic formula. The hero must refuse help so as to
emphasize his lack of care for his own safety, his devotion to his object, his
courage, and his desire not to put others in needless danger. It reminds one
of Beowulf's determination to enter the dragon's lair alone (*Beowulf*, 2532–5),
or even, ultimately, of Jesus amid his disciples at the Taking in the Garden.
No one, of course, makes the obvious suggestion, which is that Robin Hood
could easily go to church in some less conspicuously dangerous place than
Nottingham. Everyone knows that such a proposition would be quite out of
place in the heroic formula and wouldn't even begin to work.

But though Robin Hood refuses to take a company of the outlaws with
him, he says that Little John shall go with him and carry his bow till he
needs to draw it.

> 'But Litull John shall beyre my bow,
> Til that me list to drawe'.   (stanza 9)

I suppose it might be that Robin Hood thinks his mission prevents him carrying a weapon, but whatever the case Little John is having none of it, and
refuses to serve Robin Hood in what he sees as the capacity of a squire or
page.[6] He is happy to call Robin master, and does so throughout, but he

---

4 Quotation of *Robin Hood and the Monk* is from *RRH*, 115–22. 5 See stanzas 2–12 in
the edition in *RRH*, p. 261. 6 Robin offers Little John as 'knave' or 'yeman' to the

rejects the idea of another kind of relationship, one that he has not assented to, and one so redolent of the world he has rejected, being foisted upon him.

But he offers a shooting-game, presumably (as usual in a ballad, nothing in the way of motives is explained) as a gesture of friendship and good fellowship, so that Robin Hood will not feel offended, and may recognize where his true relationship with Little John lies. The ballad began with Little John trying to cheer his maser up, saying what a nice morning it was, and his affection and loyalty are stressed throughout. But Robin Hood, as if smarting under Little John's implied rebuke, now seems determined to behave badly, and he turns down Little John's offer of an even-money game with a penny-stake, and declares that he will wager three pennies to every penny that Little John shoots for. In other words, he declares himself three-to-one odds-on favourite, which is really a shockingly arrogant way of asserting his superiority. Then, when they have finished their shooting-game and Little John claims his prize of five shillings for winning fair and square, Robin Hood calls him a liar and strikes him with his hand. Little John pulls out his sword in anger, but holds his hand, and discharges himself from Robin Hood's service with some dignity.

> 'Were thou not my maister,' seid Litull John,
> 'Thou shuldis by hit ful sore;
> Get the a man wher thou wilt,
> For thou getis me no more.'   (stanza 15)

In church in Nottingham, at his prayers, Robin Hood is recognized by a fat-headed (or wide-hooded – there is some textual play here) monk, from whom he took a hundred pounds on a previous occasion. The monk rushes out and warns his sheriff and his men that they must not let this notorious felon escape. The sheriff and his men rush in, Robin Hood draws a two-handed sword and hacks his way through the thick of them, kills twelve, wounds many others, but is eventually captured.

Or at least, so we suppose, for one of the added excitements of this exciting ballad is that key bits in it are missing. Here, several stanzas are lost between the last line of fol.130v and the first line of fol.131r of the unique manuscript,[7] whether because of a lost leaf in the extant manuscript or

---

penniless knight of *A Gest of Robyn Hode* (stanzas 80–1, p. 84), and he takes no offence, but the situation is different in many ways, and the date of the poem at least fifty years later. Later still, when Robin Hood had become an earl in Munday's plays, Little John is happy to serve him as his steward (see Knight, *A complete study*, p. 126).   7 The unique manuscript is Cambridge University Library MS Ff.5.48, dated *c*.1450. The poem appears on fols. 128v–135v. Fragments of eight stanzas from the poem are reported to be found on a stray leaf among the Bagford Ballads (*Index of Middle English verse*, no.1534; *RRH*, p. 114).

because of scribal carelessness or because of an unnoticed lacuna in the exemplar. At any rate, the news of Robin Hood's capture reaches his men, who are thrown into gloom and dismay – all except Little John, who reproaches the others for being so pessimistic, expresses confidence that 'oure maister' (as he loyally still calls him, quite setting aside their little feud) has made good his escape, and proposes a plan. He has evidently heard the monk is carrying the news of Robin Hood's capture to the king, and his plan is to be, as he puts it, in the ironically understated way of the true saga-hero, the monk's guide. It doesn't sound likely to be too good for the monk's health.

The next we hear, after the briefest of narrative links, is that Little John and Much the Miller's son are lying in wait for the monk in a house belonging to Much's uncle that stands near the highway. The monk and his servant, called 'a little page', come riding by and Little John hails them, asking to hear news of Robin Hood, who has robbed him in the past. They join company and ride on talking, until Little John suddenly pulls the monk off his horse by grabbing the part of his hood round the throat, and when he's on the ground strikes his head off with his sword, replying to the monk's cries for mercy in the characteristic way of the ballad:

> 'He was my maister,' seid Litull John,
> 'That thou hase browght in bale;
> Shalle you never cum at our kyng,
> For to telle hym tale'.

> John smote of the munkis hed,
> No longer wolde he dwell,
> So did Moch the litull page,
> For ferd lest he wold tell.   (stanzas 51–2)

This is the truly shocking moment of the ballad, and it is interesting that the responsibility of disposing of the innocent witness is given to the fairly featureless Much – perhaps the reason that he is in the ballad at all. Little John stands by and is party to the deed, reminding us of a world of brutal and unsentimental saga-heroes in which decency, a respect for the lives of the innocent, what we usually call a sense of honour and fair play, are not part of the code of behaviour in the way we might expect – the world of Achilles not Hector, of Egil Skallagrimsson not Kjartan, of Heremod not Beowulf, of Dirty Harry not Philip Marlowe.

Little John and Much bear the letters to the king, explaining that the monk who should have brought them died back on the way. No one in a ballad, least of all a person in authority, ever expresses the mildest doubt at any barefaced lie that is needed by the narrative, or smells a rat, or puts two and two together. It is part of the elliptical charm of the form. The king is so delighted at the capture of Robin Hood that he gives the two outlaws twenty pounds and makes them 'yemen of the crown' (stanza 58).[8] They carry his command with his privy seal to the sheriff of Nottingham to bring Robin Hood to the king. The sheriff is as completely taken in by the outlaws as the king was; they tell him a different story about the monk – that the king was so pleased with the news that he has made the monk abbot of Westminster, and of course he can't go on taking messages round the country now. They drink deep with the sheriff and when they are all asleep the two outlaws rouse the gaoler by telling him that Robin Hood has escaped and, when the gaoler emerges to speak to them, Little John runs him through. Robin Hood makes good his escape, and when they arrive in Sherwood Forest Little John explains the plot:

> 'I have done the a gode turne for an evyll –
> Quyte the whan thou may! ...
> I have brought the under gren-wode lyne –
> Fare wel and have gode day!'   (stanzas 77–8)

Robin Hood still does not seem to grasp the point – he says that Little John should be master:

> 'Nay, be my trouth', seid Robyn Hode,
> 'So shall hit never be;
> I make the maister', seid Robyn Hode,
> 'Of alle my men and me'.   (stanza 79)

The level of his political understanding seems to be similar to that displayed by the Roman populace – the Third Plebeian, to be exact – after Brutus' winning speech: 'Let him be Caesar!', he cries (*Julius Caesar*, III.ii.51). No, says Little John, that is not how it's going to be, and might have continued (as one is always tempted to paraphrase in words the eloquent ellipses of the ballad-style), You just don't seem to understand:

> 'Nay, be my trouth', seid Litull John,
> 'So shalle hit never be:
> But lat me be a felow', seid Litull John,   [Only, just]
> 'Non oder kepe I be'.   (stanza 80)

8 The meaning of the much-disputed term is here clear. Little John and Much are raised to the rank of *valettus* in the royal household, a rank between 'page' and 'squire' for which the usual English equivalent was 'yeoman.' See *OED*, s.v. *yeoman*; *MED*, s.v. *valet*. It was the rank to which Geoffrey Chaucer ('dilectus vallectus noster') was promoted sometime before 1367: see Martin M. Crow and Clair C. Olson, *Chaucer life-records* (Oxford, 1966), pp 17, 21, 123.

What Little John wants is fellowship. If one can press the word 'fellow' a little harder, one could argue that it is not fellowship of equals that he seeks, for he still calls Robin Hood master, albeit a master whom he has voluntarily accepted and whom he feels free to throw off when the shackles grow irksome. It is, rather, a community whose members have chosen to be fellows and who have common interests and goals. It is a community that he cannot have, neither from Robin nor from the society that found itself an admiring and enthusiastic audience of the Robin Hood ballads and plays in the late fifteenth century and wanted more of them. Little John had few fellow-spokesmen in late medieval England. Walsingham mocked the idea of community that the rebellious commons had put about during the Revolt of 1381, and Froissart found no difficulty in representing John Ball's sermon on the equal brotherhood of men, which to the modern reader seems an eloquent statement of an obvious truth, as a manifest absurdity.[9] Similarly, the 'great society' (*magna societas*) invoked in a number of trial records from East Anglia and Kent after the Revolt was over cannot be seen by any of those who took the confessions and wrote the records as anything but a vast criminal conspiracy.[10] For those who generally had control over the production and circulation of writing, a Robin Hood who was a rebel against his master (the king) could not be long admired, and the history of the documents that survive is of his emasculation and progressive incorporation into the established order. To this process, Little John, in the ballad of *Robin Hood and the Monk*, is constituted as an exception.

It is inevitable that scholars should try to assemble and organize the disparate surviving early materials relating to Robin Hood so that they seem to make sense as a coherent story. It is in the nature of a fossil-record, which is how we might view the surviving Robin Hood texts, that it should demand to be read as an intelligible historical story. So, after many years of debate, there is now something approaching a consensus on the origin and development of the Robin Hood story and the cultural work that it did.[11] It is generally agreed that the story had its origin in the activities of real-life bandits and highway robbers along the roads of south Yorkshire, who may have gained some measure of popularity and hero-status because of the rough justice they meted out, among their other depredations, upon hated figures of the popular imagination such as tax-gatherers and other government officials. There may even have been a real person with a name something like Robin Hood around whom stories of an outlaw band in the forest began to gather, perhaps by association with a legendary bad sheriff of Nottingham. By the time

9 See R.B. Dobson, *The Peasants' Revolt of 1381* (1970, 2nd edn., London, 1983), pp 364–7, 371. 10 Dobson, *The Peasants' Revolt*, pp 254–6. 11 Some of the notable scholarly contributions to this debate are listed in note 2. For a recent excellent summary and survey, see R.B. Dobson, 'Robin Hood: the genesis of a popular hero', in *RHPC*, 61–77.

the story came to be set down in writing, or perhaps in the process of setting it down, Robin was being assimilated to a gentlemanly tradition in which he could stand for the values that gentlemen wished to find in the class of 'yeomen' jut below them. Whether there ever was such a class in historical reality, it pleased all ranks of society to accept it as an image of a desirable reality. So Robin Hood became the outlaw-hero of a so-called 'yeoman' culture –sturdily independent, jealous of individual freedom, opposed to self-serving government officials and fat monks, and loyal to the king and the knightly class. 'Robin Hood's band of outlaws', says David Aers, 'actually reproduces the manners, dress and food of the romances and courtesy books so popular among late medieval "gentils". His base in the forest is a model court'.[12] In the sixteenth century Robin Hood took the inevitable next step and himself became a knight, temporarily and unfairly dispossessed of his patrimony, and now dignified also with a true lady-love. The shadowy allegiance to the king became a quasi-historical loyalty to the good King Richard against the bad King John.

The ballad of *Robin Hood and the Monk* seems to have little connection with this cultural narrative. Its hero is not Robin Hood, but Little John, and what Little John stands for is fellowship, which may have been an element in the old outlaw-narrative but which has been obscured with the passage of time. Stephen Knight has done his best, in different ways at different points, to accommodate the ballad to his own *grand récit* –the 'social meaning' of the ballad, he says, is to show 'the value and structure of the outlaw band as the embodiment of a natural state opposed to a world of alien, modern, threatening acculturation'.[13] Knight recognizes the importance in the ballad of 'the securely collective world of the forest', and gives due attention elsewhere to the 'solidarity ballad',[14] but he does not pick up the precise point here: that in *Robin Hood and the Monk* it is not Robin Hood but Little John who stands for the solidarity of fellowship.

The ballad of *Robin Hood and the Monk* does not fit in readily with large narratives of the meaning of the Robin Hood tradition. It refuses the accommodation to the larger hierarchy of the estates that had given Robin Hood an almost official licence and prerogative as the outlaw who was actually the representative of the ideal values of those outside whose law he stood. The ending of the ballad is uncompromising. The king realizes how he and the sheriff have been tricked, but his grudging respect for Little John (there aren't three yeomen like him in England, he says, stanza 87) does not lessen his resentment that Little John's loyalty was greater to Robin Hood than to his king. Little John's idea of solidarity with his fellowship remains an irritant, unabsorbed.

12 David Aers, '*Vox populi* and the literature of 1381', in David Wallace (ed.), *The Cambridge history of medieval English literature* (Cambridge, 1999), pp 61–77.   13 Knight, *A complete study*, p. 54.   14 Ibid., pp 53, 82.

Nor does the ballad represent Robin Hood at all in a favourable light. His devotion to Christ and the Virgin, which leads him to risk his life on a trip to Nottingham to pay his respects, is a sign of more than usual piety but, against that, he welshes on a bet (could anything be worse?) and takes upon himself, in relation to John, the prerogatives of a lord when he asks him to act as the equivalent of his 'squire' on the journey. In fact, the values commonly ascribed to Robin Hood (contempt for established bureaucratic authority, yeoman comradeship) are represented here by Little John, not by Robin Hood, and in something like their authentic saga form and necessary casual violence. It is possible to construe this as clerical propaganda: Robin has found a higher ideal than the socially inspired greenwood. More likely, it seems that through Little John the ballad is framing a protest against the gentrification of Robin Hood, which will duly take place in the next century. Like many erstwhile rebels, Robin Hood finds himself outflanked on the left when the authority that he assumes draws him inevitably into the higher sphere.

No one, it seems, least of all myself, can resist the temptation to 'explain' things, or to draw them into an orderly narrative of development and counter-development. When the fossil record is so incomplete, it might be more realistic to accept that items in it are inexplicable erratics, bearing traces of older stories only partly absorbed into the present documentary survivals.[15] At the very least, though, there is an argument here against the idea of a 'nuclear' Robin Hood, and in favour of the view that he is in a position in a continuing debate between opposing forces, a point of intersection that keeps shifting. It is a situation that should baffle those social and cultural historians who like to believe that the writings of the past are primarily explicable as serving the cultural purposes of the society that sponsored, produced, and seemed to need them. An alternative proposal might wish to give greater prominence to the sheriff of Nottingham and recognize how he is in some ways the most important person, the mythical imperative, in this whole set of stories. Like Grendel or the dragon, he is a more archetypal figure than the odd heroes sent out to do battle against him.

---

15 It is worth remembering that the ballad stands independently in its unique manuscript, and does not appear as any part of any collection of Robin Hood poems.

The hermit and the outlaw: new evidence for Robin Hood's death?

RICHARD FIRTH GREEN

As is well known, the earliest evidence for Robin Hood's death comes from the final six stanzas of the *Gest of Robyn Hode*:

> Yet he was begyled, y-wis,
> Through a wycked woman,
> The pryoresse of Kyrkësly,
> That nye was of hys kynne:
>
> For the loue of a knyght,
> Syr Roger of Donkesly,
> That was her ownë speciall;
> Full euyll mote they the!
>
> They toke togyder theyr counsell
> Robyn Hode for to sle,
> And how they myght best do that dede,
> His banis for to be.
>
> Than bespake good Robyn
> In place where as he stode,
> 'To morow I muste to Kyrke[s]ly,
> Craftely to be leten blode.'
>
> Syr Roger of Donkestere,
> By the pryoresse he lay,
> And there they betrayed good Robyn Hode,
> Through theyr falsë playe.
>
> Cryst haue mercy on his soule,
> That dyed on the rode!
> For he was a good outlawe,
> And dyde pore men moch god.   (Child 117: sts.451–6)[1]

Though this minimally fulfills Eric Hobsbawm's requirement that the social bandit should die 'only through treason since no decent member of the com-

---

[1] The text of *A Gest of Robyn Hode* is taken from Child, vol. 3, pp 39–89; other ballad versions are taken from this same edition.

munity would help the authorities against him',[2] it is nonetheless, as Sam
Weller would say, a 'sudden pull up', and hardly surprisingly it was considerably expanded in two later ballads: the first is the powerful and frustrat-
ingly fragmentary version of *Robin Hood's Death* in Bishop Percy's Folio:

> And first it bled, the thicke, thicke bloode,
>   And afterwards the thinne,
> And well then wist good Robin Hoode
>   Treason there was within.   (Child 120A: st.17)

The second is the pedestrian eighteenth-century garland version:

> She blooded him in the vein of the arm,
>   And locked him up in the room;
> Then did he bleed all the live-long day,
>   Until the next day at noon.   (Child 120B: st.8)[3]

Typically, social bandits die fighting, betrayed to the authorities by a greedy
associate, kinsman, or beneficiary, and that Robin Hood should meet his end
by bleeding to death after the voluntary opening of a vein is surely unexpected; in this paper, however, I shall be arguing that some such version of
his end was known in England at least half a century before Jan van
Doeborch printed the *Gest* in Antwerp around 1510, for its influence can be
seen, I believe, in an earlier moral tale called *The Hermit and the Outlaw*.

   The Hermit and the Outlaw is a little known Middle-English poem of 390
lines (though it must originally have been slightly longer) dating at the latest
from the middle of the fifteenth century. The first modern edition of this
poem, by Kaluza in *Englische Studien* in 1894,[4] is based on an inferior early
nineteenth-century transcription, but the original manuscript from which this
transcription was made does in fact still survive as BL MS Add. 37492
(ff.76v–82v).[5] *The Hermit and the Outlaw* is a lively and entertaining exemplum which cleverly combines two originally distinct tale-types, known respectively as 'the penitent robber' and 'the easy penance.'[6] The first of these contrasts the instant salvation of a hardened robber, who dies immediately after

---

2 E.J. Hobsbawm, *Bandits*, rev. ed. (New York, 1981), p. 43.   3 A third, late, version
has recently come to light, in which Robin is bled by a 'fawning fryer'; see *RHFM*, pp
115–16.   4 M. Kaluza, 'Kleinere Publikationen aus me. Handschriften, I: The Eremyte
and the Owtelawe', *Englische Studien*, 14 (1890), 165–82.   5 Quotations from *The Hermit
and the Outlaw* in this paper are from my new edition of the poem in *Interstices: studies
in late Middle English and Anglo-Latin texts in honour of A.G. Rigg*, ed. Richard Firth
Green and Linne R. Mooney (Toronto, 2004), pp 137–66.   6 See G.L. Kittredge, 'The
Hermit and the Outlaw', *Englische Studien*, 19 (1894), 177–82.

a repenting his sins, with the fate of a witness to his salvation – a resentful hermit who has mortified his flesh for many years with no guarantee of any such reward. In some versions of this tale the hermit returns to the world and is subsequently damned, in others, wiser heads prevail and he is persuaded to return to his ascetic life and an ultimate salvation. In the second, 'the easy penance' tale-type, a priest is driven to his wit's end by a recalcitrant penitent (often a headstrong young nobleman, but occasionally, as here, a hardened robber) who refuses to perform any of the standard penances that are offered him; in desperation the confessor finally proposes an absurdly trivial penance which then proves unexpectedly difficult to perform. Chastened by his experience, the penitent thus learns the meaning of true contrition.

The actual plot of *The Hermit and the Outlaw* is easily summarized. It tells of two brothers living in the same forest:

> That on was an erraunt theff:
> To robben*e* & reuen hym was lef
>   And was a wylde outlawe.
> That othyr was a gode ermyte:
> Off grey clothyng was hys abyte
>   And dwellyd by wylde wode schawe,
> And ȝede barfote and nouȝt yschod;
> The heyr he weryd for loue of God
>   Hys flesche to byte and gnawe.   (28–36)

On Good Friday the outlaw encounters a contrite woman on her way to mass and, intrigued, follows her to church. There he is stricken by remorse and asks the priest for an appropriate penance, with predictably comic results:

> 'A, son*e*, thou most barfote go,
> And wolward therto also,
>   Alle these ȝerys seuene'.
> 'Syr', seyd thys owtlay, 'nay.
> Barfote ne wolward gon*e* y may,
>   Thouȝ y schulde neu*er* come in*e* heuyne'.
> 'Sone', he sayd, 'neu*er* the latyr,
> Maystu faste, brede & watyr.
>   Lustyn*e* vnto my stewne'.
> 'Nay, ywysse, that myȝt y neu*er*.
> To suffur deth me were leuer,
>   The*n*ne more therof neuene'.   (115–26)

The priest does no better with offers of Paternosters and Ave Marias, nor with a proposition that the outlaw go on pilgrimage, and in desperation he prays to God for help; presumably in answer to this prayer, he hits upon a solution just as the outlaw is about to walk away:

> 'Sone', he sayde, 'lystne ʒyt to me:
> Thorw *grace* of God sauyd maystou be,
>   That of marye was born*e*.
> Telle me', he sayde, 'w'oute bost,
> What thyng hatystou to don*e* most;
>   Telle me w'oute schorne'.
> 'Syr', he seyde, 'so haue y pr*eue*,
> To drynke watyr nas me neu*er* lef,
>   The sothe for to say.
> Neu*er* sythe y couthe sowke,
> Wat*er* wolde neu*er* in my body browke
>   For nouʒt that man do may'.
> 'Sone', sayd the vyker, 'what byfalle,
> In remyssion*e* of thy synnys alle
>   Dryng no wat*er* today,
> And I assayle the of thy synnes fre.
> Loke thys forward*es* yholde be;
>   Na more pen*a*unce y the pray'.   (156–74)

Then follow seventy-two richly comic lines in which the outlaw fights off three successive temptations to drink water: on each occasion he is offered this water by a seductive wench who is clearly a parody of that staple of sermon moralizations, the taverner who seduces men to sin by the offer of wine; here, by way of example, is John Bromyard:

> He who desires to advertise purchasable wine, that has been freshly exposed for sale in some tavern, carries a vessel of the wine through the city with a cup in his hand, crying out the price and the place where it can be obtained. To the passers-by who want to know the nature and worth of the wine, he offers a sample of it; so that they may know by that sample what it is like in the tavern, and so that, having tasted its relish in small quantity, those who are stimulated may desire a larger supply.[7]

Having valiantly resisted his startling craving for water for a whole day, the outlaw then comes to a sudden and very bizarre end:

> As he stode at the wellys brynke,
> On hys knyfe he gan to thenke,
>   That hangyd by hys syde.

---

7 Quoted in G.R. Owst, *Literature and pulpit in medieval England* (Oxford, 1966), p. 176.

He vnbotened a sleve of hys arme
And smote a veyne that was ful warme
  And made hyt blede that tyde.
Ther he dranke hys owne blode
(Hym thouʒt hyt dyd hym moche good);
  The wownde was depe & wyde.
...
The owtlawe bledde forthe wᵗ mayn*e*
(He nyst howe to stoppe hyt a gayn*e*);
  He bledde harde & sore,
Tyl he sawe that he schulde deye.
He fyll on knees & lowde gan crye,
  'Ih*e*su, m*e*rcy, thyn*e* ore!'   (259–76)

Predictably, this prayer is answered; and the rest of the poem concerns the fate of the hermit, who, at first aggrieved that the outlaw should have been saved after so short a penance, is finally convinced of the justice of God's mercy; together with the priest, he gives his brother a Christian burial and finally himself dies a good death.

Now, while both bleed to death, there are of course a number of obvious differences between the end of this outlaw and that of Robin Hood. Robin certainly offers his vein voluntarily to the knife, but his reasons for doing so are medicinal; he is not driven to it by thirst. Nor is his wound self-inflicted. Nevertheless, a flow of blood that mysteriously cannot be stanched is common to both and so is a religious setting (the proximity of a church and a hermitage in the one case, 'merry Church Lees', the nunnery, in the other), as well as a penitential tone:

'Now giue me mood,' Robin said to Litle John,
  'Giue me mood with thy hand;
I trust to God in heauen soe hye,
  My houzle will me bestand.'   (Child 120A: st.23)

Such things are not, I suggest, coincidental, for I wish to argue here that the author of *The Hermit and the Outlaw* knew some earlier version of Robin Hood's death and deliberately altered his material to make it echo a tale that he knew would be familiar to his audience. In the first place, there is internal evidence that he was familiar with outlaw tales and wished to exploit their popularity among his listeners. Like Robin, for instance, his outlaw is an archer: he meets the penitent woman who is to set on foot his own repentance with 'hys bowe bare ybent in honde' (60), and when he first enters the church, he does so with an appropriate greenwood swagger:

> To th' yȝe auter he gan wende
> And lenyd apon*e* hys bowys ende
> So wondyrly ther he wrouȝt.   (97–9)

But far more telling is the external evidence. Though both tale types, 'the penitent robber' and 'the easy penance', were extremely popular, turning up in sermon manuals and collections of exempla throughout Europe from the thirteenth century onward, in only one other version that I have found (and that from remote Temesvar in Hungary) does the easy penance involve abstaining from drinking water, and in none does the penitent robber perish by bleeding to death.

One common version of 'the easy penance' has the priest enjoin the penitent to fill a bucket from a nearby stream, but this simple task proves impossible to perform until the passage of time (in some cases as much as a year) brings the sinner to his senses, and enables him, duly chastened, to receive genuine absolution.[8] In another, he is merely required to spend a single night in a church, but finds the experience so horrendous (he is assailed all night long by demons) that he is pathetically glad to receive the priest's ministrations in the morning.[9] Other versions are clearly intended to be more humorous: both Etienne de Bourbon and Jacques de Vitry have tales in which (as in *The Hermit and the Outlaw*) an exasperated confessor is driven to his wit's end trying to find something his recalcitrant penitent is actually willing to give up. In Jacques de Vitry, the confessor, faced with a particularly depraved woman – 'who had tried out just about every kind of vice' – asks desperately, whether 'there is anything in the whole world you're able to do without', to which he receives the answer: 'I have such an abhorrence of pigs that I can never eat them, indeed I can scarcely look at them.'[10] There may be a textual corruption, however, since her counterpart (a wicked knight) in Etienne de Bourbon's version had been willing to forgo only *porros crudos* 'raw leeks' so that 'pigs' *porcos* here may simply be a slip for *porros*.[11] (In Etienne de Bourbon, the prohibition on eating leeks is, in fact, the second of two such easy penances – the first, to refrain from manual work on feast days, had led to the knight's feeling an overwhelming urge to go plowing!) At all events, the upshot of the penances in both writers is identical: the sinners find themselves unable to resist an overpowering urge to consume dishes that had earlier been abhorrent to them and return to their confessors chastened and ready to accept a more orthodox form of clerical discipline. Closer

---

8 I.e. *Du chevalier au barizel*, ed. [Étienne] Barbazon, *Fabliaux et contes des poètes françois*, new ed., 4 vols (Paris, 1808), vol. 1, pp 208–45.   **9** Étienne de Bourbon, *Anecdotes historiques, légendes et apologues*, ed. A. Lecoy de la Marche (Paris, 1877), pp 48–9.   **10** Jacques de Vitry, *The Exempla*, ed. Thomas Frederick Crane (London, 1890), pp 119–200.   **11** *Anecdotes historiques*, p. 44.

to (though far from identical with) *The Hermit and the Outlaw* is an exemplum in a sermon by the Hungarian Franciscan, Pelbart of Temesvar (died *c.*1490), in which a drunkard is forbidden to drink water and is saved by successfully negotiating this penance.[12] In none of these versions, however, is there any suggestion that the easy penance, whether observed or not, might lead, as it does in *The Hermit and the Outlaw*, to the penitent's death. However, a far closer analogue occurs in the *Dialogus Miraculorum* of Caesarius of Hiesterbach (*c.*1222): a knight, who 'always fails to perform the penance enjoined [...] is allowed to choose the penance himself, *viz.* to abstain from eating sour apples which he hates; he dies in fighting a sudden temptation to eat them'.[13] A late thirteenth-century English collection contains a similar story: a 'sheriff refuses all penance but one of his own choosing, to abstain from cod (*muluellus*), a fish which he dislikes; afterwards he almost dies in resisting a temptation to eat it.'[14] The outcome of both these versions of the tale is self-evidently far closer to the denouement of the English poem, but, as I have said, there seems to be no other version in which an injunction against drinking water leads to death.

When it is compared to tales belonging to 'penitent robber' tradition, moreover, the originality of *The Hermit and the Outlaw* is yet more apparent. In this group of tales, of course, the robber invariably dies, but there is relatively little variation in the type of death. In all but a single version, his end takes one of two major forms: in the first, the robber hurrying after a hermit to make his confession, trips and breaks his neck, but his mere good intentions prove sufficient to win him instant salvation. In the second, the robber receives absolution but is then confronted by the vengeful kinsmen of a man he had earlier murdered; in his new state of grace he offers them no resistance (though the precise motives for his passivity vary) and he is duly killed. I have found only one exception to these two categories: in a fourteenth-century Austrian version 'the robber asks the hermit to take him as a companion, but is rebuffed with scorn; he is killed in felling a tree to build himself a hermitage.'[15] Nothing remotely resembling a death from unstanched bleeding occurs in any of the versions known to me. The inference that the author of *The Hermit and the Outlaw* was consciously refashioning his hero's end to make it consonant with that of the celebrated outlaw Robin Hood, if not conclusive, is certainly persuasive.

There is one further piece of evidence that may be relevant here: a passage in *The Chronicle of Dale Abbey* which raises the intriguing possibility that *The Hermit and the Outlaw* might be more than merely the reflection of a con-

---

12 *Specimina et elenchus*, ed. Ludovicus Katona [Budapest, 1902], p. 20 (item 51).   13 See J.A. Herbert, *Catalogue of romances in the Department of Manuscripts of the British Museum*, vol. 3 (London, 1910), p. 356 (item 62).   14 Herbert, p. 484 (item 64).   15 Herbert, p. 592 (item 110).

temporary tradition about Robin Hood's death, but rather an important witness to it – that the outlaw of the poem, in other words, might be meant as Robin Hood himself.[16] I make this suggestion with some reluctance, since it can certainly be regarded as no more than an unproven hypothesis at this stage.

The *Chronicle of Dale Abbey* was written sometime after the middle of the thirteenth century, by Thomas Muskham, a canon of the house. In the course of relating a number of legends about the Abbey's foundation, Muskham tells the following story:

> There was a certain extremely well known outlaw (*uthlagus famosissimus*) frequenting these parts on account of a forest road for those traveling between Nottingham and Derby (for at that time the whole territory between Derby bridge and the Erewash was forested). Now while this outlaw was sitting one summer's day on Lyndrik (which is a hill just to the West of our monastery gates) with his comrades relaxing about him, a deep sleep overwhelmed him. And while he slept he saw in a dream a golden cross standing in the place where our church is now established [...] Roused from sleep and awaking from his dream, the man disclosed to his comrades gathered around him the vision revealed to him by God, and added: 'Truly, my most treasured comrades, this valley which you see lying below us beside this hill is a holy place [...] And because our Lord Jesus Christ has deigned to reveal such a great secret to me, a sinner, you must know that you can no longer have me for either a comrade or a master, but with the aid of his grace I shall amend my life to conform to his will.' And when he had kissed them all he turned away from them, but the place he came to was unknown to them at that time. Some said that he went to Deepdale and there continually served his Lord in secret converse, and died there a good death in the Lord.[17]

Is it legitimate to wonder whether this *uthlagus famosissimus* who, along with his band, robbed travellers on the Nottingham road might not have been one of the early incarnations of Robin Hood himself? This connection was in fact made by the Stamford antiquary Francis Peck in 1735,[18] but it is not altogether fanciful. Certainly the mystery surrounding the Dale outlaw's end ('some said he went to Deepdale') would be appropriate to such a legendary hero,[19] and Dale Abbey itself lies well within one of the Robin Hood topographical hot spots. It stands in an area once covered by Sherwood Forest,

---

16 I should like to thank David Hepworth for drawing this passage to my attention, and for his many helpful suggestions.   17 '*The history of the foundation of Dale Abbey, or the so-called Chronicle of Dale*; a new edition', ed. Avrom Saltman, *Derbyshire Archaeological Journal* 87 (1967), 28 [my translation].   18 Holt, pp 180–1.   19 See Hobsbawm, p. 51.

a couple of miles to the West of the Erewash, a river that marks the boundary between Nottinghamshire and Derbyshire; in view of its earlier spelling 'Yrewis' John Bellamy has plausibly connected this river with the Verysdale to which Richard atte Lee returns in the *Gest*.[20]

If we grant this, might not Muskham's story of a famous outlaw turned penitent hermit be seen as containing the germ of the later account of Robin's death at the hands of the Abbess of Kirklees? On this reading, such a death would represent both a secularization and a mythologizing (through the introduction of the motif of treachery) of an earlier penitential tale in order to make it conform more closely to the kind of death we expect of a true social bandit. By this account, then, *The Hermit and the Outlaw* would become, not merely a dim echo of an early account of our hero's death, but important evidence for it.

20 John Bellamy, *Robin Hood: an historical enquiry* (London, 1985), pp 79–80. Bellamy mentions Annesley Castle (which lies a few miles to the north of Dale Abbey on the Nottinghamshire side of the river) as a good fit for Sir Richard atte Lee's castle in the *Gest*, but he does not note the linguistic similarity: if Yrewis-dale might be orally corrupted to Verysdale, it is hardly a much greater stretch from the rather odd-looking 'atte Lee' to Annesley.

The literary Robin Hood: character and function in Fitts 1, 2, and 4 of the *Gest of Robyn Hode*

ROY PEARCY

The story of the debt-ridden knight and the loan-shark monk occupying Fitts 1, 2, and 4 of the *Gest* is a composite, divisible into elements which circulated independently over at least two centuries. Two of these narrative units, the stories of a knight excused payment of a fee because he is honest about his poverty, and of a monk from whom money is extorted because he is correspondingly duplicitous about his wealth, appear in isolation in *Le Roman d'Eustache*. They are linked in the *Gest* by a motif first recounted by the twelfth-century cleric, Jacques de Vitry, wherein a debt incurred with God as security is forcibly recovered from one of his secular representatives.

The romance of Eustache the Monk provides a string of episodic adventures. One concerns a merchant who honestly told Eustache how much money he was carrying and was therefore allowed to keep his money; the outlaw says that, had he lied, he would have lost everything.[1] A later, separate, episode tells a counter story: an abbot lies about the amount he is carrying and the outlaw removes most of the wealth discovered on him and returns only the small amount he claimed to possess.[2] These episodes clearly help to establish both an unconventional kind of morality for the bandit, and a claim to an alternative type of authority and moral arbitration. The second story could also be seen as a fable that implicitly exposes and punishes clerical worldliness and falseness.

The combination of narrative elements in the *Gest* is not entirely satisfactory. The monk is forced to hand over his treasure on two quite distinct bases, because he has lied about the amount he is carrying, and because, as a member of the religious community of St Mary's Abbey, he is sophistically held responsible for an unpaid debt contracted in her name. Either reason would be sufficient in itself, but each appeals to a quite different social and moral code. The issues raised by the motif derived from Jacques de Vitry are complex, and reflect an institutional clash between secular and religious authority. Tracing the evolution of this motif from Jacques de Vitry's Latin text, through an intermediary French fabliau, and then to the English popular romance provides an

---

1 *Le roman de Witasse le Moine*, ed. Denis J. Conlon, University of North Carolina Studies in Romance Languages and Literatures, 126 (Chapel Hill, 1072), ll. 972–95. A similar episode appears in the *Roman de Fouke le Fitz Waryn*: Fouke is gracious to merchants who tell the truth and to a young man who gives him something for nothing, *Fouke le Fitz Waryn*, ed. E.J. Hathaway, P.T. Ricketts, C.A. Robson, A.D. Wilshire, Anglo-Norman Text Society (Oxford, 1975), pp 27–8. 2 *Witasse*, ll. 1,746–77.

opportunity to bring some literary evidence to bear on the concept of outlawry in the *Gest*, and its relationship to established authority.

To illustrate how substantial a connection exists between the *exemplum* and the *Gest*, here is Jacques de Vitry's brief treatment:

> A poor squire was captured in war, and begged his captor to let him go in search of ransom, offering as security God and his own bond. He was released, and went and sold all his property, but could not reach his creditor on the appointed day. The latter was riding out, and saw a monk riding a very fine palfrey with worldly pomp. 'Whose man are you?' he asked. The monk replied, 'I have no other master but God.' Then the former said: 'Your master is my surety, and I wish you to make satisfaction for him', and took his horse. Soon after, the squire returned with his ransom, which his captor refused to accept, saying: 'You gave me as security, God, and I took from one of his servants this horse in discharge of your debt.'[3]

Crane's translation is a little too cryptic on the encounter with the monk, which reads in the original Latin text: 'And the knight said to his squire, "This monk, who ought to be riding a donkey, has a better horse than I do". And riding up to the monk, he seized his horse by the bridle'.[4]

In Jacques de Vitry's treatment of this theme the knight is an exemplary aristocrat, engaged in the exemplary aristocratic activity of fighting baronial wars and taking prisoners for ransom. His question to the monk, 'Whose man are you?', is sophistical, since we know that he has identified the character he is interrogating as a member of a cloistered religious community. But it is only minimally sophistical, and has in it an element of paradox. The monk's pride has secularized his order, and made God his overlord in the same mundane sense as he has become God's man. The knight's action in seizing his horse precisely repeats, from that perspective, his action in seizing the squire, and the congruity of the two events is confirmed when he releases the squire from a debt which has already been settled.

Jacques de Vitry was himself a cleric, who would have respected the absolute authority of both religious and secular institutions, but only, evidently, within their own areas of activity. Once that division has been blurred through pride, individual members of the religious community become subject to the same rules as seculars, and having, as it were, invaded the knight's territory, the monk receives a treatment which appears just in the context of the value system evoked. Since Jacques de Vitry's story is an *exemplum*, we

3 *The Exempla or Illustrative Stories from the Sermones Vulgares of Jacques de Vitry*, ed. T.F. Crane (London, 1890), p. 165. 4 De Vitry, *Exempla*, pp 30–1. 'At miles cepit armigeris dicere "Ecce monachus iste qui debuisset equitare asinum, meliorem habet equum quam ego". Et accedens tenuit equum monachi perfrenum et dixit monacho ...'

expect, even though there is an element of sophistry involved in the narrative's development, that the moral implications will be clear and unequivocal. His story assumes a medieval social order based on the three estates of aristocracy, clergy, and peasantry, in which the aristocracy and clergy at least enjoyed privileges within their own spheres of influence as long as the boundaries between them were not violated. Since the story appears in the *Sermones vulgares*, we can also assume that the audience addressed is the Christian community at large, embracing members of all three social orders.

Another exposition of the theme can be found in a thirteenth-century French fabliau called *Le povre Mercier*. Rather than being clear and unequivocal as in the *exemplum*, the issues affecting religious and secular moral authority are intricate and ambiguous. They can be brought into focus initially by following an account of the events surrounding the central episode.

A poor merchant entrusts his horse to God and the local manorial lord, and prays to God that no one should remove the horse from the pasture where he has been tethered. God, we are told, in the first intrusion of the sophistry which pervades this version of events, did not let him down. The horse did not leave the pasture, but was killed on the spot by a solitary wolf. The merchant appeals to the lord of the manor to be recompensed for his loss, estimated at three pounds, but in another sophistical twist the lord tells him that since the horse was commended to himself and to God for safe keeping, he will pay only thirty shillings. The merchant next encounters a monk, directs to him the familiar question 'A cui estes vos?' (in this context perhaps 'Who do you work for?') and is told that he is a man of God, their common Father in Heaven. The merchant claims his thirty shillings and demands, with threats of violence, the surrender of a pledge, the monk's cape, until the matter can be settled before the local court. The manorial lord, in a further and final manifestation of sophistic logic, offers the monk, who has been expecting a verdict in his favour, a choice of alternatives. He may renounce service to God and Holy Church, in which case he is acquitted of his debt, or honour his vows and pay the thirty shillings. Declaring that he would rather lose forty pounds than deny God, the monk pays up.[5]

In this morass of casuistry neither civic nor ecclesiastic authority is treated with much respect, and any genuine sense of justice is elusive. The merchant accompanies almost every statement he makes with an oath, swearing numerous times by God, the Virgin Mary, the saints, the peril of his soul, his hope for final absolution, his faith in salvation, and his fear of condemnation to the fires of hell, so that ideas of final judgement and divine justice are often evoked. But all these references pay little more than lip service to a religious system which has no perceptible influence on his conduct of a morally suspect civil suit.

5 *Recueil général et complet des fabliaux des XIIIᵉ et XIVᵉ siècles*, ed. A. de Montaiglon and G. Raynaud, 6 vols (Paris, 1872–1890), vol. 2, pp 114–22.

The character supposedly dispensing justice is the manorial lord, governor of a large feudal estate, and a draconian defender of law and order, hanging without the possibility of ransom anyone guilty of criminal behaviour. He has newly been granted licence` to hold a fair, and the fairground setting establishes the context for the narrative in a microcosmic representation of an emergent capitalist society. In the fabliau commercial values govern all matters, including the administration of justice. The manorial lord's role as judge is essentially territorial, but he may also be assuming control of the 'pie-powder' court charged with responsibility for the proper conduct of the fair, and such a role brings with it an automatic commercial bias.

The merchant fits perfectly into this context, and his portrait is a subtle and detailed depiction of one of the humbler members of his class. He cannot afford to pay for stabling, and, aware that there is free grazing available at the fair site, would naturally like to tether his pony there, but fears that it might be stolen. He will not commit to leaving it until assured by a fellow tradesman that such is the manorial lord's reputation for enforcing justice, that entrusted to his safe-keeping the pony can be left in perfect safety. Once the merchant has appealed his loss, and the lord of the manor has restored only half its value, the lord of Heaven becomes to the merchant just another bad debtor. His situation goes some way to explaining his belligerence in dealing with the monk. Caution in attempting to avoid losses, and aggressiveness in attempting to repair such losses should they occur, typify the merchant's life style, and dictate his behaviour in particular circumstances. The manorial lord seems to espouse these values. He limits his own liability by a legal quibble about the original contract, tells the merchant to take up his dispute with God, and although critical of the merchant's haste to seize pledges ultimately renders a judgement in his favour.

The monk appears in all respects to be a worthy member of his religious order, untainted with any display of pomp or vanity. Despite the obvious justness of his cause, judgement, in this mercenary world, is given against him, and in his summary the judge even denies the monk's isolation from the world of commerce, telling him that from now on he can exploit the benefits of charitable donations with greater confidence and a clearer conscience, since he has suffered the loss of thirty shillings on God's behalf. The monastic life, as far as the nobleman and perhaps the author are concerned (the latter names the monk Dan Deniers [master Moneypenny] in the closing lines) is just another form of commercial activity.

Le povre Mercier is one of the few fabliaux to preserve some evidence of oral delivery. The author announces himself as *uns joliz clers*, presumably a literate but unbeneficed cleric. He will tell, he says, an amusing story, and in an oblique reference to the minstrel's plea for silence asserts that a good tale like his deserves to be listened to. He concludes with a prayer for the well-being of those who have heard his story, and of its author, who would appreciate being rewarded with a drink. Rather than a Christian congregation, the audience for *Le povre Mercier* is a group perhaps casually assembled at a tavern, or at the drinking stall of a fair like that depicted in the fictional narrative.

Neither of the two contexts looked at, the three estates of the feudal world in the *exemplum*, or the bourgeois commercialism of the fabliau, is reflected in pure form in the *Gest*, but it incorporates elements of both in a curious *mélange*. There is, for a start, some displacement of roles in the central comic motif of the narrative. In Jacques de Vitry, the person responsible for what passes as justice, and for enforcing the forfeiture of the value of the debt, is a major member of the feudal aristocracy, and the voice of authority by virtue of his rank and privilege. In *Le povre Mercier* the sophistry, although immediately attributable to the humble merchant, is encouraged and defended by a similarly exalted nobleman, whose authority, however, is not a matter of hereditary right but bestowed on him in a civic system of distributive justice by his role as judge of both the manorial and pie-powder courts. In the *Gest* the character who most closely approximates these authority figures is the knight, but he is the debtor rather than the creditor, and implementation of the contractual ploy for recovery of the debt passes to the socially ambiguous 'outlaw' figure of Robin Hood. In place of the aristocratic hegemony of Jacques de Vitry's *exemplum*, the *Gest* presents us with an idea of the noble life which is admirable but impotent. In place of a system of distributive justice capable of governing, in a practically effective if not morally unexceptionable manner, the dynamics of a thriving commercial life, as exemplified in *Le povre Mercier*, the *Gest* depicts a profiteering conspiracy by renegade officials of church and state which can be challenged only from a position outside the recognized authority of law.

How these forces affect the portrayal of characters in the *Gest* can be seen initially in the portrait of the knight, evidently intended as an idealized figure, but presented from a perspective infused with the realities of the commercial world. The knight has an income from his estate of four hundred pounds per annum, enough, but only just enough, to maintain in properly aristocratic fashion a lifestyle commensurate with his position. Faced with an unexpected demand for blood-money incurred by his son, which amounts to a full year's income, he is plunged into economic crisis and forced to resort to moneylenders. When he first encounters Robin Hood and his men, his condition is so wretched that Robin speculates he might have been newly dubbed, but this is hotly denied, the knight claiming that his ancestors have been knights for a hundred years. He is evidently heir to a feudal estate. Land has come into conflict with money, and is momentarily under threat.

There is a commercial cast also to the following scene, wherein the greenwood fellowship unite in their desire to accommodate some of the knight's needs. Little John suggests that Robin, who is richer than any merchant in England, should provide the knight with a livery, and Robin instructs him to give the knight three yards of scarlet and green cloth. A tradesman's perspective underlies this specificity, but it is denied in the execution, since Little John measures the cloth with his bow, and adds three feet each time he gathers a measure, so that Much is prompted to ask, 'What devylles draper [...] Thynkest thou for to be?' (191–2). The real world of commerce is evoked momentarily, but only for the purpose of revealing that the greenwood company is in some manner alienated from its value system by an innate sense of aristocratic *franchise*. This is a recurrent theme in Robin Hood literature, where Robin is not averse to involving himself with the trade of various artisans (witness *Robin Hood and the Potter*, *Robin Hood and the Butcher*), but botches the job because he gives excess measure or undercharges for his goods. Once the livery has been settled, romance conventions dictate the nature of the remaining gifts, and the final act of rehabilitation is to award the knight Little John to act 'in a yeomans stede' (323).

The forces of evil, by contrast, are in the *Gest* emphatically embroiled in the world of commerce. They appear in company, hoping for the non-arrival of the knight whose lands are forfeit if he cannot discharge his debt. A fat-headed monk, the high cellarer of St Mary's Abbey, thinks the knight is dead or hanged, and rejoices in the fact that they will soon have an extra four hundred pounds per year to spend. Also present are the abbot, the high justice, the sheriff, and others who have apparently accepted part of the risk on the loan and stand to profit if the unhappy knight defaults. As a group they brusquely reject all pleas for an extension or any other merciful compromise, their only concession being to offer a token cash settlement when the knight signs over his estate. Having been funded by Robin, the knight can proudly reject this offer. Not for another thousand pounds would abbot, justice or friar be his heir. Land has now triumphed over money, and the corrupt moneylenders are left quarrelling over the final settlement.

The division between a virtuous old order of inherited land and a vicious new commercialism is articulated early in the *Gest* by the code of conduct to which the greenwood fellowship is committed. Protected are husbandmen who plough (the peasantry) and good yeoman, knights and squires (the landed aristocracy and their entourage). The clergy as a social order are not mentioned, but corrupt officials of both church and state are lumped together in common condemnation, bishops and archbishops to be beaten and bound, and the Sheriff of Nottingham to be viewed with suspicion.

A key concept in illustration of this division in the *Gest* is that of *courtesie*, associated with the vocabulary and gestures of the old order, and a touchstone for defection from old values in the commercialism of the contemporary world. When the knight first appears in the greenwood, his rank guarantees immediate respect, despite his poor appearance. Little John ('full curteyes', 93) and Robin both kneel (94, 116) and address him as 'gentyll' and 'hende' knight, and Robin 'Full curtesly dyd of his hode' to 'this gentyl

knight', a nomenclature that is repeated, just as Robin repeats 'sir,' in lines
115–133. The knight even says 'Gramarcy, sir' to Robin (134). Later, when
the knight returns with his four hundred pounds, he bares his head 'so
curteysly' (1051) and kneels to Robin, who responds with friendly respect
(1049–76). The knight wishes to add another twenty marks to his repayment
to reward Robin for his 'curteysy' (1080), but Robin rejects the offer, and
when he learns that the knight has also brought a hundred bows and a hundred peacock-feathered arrows, he orders Little John to give the knight an
extra four hundred pounds stolen from the monk. Two magnanimous characters are vying to outdo one another in *largesse*, to the credit of both parties.

For the monk, by contrast, the concept of courtesy is virtually meaningless. He responds to the knight's courteous greeting with the brutally acquis-
itive 'Hast thou brought my pay?' (411) and the knight later reprimands him
for discourteously keeping his guest kneeling (460). The phrase 'For thy cur-
tesysé' is used with ironic effect as he shows up the ruthless commercialism
of his enemies (430). The monk is equally discourteous to Robin, failing to
reciprocate when Robin doffs his hood in greeting. However, when Robin
inquires as to the cargo of a second packhorse, and the monk becomes aware
that he is to be systematically despoiled, he has the temerity to appeal to
Robin's sense of courtesy in attempting to salvage something from the deba-
cle. By Our Lady, he says, it is not courteous to invite someone for dinner
and then subject them to this kind of coercion (1023–8). But courtesy, the
mutual respect which ideally allowed the various social strata of the old regime
to co-exist harmoniously, has no legitimate place in a callously exploitative
commercial world, nor in the banditry which is the only alternative lifestyle
available to the disaffected, and Robin answers the spurious appeal to courtesy with a quip, 'It is our olde maner […] to leue but lytell behynde' (1027–9).

Only in the context of this hypocritical appeal to standards which he
himself clearly despises does the monk swear by the mother of God (1023),
and the nature of the oaths used by different characters sheds further light
on attitudes towards religious belief in the *Gest*. Unlike the indiscriminate
swearing of the merchant in *Le povre Mercier*, which had the effect of debas-
ing spiritual values altogether, swearing in the *Gest* is systematically differentiated between the different groups of characters. In the early stanzas
Robin's religious allegiances are spelled out in a statement that he always
heard three masses before dining, one to the Father, one to the Holy Ghost,
and one to the Virgin Mary, for whom he felt a particular adoration. It is a
curiously unorthodox trinity from which the son has been excluded, but the
anomaly does not end there. Throughout the romance Robin, the greenwood
fellowship, and the knight, the group representing the feudal values of an
old order, all swear by God the Father, viewed as the creator of the world
and the shaper of man's destiny. Swearing by God among the commercial
fraternity has reference always to God the Son. The high cellarer swears 'by

God that bought me dere', the abbot rejects the knight's appeal for an extension with a similar oath, 'By God that dyed on tree', and the high justice later uses the same oath during the quarrel between the creditors. The distinction is too systematic to be coincidental, but if its reality needed confirmation it can be found in Robin's exchanges with the knight prior to the agreement for a loan. The idiosyncrasy of his attitude towards the trinity emerges forcefully when he asks the knight to suggest a sponsor for the loan, and the knight says he has none, 'But God that dyed on tree'.

> 'Do away thy japis,' than sayde Robyn,
> Thereof wol I right none;
> Wenest thou I wolde have God to borowe,
> Peter, Poule, or John?'   (249–52)

Robin swears 'by Hym that me made, / And shope both sonne and mone' (254), that no money will be forthcoming unless the knight can propose a better sponsor. The knight can suggest only 'Our dere Lady', who suits Robin much better, since he could hope for no better guarantor.

There is a clarity about the attitude towards religious belief that imposes itself on the narrative, although only by assuming some play of irony on the author's part would it be possible to reconcile the fictional system with Christian orthodoxy. Among the greenwood fellowship commitment is to God the Father, creator and ruler of the world, and the figure associated historically with the biblical era of justice and the Old Law. Among the renegade representatives of an emergent profit-based economy allegiance appears to be to God the Son, whose death on the cross initiated the New Covenant and salvation by grace. If there is a connection, it would seem to rest on association of the ideas of original sin and debt, of the redemption of mankind and the redeeming of a loan, but if that is the case the intention must be profoundly ironic, since Christ's sacrifice on the cross is the definitive act of charity, a quality singularly absent from the commercial activities of the abbot and his colleagues.

What certainly emerges with great clarity from the *Gest* is the important role played in such a religious schema by the Virgin Mary. Robin is devoted to her worship, and she plays a part which has no equivalent in the *exemplum* or the fabliau. In both these versions, the theme of recovery of a defaulted loan from a servant of the God invoked as sponsor is pure sophistry. In neither instance is there the remotest suggestion that the monks are agents of the divine will, and that God is settling legitimate claims against Him through their agency.

But that is not the situation with the *Gest*, where the very idea that sophistry is a feature in the despoiling of the monk of St Mary's Abbey is deliberately obfuscated, and the idea allowed to emerge that divine intervention plays a part in the recovery of the loan. While Robin awaits the overdue knight, he expresses concern that anger against him may explain the Virgin's failure to ensure that the money is restored. When the two Benedictine monks and their entourage are first spotted, Little John speculates that they might have brought their pay. The surviving monk acknowledges that he is high cellarer of St Mary's Abbey and a servant to the Virgin, and, since he has appeared on the day that the four hundred pound loan was due to be repaid, Robin is convinced that he is the Virgin's messenger. When Little John discovers that the monk, although claiming to have only spending-silver, is in fact carrying eight hundred pounds, he says the Virgin has doubled Robin's investment, and when the delayed knight eventually shows up prepared to honor his debt, Robin tells him to keep the money and use it well, 'For Our Lady, by her selerer / Hath sent to me my pay' (1083–84). By a strange twist for which no precedent exists in the two earlier versions examined, repayment of the debt has become less a matter of sophistical expediency, and something approaching a *miracle de la vierge*.

In following the theme from Jacques de Vitry's *exemplum* through the anonymous French fabliau we have established a literary context from which to view its appearance in what generically should be classified as pastoral romance. The vision of the greenwood fellowship which emerges is not radically different from that expected had we begun with the conventions of that particular literary genre, which dictates to a large extent the nature of Robin Hood's 'outlaw' society. There is about it an element of criminality, as there is in the *exemplum* an element of autocracy, but both tend to be subsumed into paradox. In a society where legal institutions have become irremediably corrupt, true justice may find its expression only in what would otherwise be an outlaw band. In a religious system similarly corrupted by the concupiscence of its secular representatives, true faith may require direct correspondence through prayer with a divinity conceived as actively participant through miracle in everyday human affairs. In a commercialised society, true 'curtesye' is found in the outlaws: the disguised Little John calls his master, 'A curteys knight' (602), deceptively but also with deep truth. Robin Hood and the greenwood fellowship exhibit some qualities of an outlaw band, but their significance is probably better understood as a kind of government in exile. As such they are certainly not revolutionaries preparing the way for the implementation of some new order but profoundly conservative proponents of an anachronistic social system. As yeomen they support the ideals of what, in normal circumstances, would be their aristocratic masters, but the corrupt officialdom of a burgeoning profit-based economy has driven them into exile, where they wage guerilla warfare against the current regime and await the restoration of a system sympathetic to the ideals of a statically hierarchical society. It is within the households of the lesser landed aristocracy that such a vision would elicit the most enthusiastic response, and it is to such an audience that *The Gest of Robyn Hode* was probably directed.

Merchant adventure in *Robin Hood and the Potter*

THOMAS H. OHLGREN

After opening with the traditional springtime theme and a request for the audience to 'Herkens', the poet-narrator of *Robin Hood and the Potter* offers a variation of 'Robin Hood meets his match'.[1] Observing the approach of a 'prowd' potter on the road, Robin reports that this frequent traveller has failed to pay the road-toll ('pavage,' literally paving toll) charged by the outlaws. Little John responds that when he previously tried to exact payment ('wed') he was soundly beaten, and he wagers 40 shillings that no one can make him pay up. Robin accepts the wager, stops the potter on the road, and demands payment. The potter refuses, grabs his staff, and knocks Robin and his buckler to the ground. After offering the potter a 'felischepe', which is the customary resolution of the meets-his-match episode, Robin next proposes that they exchange clothing so that he can venture undetected into Nottingham, ostensibly to sell the potter's pots. After Little John warns him about the sheriff, Robin proceeds to Nottingham, where he stables his horse and sets himself up next to the sheriff's gate in the marketplace. Robin-the-Potter shows his wares, shouting: 'Pottys! Pottys! [...]Haffe hansell for the mare' ('Get a free gift the more you buy!'), 127–8. The wives and widows quickly gather around him and purchase the pots at a bargain. Everyone says he must not have been a potter long because he is selling pots worth five pence for only three. Men and women privately observe 'Ywnder potter schall never the', 140.

At first sight this scene appears to be, as Stephen Knight has suggested, a parody of mercantile practices; that is, Robin is 'a comically bad marketeer' in selling the pots at a ridiculously low price and the folk of Nottingham are 'canny' in taking advantage of such an incompetent fool. The poem then reveals, opines Knight, the poet's distrust of the new social formation of towns and trades.[2] While I agree that there is humour in this scene, I think that it is self-directed and self-deprecating rather than imposed from outside. That is, the minstrel/poet of this version of the story has refashioned a traditional 'ryme' for an audience interested in mercantile matters. And, as I have argued elsewhere, some of the early Robin Hood poems were very likely recited aloud at the social events sponsored by a merchant guild, possibly as entertainment at its annual election dinner. These recited poems, with their carnivalesque irreverence towards guild leaders, policies, and practices, remind readers of the modern-day celebrity 'roast' at a fraternal or

---

1 Text in *RHOOT*, pp 57–79.   2 Knight, *A complete study*, pp 54–5.

charity dinner, such as the man-of-the-year award given by the Hasty
Pudding Theatricals at Harvard University.[3] It is easy to miss the poet's
ironic tone because he lets us see Robin's salesmanship only from the point
of view of the wives and widows crowding around his stall (too?) eager for
a bargain.[4] What appears to be incompetence is in fact premeditated merchant craftiness, an essential element of merchant adventure. By knocking
down the price of the pots, Robin sets in motion a series of events calculated
to humiliate his enemy, the Sheriff of Nottingham. The ruse begins when
Robin, disguised as the potter, gives the five remaining pots to the sheriff's
wife, who, obviously impressed with his generosity, invites him to have dinner
with the sheriff and her. After dinner follows a shooting match, which Robin-
the-Potter wins by splitting the target into three pieces. When he brags that
he has one of Robin Hood's bows in his cart, the sheriff takes the bait and
eagerly follows him into the forest the following day. Once they arrive in the
forest, Robin-the-Potter reveals his true identity and robs the sheriff of his
horse and other gear. To add insult to injury, Robin-the-Potter further humil-
iates the sheriff by courting his wife right under his nose. While the poem
only hints at their romantic relationship, the fact that he not only gives her
three sets of gifts (the five pots, a gold ring, and a white palfrey) but twice
declares his 'loffe' for her, strongly suggests that the sturdy outlaw is appropriating the role of the aristocratic courtly lover.

The marketplace scene in *Robin Hood and the Potter* has broader significance because it is but one example of merchant adventure that underlies
the entire poem. In *Ideology of Adventure*, cultural critic Michael Nerlich
describes how the concept of adventure evolved over time from the French
medieval court of Chrétien de Troyes to the capitalist economies of western
Europe in the eighteenth century.[5] Nerlich marks the decisive moment when
the knightly *queste d'aventure*, as idealized in the courtly romances of the

---

3 See Thomas H. Ohlgren, 'The "Marchaunt" of Sherwood: mercantile ideology in *A
Gest of Robyn Hode*,' in Hahn, pp 175–90.   4 This reading is reinforced by the Percy
version of *Robin Hood and the Butcher*, which is based on the earlier *Robin Hood and the
Potter*. Like Robin-the-Potter, Robin-the-Butcher knocks down the price of his meat to
attract buyers and his customers 'drew about the younge bucher / Like sheepe into a
fold'. For the text, see Child, vol. 3, no. 122, pp 115–20. Crafty tradesmen and gullible
consumers also figure prominently in the Latin poem, *Descriptio Norfolciensium*, which is
a satirical attack on the people of Norfolk who had a reputation for being simpletons. Of
the various examples of gullibility and stupidity, several concern marketplace activities.
In one episode a father and son go to the market, and when the son sees a meal cake, he
asks his father what it is. The father replies that it is food for the sick and it does no
good to those who are well! In another episode a Norfolk man's dog eats a jar of honey.
The man squeezes the dog until it vomits up the honey which he places in a jar and offers
for sale in the market. When a customer tells him it is putrid, he replies that it has been
in a smelly jar. Since the *Potter* manuscript was very likely written in Norfolk, it may
reflect this local tradition.   5 Michael Nerlich, *Ideology of adventure: studies in modern
consciousness, 1100–1750*, vol. 1 (Minneapolis, 1987).

twelfth and thirteenth centuries, was transformed into merchant adventure in the fourteenth and fifteenth centuries. The transformation from feudal to mercantile culture involved the gradual refashioning or 're-functioning' of the virtues celebrated in courtly ideology: martial prowess, voluntary daring, quest for unpredictable risk, loyalty to a revered lady, solidarity of the group, and largess. These behaviours and values were conserved, imitated, and appropriated by the urban merchant and artisan classes, not as class flattery or emulation, but as part of a complex dialectical process whose goal was competition with and domination of the feudal nobility.[6] Robin Hood acts as if he were knightly by undertaking the risky adventure in Nottingham, by showing his martial prowess in the archery match, by displaying his largess in extravagant gift-giving and in presenting the real potter ten pounds for pots worth much less, and by pursuing the romantic encounter with a married woman, the sheriff's wife. And he proves his superiority to the sheriff – the poem's representative of the lesser nobility – by cleverly enticing him into the forest where he is humiliated and robbed. The poem then is not only an artistic depiction of the struggle between bourgeois and courtly ideologies but an exploration of the values that underlie both, and these values are expressed and developed primarily in the following economic terms: the language of the marketplace, arithmetic specificity, the doctrine of just price, mercantile speculation, and the exchange value of commodities.

The language of the marketplace permeates the poem. There are over fifty words denoting money, buying, selling, merchandise, and other forms of exchange. The nouns include denominations of currency [*pens* and *peney* (both are used), *nobellys, shillings, ponde*]; money [*money*, 33, 317]; merchandise [*ware*, 126, 132, 263], goods [*goddes, god*, 281, 298, 307], trade [*chaffare*, 130, 267]; bargain [*chepe*, 133]; payments [*wed*, 28, 32, 48, 49], toll [*pavage*, 20, 44, 46, 50]; gambling [*ley*, 25, 32, bet [*wager*, 80, 168, 172]; profits [*gayne*, 172, *won*, 80, *the* (thrive), 140]; reward [*queyt*, 230]. The verbs include: buy (*bey*, 148, *chepe*, 104, 132); gain (*gayne*, 172); give (*geffe*, l. 161); *leyde*, i.e. pay (33); *pay* (20, 26, 28, 32, 44, 50, 304); purchase (*chepyd* 132); *sell* (99, 114, 135, 141, 263); *show* goods (126, 130); and *spende* (251). There is even the cry of the seller in the marketplace: '"Pottys! Pottys!" he gan crey foll sone' and again, '"Pottys, gret chepe!" creyed Robyn' (127, 133).

How many pots did Robin sell? And how much were they worth? The answers to both questions can be easily calculated given the arithmetic details in the poem. Robin sells pots worth 5 pence for 3 pence (137–8), which represents a forty per cent reduction in the retail price. He quickly sells all but five pots which he 'gives' to the sheriff's wife as part of his plan to avenge himself on the sheriff. We later find out from the potter in line 312 that the pots were worth a total of 2 nobles (a noble being a gold coin worth 6*s*., 8*d*.)

6 Nerlich, *Ideology*, pp 51–75, esp. pp 60–7.

or 13*s*. 4*d*. If we assume that each pot is worth 5 pence, then Robin had a total of 32 pots (160*d*. divided by 5 = 32). Of these 27 were sold in the marketplace for 81*d*. (27 x 3*d*. = 81), and the remaining 5 pots, worth 25*d*., were given to the sheriff's wife. The inclusion of such monetary details would of course be lost on an audience not interested in such matters.

The poem also explores a number of economic concepts. By selling his pots at forty per cent below the fixed market value, Robin is violating the doctrine of just price, which was the 'scholastic notion that the 'value' of a commodity was the price at which it *ought* to sell on the market in favour of the idea that it was the price at which it actually *did* sell.'[7] Based ultimately on the political philosophy of Aristotle, this doctrine, along with prohibitions against usury, formed the cornerstone of medieval economic theory as expounded by Thomas Aquinas in the *Summa Theologica*: 'To sell for more or to buy for less than a thing is worth, is, therefore, unjust and illicit in itself.'[8] By selling pots worth five pence for three pence, Robin challenges the right of the local authorities to engage in anti-competitive and monopolistic price-fixing. He furthermore recognizes that competition based on lower prices will attract more customers, and he is right: 'Weyffes and wedowes abowt hem drow, / And chepyd fast of hes ware' (131–2).

Robin also undertakes a speculative business transaction – selling the pots at a loss – in the anticipation of greater gain – the robbery of the sheriff. His gain is so great, in fact, that he can afford to repay the potter ten pounds for pots worth only two nobles (316). Knight sees in Robin's generosity a reminder of feudal consciousness, which is an accurate observation, but I think the virtue of largess has been fully appropriated by the successful merchant in this poem.[9] The 'gift' of ten pounds is in fact a repayment with interest of the initial exchange of identities and pots. It is not usurious because the lender (the real potter) asked for no more in return than his original investment. For an economic exchange to take place there has to be reciprocal giving and receiving of a commodity of equal value. Since the change of identity leads to such a large return on his investment, Robin is simply completing the transaction with the real potter.

That this speculation is pre-meditated is seen at the moment when Robin switches identities with the real potter:

> 'And then Y bescro mey hede,
> Yeffe Y bryng eney pottys ayen,
> And eney weyffe well hem chepe'.   (102–4)

---

7 Phyllis Deane, *The evolution of economic ideas* (Cambridge, 1978), p. 3.   8 St Thomas Aquinas, *Summa Theologiæ*, ed. Marcus Lefébure, OP, vol. 38 (London, 1975), quoted in Robert B. Ekelund, Jr. and Robert F. Hebert, *A history of economic theory and method* (New York, 1975), pp 26–7.   9 Knight, *A complete study*, p. 55.

Knightly adventure also involves risk-taking but it is often unpremeditated and based on fate or blind luck; that is, knights often search for adventure not knowing what will happen next.[10] It is a form of speculation or gambling without figuring if the odds are in your favour. Robin in fact fails at gambling at the beginning of the poem when he hastily bets Little John 40 shillings that he can make the potter pay road toll. After he is defeated by the potter, Little John asks him: 'Schall Y haffe yowre forty shillings?' (81). Robin thus learns an important economic lesson – merchant adventure or economic speculation must be accompanied by a reasoned calculation of the risks involved. Robin-Potter later puts theory into practice when he enters and wins the archery match. Like the previous encounter, there is a wager, but this time Robin relies on his self-confidence and skill and wins the prize of 40 shillings, which is the exact amount lost in the first failed wager. While the outcome of the tournament is uncertain, Robin greatly increases his odds of winning by relying upon his archery prowess rather than on blind luck. Gambling then becomes a metaphor for describing the diffuse operations of the speculative marketplace.

Another economic concept concerns the exchange value of commodities. As defined by the *OED*, exchange refers to the 'action, or an act of reciprocal giving and receiving'. That is, something (money or commodity) is exchanged for something else of equal value. Like the theory of just price, the concept of exchange value was formulated by Aristotle (*Politics* Book I, Chap. 9):

> Of everything which we possess there are two uses; both belong to the thing as such, but not in the same manner, for one is the proper, and the other the improper or secondary use of it. For example, a shoe is used for wear, and is used for exchange; both are uses of the shoe.[11]

Likewise, pots can be used for use, i.e., cooking or storing food, or they can be used for exchange, i.e. sold or bartered for money or another commodity of equal value. And, as we have seen, Robin recognizes that the pots, particularly those given to the sheriff's wife, have greater value in exchange than in use because they result in a greater return on his investment. This return is two-fold. First, as we have seen, the gift of pots leads to Robin's capture and robbery of the sheriff in the forest. When Little John asks Robin 'How haffe yow solde yowre ware?', he answers 'Ye' and adds 'Y haffe browt the

---

10 At the beginning of 'A Noble Tale of Sir Lancelot du Lake' Lancelot sets forth from Camelot with no apparent purpose in mind other than 'hymself to preve in straunge adventures'. Accompanied by his nephew, Sir Lyonell, 'they mounted on their horses, armed at all ryghtes, and rode into a depe foreste and so into a playne', Malory, *Works*, ed. Eugène Vinaver (Oxford, 1971), p. 149. 11 *Aristotle's Politics and Poetics*, trans. Benjamin Jowett and Thomas Twining (New York, 1957), p. 15.

screffe of Notynggam, / For all howre chaffare', 263, 266–7. The word 'chaffare' here means 'trade' or 'business.' The sheriff is being viewed in economic terms – he is one of the commodities that Robin exchanged the pots for. Second, the other commodity is the sheriff's wife. Upon receiving the five pots, the wife invites Robin-Potter to dinner: 'Foll corteysley sche gan hem call, / Com deyne with the screfe and me', 151–2. Afterwards, he spends the night in the sheriff's house before taking him into the forest the next morning. When one considers similar plot elements in Chaucer's *Reeve's Tale* – in which the Cambridge students avenge themselves against the crooked miller by sleeping with his wife and daughter – the likelihood of a sexual encounter in the poem was probably assumed by the audience.[12] Interestingly, both works feature a parody of the *aubade* – song celebrating the lovers parting at dawn. When Aleyn awakened in the morning after having 'swonken al the longe nyght', he bids Malyne 'Fare weel, Malyne, sweete wight! / The day is come; I may no lenger byde; / But everemo, wher so I go o ryde, / I is thyn awen clerk, swa have I seel', 4235–9. Likewise, when Robin 'toke leffe of the screffys wyffe' in the morning (238) he gave her a gold ring 'for mey loffe'.[13] And after robbing the sheriff, Robin asks him to greet his wife and sends her a white palfrey as another gift. He reminds the sheriff that his sorrow would have been worse if it had not been 'for the loffe of yowre weyffe', 288. The equation between money and sex culminates when the sheriff, stripped of his goods, returns home and is greeted by his wife who offers herself to him as 'goods' – 'Ye schall haffe god ynowe' (307). The use of such puns reminds us of the end of Chaucer's *Shipman's Tale* when the adulterous wife, in an attempt to pacify her cuckolded merchant husband, offers to repay him with sex: 'I am youre wyf; score it upon my taille, / And I shal paye as soone as ever I may', 416–17.[14]

To account for the dominant theme of merchant adventure in *Robin Hood and the Potter*, we only have to consider its manuscript context. The unique text of the poem is located on folios 14v to 19v of Cambridge University Library MS Ee.4.35.1, a slender miscellany of secular and religious texts, a

---

12 In *The Reeve's Tale* the Cambridge students, John and Aleyn, are forced to spend the night in the cramped quarters of the miller's house. To avenge the miller's outrageous theft of half a peck of corn they have sex with his wife and daughter, Malyne. Here the revenge is clearly motivated by the miller's flagrant dishonesty, while in *Robin Hood and the Potter* the cause of Robin's animosity towards the sheriff is not specified. Little John, however, alludes to a prior confrontation when he warns Robin to 'be well ware of the screffe of Notynggam, / For he ys leytell howr frende'. See *The Riverside Chaucer*, ed. Larry D. Benson (Boston and Oxford, 1987), I(A), ll. 107–8. **13** See ll. 4234–40. **14** Under the entry for *chaffare* ('goods' or 'wares'), Thomas W. Ross observes, 'Chaucer's most amusing use of the word is in the "Shipman's Tale" (B 1475), when the rich merchant promises not only his gold to Daun John but his "chaffare" as well. As a matter of fact, the good monk gets both: the money and the wife herself, a nice piece of the merchant's "chaffare"', *Chaucer's bawdy* (New York, 1972), p. 55.

number of which also have strong mercantile themes.[15] At the bottom of folio 5v, for instance, is a four-line poem in the form of a word puzzle warning against loaning money to a friend:

> I had mey god and mey ffrende   *goods*
> lent mey good to mey ffrende
> axyd mey god off mey ffrende
> I lost me good and mey ffrende.[16]

On folio 21 is an arithmetical problem in prose:

> In Ynglond ther ys a schepcote the wyche schepekote hayt ix dorys and at yowy dor standet ix lamys and ewy ram gat ix ewys and yony ewe hathe ix lambys and yeny lambe hayt ix hornes and eny horne hayt ix tyndes and what ys the some of all thes bestes?

> [In England there is a sheepfold which has 9 doors and at each door stands 9 lambs (rams?) and each ram has 9 ewes and each ewe has 9 lambs and each lamb has 9 horns and each horn has 9 tines and what is the sum of all these beasts?][17]

On folio 14v is a full-page inventory of the foodstuffs served at the wedding banquet 'off mey ladey margret that sche had owt off eynglonde'. The Cambridge library catalogue identifies the event as 'the marriage of Margaret Tudor, sister of Henry VIII, which took place at Edinburgh, August 8, 1503', but this attribution is incorrect. There is another royal marriage that has much closer ties to the manuscript and to its owner, whom I have identified as Richard Call, grocer and bailiff of the gentry family in Norfolk, the Pastons. The marriage being described is that of Charles Duke of Burgundy and Margaret, the youngest sister of King Edward IV, on July 3, 1468 in Bruges. The Paston brothers, both named John, attended the wedding as

15 For descriptions of the manuscript, see *A Catalogue of the Manuscripts Preserved in the Library of the University of Cambridge*, 5 vols + index (Cambridge, 1856–67); vol. 2 (1867), pp 167–9. There is also an unpublished handwritten description by Mr Pink, a former librarian at Cambridge University Library. I have also consulted Melissa M. Furrow's description in her edition of *Jack and his Stepdame, ten fifteenth-century comic poems* (New York & London, 1985), pp 75–7. For more detailed discussion of the Cambridge manuscript and its connection to the Pastons, see my article, 'Richard Call, the Pastons, and the manuscript context of *Robin Hood and the Potter*', *Nottingham Medieval Studies* 45 (2001), 210–33.   16 For a list of the six other versions of this word puzzle see Carleton Brown and Rossell Hope Robbins, *The index of Middle English verse* (New York, 1943), no. 1297. The Harley 116 version adds the two verses: 'I made of my ffrend my ffoo:/ I will be war I do no more soo'; see Rossell Hope Robbins, *Secular lyrics of the XIVth and XVth centuries*, 2nd ed. (Oxford,1955), no. 87.   17 This is an exercise in multiplication and addition; the answer is 7380.

members of the retinue of the Duchess of Norfolk, who served as the chief lady attendant of the princess. The Pastons became acquainted with the young princess in 1461 when she and her brothers lived in the Paston's property in Southwark. While it is not clear if Richard Call actually attended the wedding, the surviving inventory of foodstuffs and livestock taken to Bruges is precisely the type of record that he was required to keep in his own hand as estate agent for the Paston family.[18]

The identification of Richard Call as the manuscript's owner is confirmed by the presence of the inscription, *Iste liber constat Ricardo Calle*, and the large merchant's mark on folio 24b. An early form of trademark, and later coat of arms, the merchant's mark uniquely identified a tradesman's merchandise. The identical mark is inscribed on a house in Norwich, Norfolk, dated 1566, but it can be traced back to Richard Call through the marriage of his niece, Alice Call, to Henry Bacon.[19] That Call was considered too bourgeois for the family is seen in the letters condemning his secret marriage to the 'boss's daughter' Margery Paston. Expressing the family's outrage, John Paston III wrote that Call 'shold neuer haue my good wyll for to make my sustyr to selle kandyll and mustard in Framly[n]gham' (Davis no. 332).

In addition to *Robin Hood and the Potter*, two other verse tales in the manuscript concern flattering portraits of tradesmen or merchants. F.J. Child describes a dozen or so versions of one of them, *The King and the Barker*, noting that next to Robin Hood 'the most favorite topic in English popular is the chance-encounter of a king, unrecognized as such, with one of his humbler subjects'.[20] The poem follows the familiar pattern: out hunting and separated from his entourage, the King of England encounters a commoner, strikes up a conversation with him, invites him to ride with him, and pumps him for information about one of the local lords. After meeting Lord Bassett, the king proposes that they go hunting, and requests that they exchange horses. The tanner, unable to control the king's stallion, is thrown off, which greatly amuses the king. In the end the king thanks the tanner for his service and gives him 100 shillings. A good deal of the humor lies in the fact that the tanner is unaware of the real identity of his companion, and his pugnacious replies to questions put to him by the king would have been shocking to the audience. For instance, when the king asks that the tanner show him the way, he rudely replies 'What, devell! art þou owt off they wet? Y most hom to mey deynere, ffor y am ffastyng yet'. And when the king promises to give him dinner if he accompanies him, he responds, 'Y trow Y hafe mor

18 Call not only kept similar accounts himself (Davis, no. 645, no. 703) but he used the same listing technique by Item (Davis no. 683, no. 759). For the documents see Norman Davis, *Paston letters and papers of the fifteenth century*, 2 vols (Oxford, 1971).   19 For a reproduction of the mark, see Edward M. Elmhirst, *Merchants' marks* (London, 1959), p. 17.   20 Child, vol. 5, pp 67–75. Child includes the text of *The King and the Barker*, 78–81.

money yn mey pors / nar thow hast yn theyne'. There are also several mercantile elements in the tale. When the king inquires about any tidings or news
that he might have, he answers in specifically commercial terms: 'I know no
tidings other than cow-hides are the dearest merchandise'. The king then asks
if the tanner knows Lord Bassett, and he answers that such a person never
bought any shoe leather from him. The tanner also zealously guards his merchandise – when the king proposes that they exchange horses, he transfers
the cow-hides to the king's saddle, which is a source of great amusement to
the king. While some humour is directed at the tanner, all in all the poet finds
admirable his independence, resourcefulness, and self-confidence.

The other piece is *The Cheylde and hes Stepdame*, on ff. 6v–13v, also
known as *The Frere and the Boy* and *Jack and his Stepdame*. It survives in
five manuscripts and in five early prints.[21] The story relates how Jake is mistreated by his malevolent stepmother, who begrudges the poor boy a decent
meal. When the boy is forced to work in the fields, he shares his meager food
with an old man who responds by giving him three magic gifts: a bow that
will never miss the mark; a musical pipe that causes those hearing it to dance;
and the ability to make his stepmother fart when she menacingly stares at
him. Jake uses the three gifts to avenge himself against his stepmother and
her accomplice, the friar Capias, who plots to beat him. The friar orders the
boy to appear in ecclesiastical court. Standing before the official, the friar
accuses Jake of necromancy, while the stepmother adds that the boy is a
witch. All of a sudden the stepmother's tail begins to blow loudly, and the
onlookers laugh. The friar then explains to the official that the boy has a
pipe that causes people to dance. Asking to see the pipe, the official tries to
blow it but it doesn't make a sound. He then orders Jake to play the pipe,
and upon doing so they all begin dancing wildly. The official begs Jake to
stop playing, promising to give him whatever he wants. After Jake stops playing, the official blesses him and gives him twenty shillings. Jake goes home
never to be mistreated by his stepmother again, and he grows up to become
a worthy merchant: 'a man of gret degre'. It is interesting to note that the
ending is unique to the Cambridge version of the story, which suggests that
the poet/scribe modified the ending of his copy text to reflect the mercantile interests of his audience.[22]

Robin Hood's robbery of the sheriff reminds us, finally, that thievery
itself is a form of economic activity. This idea appears to lie behind one of
the dozen or so proverbs collected by Joseph Ritson: 'To sell Robin Hood's
pennyworths'.[23] As Dobson and Taylor suggest, the saying refers generally
to a bargain, but it also implies that the commodity being sold was stolen.[24]
Seen in the context of mercantile adventure, robbery symbolizes capitalist

21 Text in Furrow, *Ten fifteenth-century comic tales*, pp 67–154. 22 See Furrow, *Ten fif-teenth-century comic tales*, pp 144–8. 23 Ritson, pp 85–6. 24 *RRH*, 291.

competition and exploitation, thereby anticipating Karl Marx by some four hundred years.

Because other versions of the outlaw's potter disguise survive, the basic storyline was not original to our poet. Other heroes such as Hereward the Wake, Eustache the Monk, and William Wallace used the disguise in order to infiltrate the enemy's base of operations, but *Robin Hood and the Potter* differs from the other stories in configuring 'god yeomanry' as merchant adventure.[25] As the *novus homo*, Robin Hood competes with and dominates the petty nobility – represented by the Sheriff of Nottingham – by using his brain rather than brawn. The new battlefield in English culture is the marketplace.

25 For translations of the thirteenth-century Latin *Gesta Herwardi* and the Old French romance, *Li Romans de Witasse le Moine*, dated 1284, and the Middle Scots *Acts and Deeds of Sir William Wallace*, dated 1488, see *Medieval outlaws: ten tales in modern English*, ed. Thomas H. Ohlgren (Stroud, 1978). The potter episodes occur on pp 47–9, 80–1, and 272–3.

'Oublïe ai chevalerie': Tristan, Malory, and the outlaw-knight

TIMOTHY S. JONES

Most histories of medieval outlaw narratives have concentrated on Robin
Hood and the expression of peasant discontent, to the exclusion of other
texts. Stories concerning the Anglo-Saxon Earl Godwin who was outlawed
by Edward the Confessor in 1051 are a striking example of an omission, as
are the various versions of the Tristan story. Maurice Keen makes passing
reference to the former in his *The Outlaws of Medieval Legend*, but apparently disregards him because of the lack of a single substantial text narrat-
ing his outlawry.[1] Tristan, on the other hand, is snubbed because he seems
too clearly the fictional product of courtly romance, and, without a clear basis
in history, his story stands apart from the *Gesta Herewardi*, *Fouke le fitz
Waryn*, *Eustace the Monk* and Blind Hary's *Wallace*. Moreover, as a romance
with all the trappings of chivalry and courtly love Tristan is a part of the
cultural machinery of the nobility, a distinct drawback when modern readers of outlaw tales prefer more radical protagonists. Yet it is Robin Hood
who is the exception within medieval outlaw tradition: Godwin, Fouke,
Hereward, and Eustace are all members of the nobility and their grievances,
the ownership of property and ancestral privilege, are those of the nobility.
In their stories we see that outlaw narratives are not the sole preserve of
oppressed classes and marginal communities, but rather a literature which
develops along all sorts of boundaries of value, within as well as between,
social classes. From this perspective, we should not ignore Tristan but ask
how the narrative of outlawry complies with the discourse of romance and
the desires, interests and anxieties of its audience.

In his discussion of *Fouke le Fitz Waryn*, Keen also comments that by
the thirteenth century the elements of the outlaw legend, the solitary hero
in the forest, or the outlawed band, living and fighting by cleverness and
deception, in opposition to the forces of authority in their society, and those
of romance, knights living and fighting within a courtly society according to
the rules of chivalric behaviour, 'are beginning to find literary partnership

---

1 Keen, pp 1–2, considers that to knights in romance the forest is 'dangerous no-man's
land' while for Robin Hood it is 'sanctuary'. Other histories of the subject include Joost
de Lange, *The relation and development of English and Icelandic outlaw traditions* (Haarlem,
1935), Ingrid Benecke, *Der Gute Outlaw* (Tübingen, 1973), and Holt. Thomas Ohlgren's
recent anthology, *Medieval outlaws: ten tales in modern English* (Stroud, 1998), includes
Godwin but not Tristan.

uncomfortable.'² After *Fouke*, he claims, the two part company and become separate genres, romance being the literature of the court, the outlaw story that of the countryside. An initial glance at the development of the Tristan story would appear to support this claim. In the twelfth and thirteenth-century poetic versions of the Tristan story we discover similarities of narrative structure and characterization with the outlaw stories of Godwin, Hereward, Fouke, Gamelyn and Robin Hood.³ The cleverness of the outlaw, the deception of the ruler, and the flight to the forest are all primary motifs, many of which derive from older folk literature. But when we turn to the prose *Roman de Tristan*, which appeared shortly after the poetic versions (probably around 1230–40) and culminated in England with Sir Thomas Malory's *Morte Darthur* ('The Book of Sir Tristram de Lyones'), we find that many of these elements are lost or subdued. But rather than exposing a gradual divorce between the literature of romance and outlawry over time, as Keen argues, this essay contends that the history of the Tristan story chronicles a rewriting of the outlaw narrative to interrogate competing chivalric values.

Although the earliest evidence of the Tristan story is the name of a Pictish king, Drust, son of Talorc, who ruled in the north of Scotland in the late eighth century,⁴ the prototype for subsequent romances emerged in the middle of the twelfth century.⁵ Between 1150 and 1210 several poems were composed which are commonly divided into two families: the *version commune*, including the poems of Eilhart von Oberg and Béroul; and the *version courtoise*, including those of Thomas d'Angleterre and Gottfried von Strassburg.⁶ These two versions differed significantly in their treatment of the love potion and the adulterous relationship of the lovers.⁷ Unlike Béroul

---

2 Keen, p. 39.   3 The tricks of Tristan have been commented on most recently by Merritt R. Blakeslee, *Love's masks: identity, intertextuality, and meaning in the Old French Tristan poems* (Cambridge, 1989) and Maureen Fries, 'Indiscreet objects of desire: Malory's "Tristram" and the necessity of deceit', in *Studies in Malory*, ed. James W. Spisak (Kalamazoo, 1985), pp 87–108.   4 This material has been often repeated and summarized, notably by Helaine Newstead, 'The origin and growth of the Tristan legend', in R.S. Loomis (ed.), *Arthurian literature in the Middle Ages* (Oxford, 1959), pp 122–33; Robert J. Blanch in 'The history and progress of the Tristan legend: Drust to Malory', *Revue des langues vivantes* 35 (1969), 129–35; and Sigmund Eisner, *The Tristan legend: a study in sources* (Evanston, 1969).   5 Joseph Bédier proposed the existence of this text in *Le Roman de Tristan par Thomas*, Société des anciens textes français 53, 2 vols (Paris, 1902–5) and attempted to reconstruct it from the poems of Béroul, Thomas and Eilhart (vol. 2, 194–306). He concluded that Eilhart had best preserved what has come to be called the *Estoire*, but that both Eilhart and Béroul depended on an intertext (y) which limited the effect of the potion. For a summary of criticism, see Frederick Whitehead, 'The early Tristan poems' in Loomis, *Arthurian literature*, pp 134–44.   6 Eilhard von Oberg, *Tristrant*, ed. Danielle Buschinger, (Göppingen, 1976); Eilhart von Oberge, *Tristrant*, trans. J.W. Thomas (Lincoln, Nebraska, 1978); Beroul, *Tristan and Yseut*, ed. and trans. Guy R. Mermier, (New York, 1987); Thomas, *Les fragments des Roman de Tristan, poème de XIIᵉ siècle*, ed. Bartina Wind (Geneva, 1960).   7 See Jean Frappier,

and Eilhart, Thomas placed no limitation on the duration of the potion. Thus while Eilhart's Tristrant is overwhelmed by his sin and repents as soon as the four years are up, Thomas' hero feels no such remorse. The love affair of the *version courtoise* seems much more acceptable to the poet, probably because of its accord with the rules of courtly love.[8] But the *version commune* is generally more coarse than the *courtoise* in many ways. The lovers are clever rather than courtly characters, and they resort to many more mean tricks. At the trial of Isolt, for instance, Beroul describes Tristan getting revenge on some of the jealous nobles by dunking them in the bog (lines 3788–878) and later ambushing Denoalen in a thicket (lines 4381–93). In contrast, the *courtoise* grants revenge in a tournament.

These clever deceptions, especially verbal tricks and disguises which Keen equates with the outlaw tale and finds antithetical to the spirit of romance, appear frequently in the twelfth-century versions of the story and, as Gertrude Schoepperle has shown, are echoes of wide-spread 'popular traditions'. The story of the blades around the bed and the footprints in the flour, for instance, are common in folktales of the 'master thief' variety, appearing as early as Herodotus.[9] In these stories, when the thief discovers that he has been marked, he marks all the others to hide his guilt. Given this relationship to popular tradition, it does not surprise us to find the same sorts of episodes associated with Tristan, the historical outlaws, and Robin Hood.

A common trick, for instance, is the deception of the authoritarian antagonist through the play of ambiguous, often figurative, language. In Béroul's poem, for instance, when the barons begin to plot against her, Isolde arranges a trial by ordeal in order to prove her innocence. She sends word to Tristan to disguise himself as a leper and wait at the ford near the site of the ordeal. On the appointed day she orders the leper to carry her across the stream and then swears,

> Q'entre mes cuises n'entra home,
> Fors le ladre qui fist soi some,
> Qui me porta outre les guez,
> Et li rois Marc mes esposez.
>
> (4205–8)[10]

'Structure et sens du *Tristan*: version commune, version courtoise', *Cahiers du Civilisation Médiévale* 6 (1963), 255–80, 441–54. **8** An interesting alternative is posed by John H. Fisher, 'Tristan and courtly adultery', *Comparative Literature* 9 (1957), 150–64, who believes the adultery is evidence of matrilineal succession in the Pictish society which gave birth to the legend. **9** Gertrude Schoepperle, *Tristan and Isolt: a study of the sources of romance*, 2nd ed., 2 vols (New York, 1963), vol. 1, 213–21. For a more complete discussion of Tristan as a trickster see Blakeslee. **10** 'that between my thighs no man entered, / Except for this leper who acted as a beast of burden, / Who carried me beyond the ford, / And King Mark, my husband'.

She repeats this duplicity when she protests her innocence after the infamous tryst under the tree: the Middle English version, *Sir Tristrem*, says, 'Y loued neuer man wiþ mode / Bot him þat hadde mi maidenhede' (lines 2133–4). She had indeed given herself first to Tristan, but because she had arranged for Brangwine to take her place in Mark's bed on the wedding night, he interprets her oath differently. Such deceptive play with language contrasts strongly with the chivalric ideal of truth, but is clearly consonant with Godwin's acquisition of Bosham, Fouke's promise to lead King John to a horned beast, and Little John's guile in leading the Sheriff of Nottingham to a noble hart.[11]

While such episodes are more infrequent in Malory and the *Prose Tristan*, they are not entirely absent. What is more, other notable features of the outlaw narrative – an account of the causes and process of outlawry, a complex treatment of the king, and the alienation of the hero in the wilderness – continue to be prominent. The continuing presence of these elements of the outlaw narrative indicates that the romance mode is not as monolithic as Keen imagined it.

Tristan, for his part, endures a number of periods of outlawry, once with Isolt and several on his own, and often these periods are described with language which intentionally identifies Tristan's legal condition. In *Sir Tristrem*, a Middle English poem in the *courtoise* tradition, this first occurs after the blades at the bed trap incriminate Tristan. When Mark saw the bloody sheets, 'He told þo brengwain / Tristrem hadde broken his pes' (lines 2218–19). His choice of language here immediately defines Tristrem's act in legal terms: he has broken the 'king's peace', a felony punishable by death.[12] Eilhart also presents the transgression as a political crime, depicting the angry king summoning 'those who wanted to support the country' to come to the trial and execution (93). Tristrem's decision to flee thus makes him an outlaw: again, *Sir Tristrem*, 'Anon of lond he ches / Out of markes eige sene. / Tristrem was fled oway' (lines 2221–3). And again after a brief reconciliation Mark 'flemed hem boþe, y wis, / Out of his eige sene / Away' (lines 2449–51). These phrases, 'fled away' and 'flemed [...] Away', are a legal expression derived from the Anglo-Saxon *flieman*, 'to exile or outlaw', and thus describe a legal and not merely spatial relationship between Tristan and the court. Beroul also adds a legally significant detail: when Isolt is restored and Tristan

---

11 Walter Map, *De Nugis Curialium*, ed. and trans. M.R. James, rev. C.N.L. Brooke and R.A.B. Mynors (Oxford, 1983), p. 418; *Fouke le Fitz Waryn*, ed. E.J. Hathaway, P.T. Ricketts, C.A. Robson and A.D. Wilshere, Anglo-Norman Text Society 26–8 (Oxford, 1975), p. 49; *The Gest of Robyn Hode*, in *RHOOT*, pp 80–169.   12 See Bracton, *On the laws and customs of England*, ed. George E. Woodbine, trans. Samuel E. Thorne, 2 vols (Cambridge, 1968), who observes that outlawry may be declared in the case of any crime 'contra pacem' (359); also Frederick Pollack and Frederic Maitland, *The history of English law before the time of Edward I*, 2nd ed., 2 vols (Cambridge, 1969), vol. 1, p. 476.

exiled, he is escorted toward the sea, but when the escort turns back he immediately leaves the road and takes a path into the woods. This action, according to English law, makes him an outlaw, for anyone abjuring the realm had only a few days to proceed by the most direct route to the coast and to sail from the shore before the king's favour expired.[13]

While the legal practice of outlawry establishes the conflict between the outlaw and the king, in most of the surviving English outlaw narratives the characterization of the king is ambiguous. In the *Gesta Herewardi*, the outlaw's enemies are a handful of Norman lords, not William I, who is held at a distance from the action and responds with admiration to accounts of Hereward's accomplishments. Similarly, in the *Vita Ædwardi Regis*, Godwin's conflict is with Edward's Norman advisors, especially Robert of Jumiéges, not the king himself. And of course Robin Hood is notably at odds with the corrupt sheriff of Nottingham yet supports the king. The same is true of the Tristan tales. Eilhart, for whom the love of Tristan and Isolt is entirely illicit and the product of the fatal potion, treats Mark sympathetically. Of course he is quick to anger, as when he finds the lovers embracing in his own bedroom, but he is also quick to forgive. At the end of the poem, Mark laments,

> God knows [...] I would gladly have treated Queen Isalde and my nephew Tristrant kindly so that the knight would have stayed with me always. I shall forever regret having driven him away. It was very foolish of them not to tell me that they had drunk the fatal potion and, against their will, were forced to love each other so. Oh, noble queen and dear nephew, Tristrant! I would give you my whole kingdom, people and land, forever for your own if this could bring you back to life. (Thomas, 155)

This sentiment suggests that Mark is a merciful and just judge, as a king ought to be. Indeed, throughout the poem he desires to believe the best about his wife and nephew, but the evidence always points the other way. If only he had known of the potion he would have been able to rest his case. Instead, Eilhart's criticism falls on the seven noblemen who are anxious to present evidence against the lovers because they are jealous of Tristan's kindness, deeds of prowess and desire for fame and glory.

The alienation of the outlaw from the human community is represented for Tristan and Isolt as for our other outlaws in the poets' descriptions of the forest. While the quality of the forest life varies between the *version commune* and the *courtoise*, both succeed in setting the lovers apart from the world of Mark and the court. In the poems of Béroul and Eilhart, the forest is a harsh, primitive and uncomfortable environment, but Tristan and Isolt are

13 Bracton, p. 382.

oblivious to this as long as they are deluded by the potion of love. But when the potion loses its efficacy after three years, Tristan's attitude changes. While chasing a deer through the forest one day, the rigours of the forest life overwhelm him and he regrets leaving the civilized life of court and dragging Isolt into the wilderness:

> 'Ha! Dex,' fait il, 'tant ai traval!
> Trois anz a hui, que riens n'i fal,
> Onques ne me falli pus paine
> Ne a foire n'en sorsemaine.
> Oublïé ai chevalerie,
> A seure cort et baronie;
> Ge sui essillié du païs,
> Tot m'est falli et vair et gris,
> Ne sui a cort a chevaliers.
> Dex! tant m'amast mes oncles chiers,
> Se tant ne fuse a lui mesfez!
> Ha! Dex, tant foiblement me vet!'   (2161–72)[14]

The forest in these poems becomes a period of expiation during which Tristan is brought to a recognition of his sin.[15] Like the prodigal son sitting among the hogs in Egypt, he is reminded of the life he gave up in order to pursue illicit desires.

On the other hand, Thomas and his followers express little realistic recognition of the hardship of forest life. Any difficulty is negated by the joy of the lovers in each other's presence, so even the condensed and aesthetically limited description of *Sir Tristrem* conveys a pleasant idyl. But when Tristan must flee alone, the description is quite different, even in the *versione courtoise*. Consumed now with concern for his life, he complains in *Sir Tristrem*:

> For dout of deþ y fle,
> In sorwe and wo y wende.
> Y fle for dout of deþ,
> Y dar no leng abide

---

14 'Oh God', he laments, 'How distressed I am! / It has been exactly three years to the day / That I was not spared any suffering / Whether on feast days or during the week. / I gave up chivalry, / Court life and the company of noble men; / I am banned from the kingdom, / I lost everything, / I am no longer at the Court with the other knights. / God! My dear uncle would have loved me, / If I had not wronged him so! / Oh! God, Everything goes wrong for me!'   15 See Frederick Whitehead, 'Tristan and Isolt in the forest of Morrois' in *Studies in French language and medieval literature presented to Professor Mildred K. Pope* (Manchester, 1939), among others. Whitehead notes the similar thematic use of the forest in the Old French epic *Girart de Roussillon*.

> In wo mi liif to lede
> Bi þis forestes side. (2595–600)

In these texts, the forest is a place of refuge for the lovers when they share it, but a burden when Tristan is there alone. Thus the forest here reflects their psychological state with respect to each other more than their relationship to the courtly community from which they are exiled. Schoepperle once noted that Tristan and Isolt are unique in medieval French literature:

> But Tristan and Isolt, alone of the lovers that we know, have made the wilderness their home, have had no thought of seeking beyond it a more friendly society. These alone establish themselves in the desert, wrenching their scanty sustenance and shelter from reluctant nature. These alone are cut off for years from the world, living without intercourse with any, deprived of every activity and every responsibility. In the closely woven fabric of feudal society, they alone have no relation, no place. (II.392)

This observation has been taken a step further by Donald Hoffman, who argues that the forest defines a space outside the law of the court where Tristan and Isolt are free to love each other apart from the obligations which limit their behavior in human society.[16] Here is an outlawry consistent with the codes of romance.

When we turn to the 'Book of Sir Tristram de Lyones' in Malory's *Morte Darthur*, written three centuries after the poems of Béroul, Eilhart and Thomas, we find a version of the story which joins the matter of Tristan with the Arthurian world and forgets much of the tragic love story which animates the earlier poems.[17] In the section titled 'Isode the Fair', which tells Tristram's story from his birth until his marriage to Isode of the White Hands, only the final quarter describes the life of the lovers after drinking the potion, and only a few lines are devoted to their time together in the forest before Mark takes Isode back home. The details of the affair are rarely described: Tristram is

16 Donald L. Hoffmann, 'Cult and culture: "courtly love" in the cave and the forest', *Tristania* 4 (1978), 17–20. 17 *Le Roman de Tristan*, ed. Renée L. Curtis, 2 vols (1963 Cambridge, 1985). The exact text used by Malory is unknown. More than seventy-five manuscripts are extant with numerous fragments. See Curtis, *Tristan*, vol. 1, pp 12–16; Eugene Vinaver, *Etudes sur le Tristan en prose* (Paris, 1925), pp 37–58; B. Woledge, *Bibliographie des romans et nouvelles en prose française antérieurs à 1500* (Paris, 1950), pp 122–5; Emmanuèle Baumgartner, *Le Tristan en prose* (Geneva, 1975), pp 18–21; P.J.C. Field, *Bulletin bibliographique de la Société Internationale Arthurienne* 41 (1989). Vinaver attempts a detailed comparison of Malory's book with the French Prose *Tristan* in his notes, using those manuscripts which are closest to Malory's narrative: MSS BN fr.103, 334, 99; Musée Condé Chantilly 646; Pierpoint Morgan Library MS. fr.41; and Leningrad Public Library MS fr. F.v.XV–2 (3, 1443–1533).

'takyn nakyd a-bed with La Beale Isode' one night, but more often the lovers
are only acknowledged in dialogue between other characters. Instead, a much
greater emphasis is placed on Tristram's solitary exile, which includes a secret
visit to Isode, a period of madness in the wilderness, and a second banishment
from Mark's court. Almost the entire remainder of the 'Book of Sir Tristram'
is composed of acts of knight errantry in which Isode barely appears. Yet the
basic structure of the outlaw narrative is not negated. Here too Tristan finds
himself on the margins of society: estranged from Mark and the court of
Cornwall, he too often finds that his past prevents him from settling into a
community, especially the court of Arthur and the fellowship of the knights
of the Round Table. Here is an outlaw more reminiscent of Icelandic outlaws
like Grettir Asmundarson or the tragic Robin Hood of the *Gest*, who finds his
own longings incompatible with the life at court.

In the *Morte Darthur*, as in the French prose romance, Tristram's trouble begins early. His father, King Melyodas, is taken prisoner by a lady
through enchantment. In a fit of despair, his pregnant wife runs into the
forest, where the pains of labor overtake her and she delivers her son, 'but
she had takyn suche colde for the defaute of helpe that the depe draughtys
of deth toke hir' (I. 372.6–8).[18] Sensing her own death, Elyzabeth laments
over her newborn son:

> 'A, my lytyll son, thou haste murthered thy modir! And therefore I
> suppose thou that arte a murtherer so yonge, thow arte full lykly to
> be a manly man in thyne ayge; and bycause I shall dye of the byrth
> of the, I charge my jantyllwoman that she pray my lorde, the kynge
> Melyodas, that whan he is crystened let calle hym Trystrams, that
> is as muche to say as a sorowfull byrth.'   (I. 372.19–26)

This charge of murder at birth defines the ambiguity of Tristram's character for the remainder of the romance. It seems, on the one hand, to be a sign
of male virtue, the likelihood of becoming a 'manly man.' On the other hand,
the identification as murderer leads to his name, 'Tristram', and the legal
consequences of the charge would necessitate either his execution or
exile/outlawry. A sort of execution is almost carried out by the barons who
find the baby and the handmaid, although their motivation is personal gain
rather than justice: 'sertayne of them wolde have slayne the chylde bycause
they wolde have bene lordys of that contrey of Lyonesse' (I. 372.33–5). This
failing, we can see Tristram as serving a life of exile and outlawry, cursed
by the circumstances of his birth.

His conflict with the king begins when his stepmother attempts to poison
him in order to ensure the inheritance for her own child. Melodyas discov-

18 Thomas Malory, *Works*, ed. Eugene Vinaver, rev. P.J.C. Field, 3rd ed. (Oxford, 1990).

ers her treachery and orders her to be burnt, but with a characteristic sense of mercy young Tristram asks for her life, 'for Goddis love'. Melodyas is reluctant to agree but keeps his promise. Afterward, Tristram succeeds in making 'the kynge and hir accorded', but he has created a distance between himself and his father: 'but than the kynge wolde nat suffir yonge Trystrams to abyde but a lytyll in his courte' (I. 375.3,4). Here is an echo of the tension between Hereward and his father which also arises from the son's generosity and initiates the outlawry in the *Gesta Herewardi*. Melodyas' thoughts remain hidden, but the reader wonders if he feels threatened by his son or embarrassed because he has been upstaged: the intended victim of the queen's plot can forgive her, but he cannot. This may foreshadow the love that Tristram can give to Isolde which Mark cannot, but certainly Mark steps in as another father figure to clash with Tristram.[19]

In Malory's work too Tristram falls in and out of favor with King Mark often. The first conflict involves their shared love for the wife of Sir Segwarydes and a fight in which Mark is embarrassed, and 'aftir that, thoughe there were fayre speche, love was there none [between them]' (I. 396.9,10). This preliminary dispute over a woman leads directly to the primary dispute as it provokes Mark to plot a marriage with Isolde:

> So whan this was done kynge Marke caste all the wayes that he myght to dystroy sir Trystrames, and then imagened in hymselff to sende sir Trystramys into Irelonde for La Beale Isode. For sir Trystramys had so preysed her for hir beaut and hir goodnesse that kynge Marke seyde he wolde wedde hir; whereuppon he prayde sir Trystramys to take his way into Irelonde for hym on message. And all this was done to the entente to sle sir Trystramys.
>
> (I. 403.12–19)

This passage is not found in the French prose romance and seems to be part of Malory's effort to characterize Mark as a thoroughly unchivalrous and unsympathetic character. When once, for the sake of sport he orders Tristram to joust with the exhausted Sir Lameroke, Tristram responds, 'ye bydde me do a thynge that is ayenste knyghthode' (I. 428.16,17). Elsewhere he is upbraided by others for his treatment of Tristram:

> 'A, false knyght!' seyde sir Palomydes, 'hit ys pité thou haste thy lyff, for thou arte a destroyer of all worshipfull knyghtes, and by thy myschyff and thy vengeaunce thou haste destroyed that moste noble knyght, sir Trystramys de Lyones.' (II. 497.25–9)

19 Remarkably little has been said about the Oedipal possibilities in the Tristan legend. One critic who has thought about the issue is Gerald A. Bertin in 'The Oedipal complex in *Tristan et Iseult*', *Kentucky Foreign Language Quarterly* 5 (1958), 60–5.

At times he even becomes comically inept in contrast to Tristram's prowess. For instance, when alerted to a rendezvous between Tristram and Isode, he tries to confront the lovers: 'Than kyng Mark toke a swerde in his honde and cam to sir Trystrames and called hym "false traytowre", and wolde have stryken hym, but sir Trystrames was nyghe hym and ran undir his swerde and toke hit oute of his honde' (I. 426.12–17). When no one comes to the king's aid, Tristram chases him, hitting him with the flat of the sword and causing him to fall on his nose.

Tristram is no more successful in finding a place to settle down outside of Cornwall. Often his prior displays of chivalric excellence stand in his way. King Angwyshe of Ireland is thankful that Tristram has successfully defended him in a trial by combat, but he cannot offer him a position in his court because he has killed Morholt (I. 391.17–22). He is likewise deserted by his kinsman Andrete, who conspires to have him exiled in order to receive his inheritance for himself (I. 431). And perhaps most disappointing to him is Sir Segwardes' wife's choice to continue to accompany her abductor, Sir Bleoberys, after Tristram has rescued her (I. 401,2). He even falls out with his friend and brother-in-law when he discovers that Kahydyns has sent a love letter to La Beale Isode (II. 493,4).

It is after this last incident that Tristram reaches his nadir: 'he made such sorow that he felle downe of hys horse in a sowne, and in such sorow he was inne three dayes and three nyghtes' (II. 495.10–12). Awaking from unconsciousness, he behaves like a madman, running naked in the forest and in the company of shepherds. In this simple foolish state he seems to rediscover some of the essence of knighthood: the fellowship of a community and the service of noble deeds. When a passing knight is attacked by the giant Tauleas, 'Sir Tristram was ware of the swerde of the knyght thereas hi lay, and so thydir he ran and toke up the swerde and smote to sir Tauleas, and so stroke of hys hede' (II. 500.18–20). It is the news of this event reaching the court which facilitates Tristram's return to civilization, and as long as he remains in his natural, childlike state he is welcome there. When his sense returns and his identity with it, he is banished once more.

At this point Tristram begins in earnest his quest for the fellowship of the Round Table. Now, however, he is prevented more by his own feelings of inadequacy than the ill will of the company. Sir Brandiles, for instance, makes an offer:

> 'And wyte you well that we be ryght glad that we have founde you, and we be of a felyship that wolde be ryght glad of youre company, for ye ar the knyght in the worlde that the felyship of the Rounde Table desyryth moste to have the company off'.   (II. 489.24–7)

But Tristram declines politely, arguing that 'as yet I fele well that I am nat able to be of their felyship, for I was never yet of such dedys of worthynes to be in the companye of such a felyship' (II. 489.24–32). Shortly thereafter he rescues King Arthur himself from the sorceress Aunowre, but refuses to identify himself and leaves his company as soon as they meet Sir Ector (II. 491,2). Even when he is finally brought to Camelot by Lancelot and offered a place at the Round Table, Tristram replies, 'thereto me is lothe, for I have to do in many contreys' (II. 572.5,6). Moreover, we have yet covered less than half of the 'Book of Sir Tristram'. During the remainder of the book, Tristram is constantly reminded of his past. Isode and Mark continue to haunt him and it becomes clear that his period in the wilderness has brought neither expiation nor forgiveness. He ends the story not at Arthur's court but at the 'Joyous Gard' of Sir Lancelot. Although this seems to be a place of refuge for the lovers, like the forest it is outside the mainstream, and because of its attachment to Sir Lancelot it is a reminder of the forces of decay at work in Arthur's kingdom. Indeed, it is a reminder that Sir Tristram is ultimately an Arthurian outsider, like two other prominent characters in his book, Sir Palomydes the Saracen and Sir Dynadan the anti-knight. Like Godwin, Hereward, Fouke, and Robin Hood he has his own agenda which alienates him from the company of kings.

It does not come as a real surprise when Lancelot reports to the knights of the Round Table that Tristram has been killed treacherously by Mark. This fate has been lying in wait for him since his birth. That he is unable to rise triumphantly from his outlawry like Godwin, Hereward, and Fouke does not remove him from their company. In fact, the tragic end may bind him to them more than to other heroes of romance. Joan Ferrante has observed that while the poems of Thomas and Gottfried follow the rise, fall, rise structure of romance, Eilhart's poem traces the rise and fall of heroic epic.[20] The former pattern also describes the structure of the *Vita Ædwardi Regis*, the *Gesta Herewardi*, and *Fouke le Fitz Waryn*, but we should remember as well the stories of Godwin's death told in the *Liber de Hyde* and the *Estoire de Seint Aedward le Rei* and of Hereward's bloody end in Geoffrey Gaimar's *Lestoire des Engles*.[21] Given Godwin's black record among the Normans, it made sense for them to give him an ignominious death. Given Hereward's many enemies, it was impossible for a royal pardon to reconcile completely the outlaw with the community. Robin Hood too dies at the end of the *Gest* in the hands of a treacherous cousin, reconciled with the king but still roaming the greenwood.

20 Joan Ferrante, *The conflict of love and honor: the medieval Tristan legend in France, Germany and Italy* (The Hague, 1973), pp 59, 60.   21 *Liber Monasterii de Hyda*, ed. Edward Edwards, Rolls Series 45 (London, 1866), p. 289; *La Estoire de Seint Aedward le Rei*, ed. Henry R. Luard, *Lives of Edward the Confessor*, Rolls Series 3 (London, 1958), ll. 3277–340; *Lestorie de Engles*, ed. T.D. Hardy and G.T. Martin, Rolls Series 91, 2 (London, 1888).

While Malory's version of the Tristan story corroborates Keen's thesis on one level, since the outlaw narrative defined as a tale of the forest-dwelling trickster fades from view, yet the outlaw as a representation of alienation, of conflict in value systems, even of criticism of structures of authority, does not become incompatible with romance either in terms of narrative structure or thematic interest. The overall structure of the outlaw narrative, its cycle of loss and recovery, and the fascination with reconfiguration of identity in a liminal, extra-legal space, are both common features of romance. After all, what is outlawry but a change in fortune and social context? Who is the outlaw but someone who has been deprived of all his property, evicted from the social order and cast into the wilderness? And what is an errant knight but one who leaves the certainty of the feudal community for the uncertainty of the forest? All romances of *aventure* challenge and reconstruct the identity of the knight, and frequently Middle English romances detail the fortunes of knights who succumb to periods of madness, debauchery, and paganism.[22] What is more, medieval legal records suggest that English knights and nobles of the fourteenth and fifteenth centuries frequently opted to undertake periods of lawless behaviour when expedient.[23] It should not surprise us, then, that the literature of the nobility might portray characters who display the attitudes or behaviour which were used to typify outlaws.

Yet Tristan is different from the other noble outlaws. While Hereward, Fouke, and Godwin are all confronted by conflicting social obligations, such as loyalty to family versus loyalty to lord, for Tristan the struggle is between loyalty to his lord and his own erotic desire. Fouke le fitz Waryn, for instance, responds to a dilemma – respect the authority of King John and give up the family property or respect the family heritage and give up fealty to the king – by stepping into the flux outside the law. Free of his identity in the feudal hierarchy, Fouke can rediscover and refashion himself as both a valuable vassal and the head of the fitz Waryn family. Tristan, likewise, is free to love Isolde when he steps away from his identity as Mark's vassal and into the forest. Unfortunately a new identity evades him. In pursuing an individual desire rather than a communal value, Tristan, unlike other noble outlaws, finds himself without a community to support him, without an outlaw band. 'Once I was a knight,' he complains, but what has he become? He is caught on the border between competing definitions of chivalry and masculinity: the loyal warrior-retainer versus the courtly lover. In this position he not only looks back to the noble outlaws of twelfth century historical romance, but also forward to the individualistic protagonists of the novel.

---

22 See Andrea Hopkins, *The sinful knights* (Oxford, 1992), 20–3, who lists the following stages of loss and recovery: stability and prosperity, revelation, separation, journey to solitude, repentance, atonement and forgiveness.   23 See J.G. Bellamy, *Crime and public order in England in the later Middle Ages* (London, 1973).

A grave tale

DAVID HEPWORTH

One of the continuing arguments in Robin Hood studies is whether the entire early corpus is fictional or based, in some degree, on fact. The split in academic circles, particularly since studies into the literary history of the works have taken over from empirical history, seems to come down in favour of fictional origins. However, within the early ballads, particularly the *Gest*, are several site-specific indicators that seem to point towards some factual bases, whatever these may be.

My interest in Robin Hood studies arose from research into the post-Conquest history of the former West Riding of Yorkshire, particularly the manor of Wakefield and honour of Pontefract, and a specific study on Kirklees Priory. In the course of this, I encountered many historical factors that seem to tie into the Yorkshire elements of the early ballads. These elements are worth investigating to see if they offer insight, and open up future study on the local contexts of the ballads.

The association of the Robin Hood legend with Kirklees

From the earliest surviving copy of the *Gest of Robyn Hode, c.*1506,[1] to the most recent studies of the Robin Hood corpus, writers, antiquarians, academics, archaeologists, and local historians have alluded to the Robin Hood grave at Kirklees. Little actual research of the grave has occurred in the last century. This paper aims to shed light on what Maurice Keen called 'endless confusion' about the grave and answer the following questions.[2]

Does the gravestone have a traceable history?

Does it even have a relationship to the ballad Robin?

What are the facts in the published corpus of work, and what is merely conjectural or misinformed?

What remains today are an enclosed stone fragment at Kirklees with an epitaph,[3] numerous allusions by those in the past who visited the site, and

1 Masa Ikegami, 'The language and date of *A Gest of Robyn Hode*', *Neuphilologische Mitteilungen*, 96:3 (1995), 271–81; p. 280 n. 1b refers to Wynkyn de Worde's edition (Cambridge University Library MS. Sel. 5.18) and virtually dates it to 1506. However, Ikegami used the version of the *Gest* in *RRH*, pp 71–112, a composite of the Lettersnijder and Wynkyn de Worde texts.   2 Keen, p. 180.   3 OS Grid Ref. SE17442151.

drawings of the grave, the most famous of which is that attributed to Johnston.[4]

The body of work on Robin Hood's grave contains many inaccuracies and conflicts, and this paper attempts to clarify the reliable sources and possibly identify the provenance of some of the errors. To formulate any history of the grave, it is also necessary to consider the history of the Armytage family, owners of the grave site for much of its recorded history, and their developing interest in the Robin Hood legend and Robin Hood artefacts.

The connections between Kirklees and the ballad Robin Hood go beyond the physical monument of the grave. Robin's decision to be buried where his last arrow lands is, in Dobson and Taylor's words, 'one of the most celebrated episodes in the entire Robin Hood saga',[5] and the arrow was shot from the 'gatehouse,' a largely Tudor building adjacent to the old Priory site.[6] As discussed later, although the obvious assumption might be that the identification and fame of the Robin Hood grave followed the existence and dissemination of the famous story, an alternative hypothesis may be that the grave predated the poignant story of the arrow-shot, which was created to explain the location of the grave.

Twentieth-century historians

Modern historians, including Keen, Dobson and Taylor, refer to the present grave, though Keen outlines the history of four possible tombstones for Robin at Kirklees, basing his conclusions on texts alone.[7] Holt comments that, 'a spurious inscription based on Gale's epitaph was erected in the nineteenth century when the slab was enclosed by iron railings. By then it was badly damaged. Labourers constructing the Yorkshire and Lancashire railway took fragments from it as a cure for toothache'.[8] Holt's comments, however, are based on those of J.W. Walker who, in turn had expanded those of local historian Horsfall Turner in 1893.[9]

Plausible as this explanation of the enclosure may sound, Walker's statements should be read alongside his other sweeping comments concerning the fourteenth-century Robert and Matilda Hode of Wakefield, which have attracted criticism from virtually all scholars. Unfortunately, most commentators on the grave have used printed source material, because they have not known what else was available to shed light on the subject. Walker must have known about local source material, which could have told a different story,

Photographs can be seen at http://groups.msn.com/YorkshireRobinHood.   **4** *Yorkshire Archaeological Journal* (hereafter *YAJ*), 16 (1902) opposite 336.   **5** *RRH*, p. 134.   **6** Royal Commission for Historical Monuments 49301, 4/123.   **7** *RRH*, p. 309; Keen, pp 178–83. **8** Holt, pp 41–2.   **9** J.W. Walker, *The true history of Robin Hood*, (Wakefield, 1952), p. 120; J. Horsfall Turner, *The history of Brighouse, Rastrick and Hipperholme* (Bradford, 1893), pp 203–4.

through his contacts within the Yorkshire Archaeological Society, but he was a highly influential amateur local historian who was passionate about Wakefield and possibly desperate to find the true Robin Hood in Wakefield.[10] His argument for a Wakefield Robin Hood and naming of Elizabeth de Stainton as the prioress who murdered Robin Hood are founded on poor understanding of the available information. Yet he was in contact with respected academic historians of the time and at least some of his research was sound and his theories supportable.[11]

Textual references to the grave and death of Robin Hood at Kirklees

Kirklees Park has been linked to Robin Hood since the now lost original version of the *Gest,* composed probably in the mid fifteenth century.[12] The *Gest* says that the prioress of Kirklees was 'hys kynne,' that she was having a relationship with a Sir Roger of Doncaster, that Robin went to Kirklees to be bled and was betrayed, being bled to the brink of death (ll. 1801–24). Evidence of earlier stories of his death could be couched in the oblique reference by the Scottish chronicler Walter Bower, to 'tragedies and comedies' of Robin.[13] This phrase, from Bower's continuation of John of Fordun's *Scotichronicon* of *c.*1440, may suggest the death story, perhaps already linked to Kirklees, was widely known some two decades before the *Gest*'s composition. Robin's death may never have been a popular story in terms of printed ballads and its popularity was perhaps greater in the north of England. The earliest imperfect surviving text of the ballad *Robin Hood's Death* is in the Percy Folio, mid seventeenth century, and the earliest full text, of a variant version, is late eighteenth-century, printed in York.[14] The death story is rarely connected with anywhere except Kirklees, variously spelled, and some texts in which it appears also locate Robin's other activities in the north. The *Gest*

10 He was president of Yorkshire Archaeological Society, as well as a fellow of the Society of Antiquaries and the Royal Historical Society.   11 His associates included Powicke and Trevelyan in Oxford and Dr Flower at the Public Record Office.   12 Thomas Ohlgren, personal communication, links it to the Draper's Company and specifically 1439, the year the Company obtained its coat of arms; see also Ikegami, 'Language and Date', p. 279; Knight, *A complete study*, pp 47–9; Holt, pp 56, 188; Holt, 'Robin Hood: the origins of the legend', in Kevin Carpenter, *Die vielen Gesichter des edlen Räubers Robin Hood: the many faces of that celebrated English outlaw* (Oldenburg, 1995), 27–34, p. 30.   13 *RHOOT*, pp 25–6. See Richard Green's '*The Hermit and the Outlaw*: New Evidence for Robin Hood's death' in this volume. The passage in the *Chronicle of Dale Abbey* (BL MS Cotton Vespasian E.XXVI), written before the mid thirteenth century, in which Thomas Muskham, a canon of the house, related a legend concerning the Abbey's foundation, tells a similar tale. Were Bower, the chronicle and *The Hermit and the Outlaw* linked to a death legend of either Robin Hood or a similar outlaw?   14 *RRH*, pp 133–4; *RHOOT*, 592–3, summarizes reasons for thinking the original composition was medieval.

locates him in Barnsdale. Drayton's *Poly-Olbion* (1622) in its Song 28 (67–70) talks of his death and burial at 'Kirkby', though setting his activities in Sherwood. Parker's *True Tale of Robin Hood* (*c.*1631) says his bandit activities were in 'Yorkshire woods … And Lancashire also' (49–50); it has a different murderer, a friar, doesn't locate the murder, but the epitaph it includes says 'These northerne parts he vexed sore'.[15] Grafton's *Chronicle at Large* (1569), one of Parker's sources, says he operated in 'the Forestes or wilde Countries', was murdered at a Yorkshire nunnery called 'Bircklies', and describes the gravestone and inscription (see below).[16]

The *Gest* gives Kirklees a role in Robin Hood legend for five and a half centuries. If Bower's reference to 'tragedies' does refer to Robin's death, the priory was linked to Robin for 64–100 years before its dissolution in November 1539.[17] Of five earliest surviving copies, four pre-date the dissolution of the Priory and the fifth John Armytage of Farnley Tyas' purchase of the estate in 1565.[18]

Antiquarian references to Robin Hood's grave

The earliest known 'historical' reference to Robin's grave at Kirklees appears in John Leland's *Collectanea*:

> Ebor. Kirkley monasterium Monialium, ubi Ro: Hood nobilis ille exlex sepultus'

> York[shire]: Monastery of Kirkley[s], where the noble outlaw Ro[bin] Hood is buried.[19]

This entry must date from Leland's Royal Commission to visit religious houses in the early 1530's, probably 1534 when he visited York.[20] Leland visited Yorkshire again whilst undertaking his *Itineraries*, visiting Nostell Priory on the point of its Dissolution on 20 November 1539, four days before the surrender of Kirklees.[21] The brevity of the *Collectanea* entry, its position in a group of Yorkshire monastic houses, and the lack of reference to Kirklees or other local towns in the *Itinerary*, suggest Leland did not visit Kirklees Priory

15 *RHOOT*, pp 606, 625. 16 *RHOOT*, pp 28–9. 17 *RHOOT*, p. 592. David Knowles & R. Neville Hadcock, *Medieval religious houses: England and Wales*, 2nd ed. (Harlow, 1971, 1996), p. 274. 18 *RRH*, pp 71–4; *RHOOT*, p. 80. 19 John Leland, *De Rebus Britannicis Collectanea*, ed. Thomas Hearne, 2nd ed., 6 vols (London, 1770), I. 54. 20 See John Chandler, 'John Leland in the West Country', in *Topographical writers in south-west England*, ed. M. Brayshay, Exeter Studies in History (Exeter, 1996) 34–49, pp 36, 38; Chandler, *John Leland's itinerary travels in Tudor England*, (Gloucester, 1997), pp xiv–xv, xviii, xxvii–xxxi, 521–2. 21 Knowles and Hadcock, *Medieval religious houses*, p. 169; *Yorkshire monasteries' suppression papers*, ed. John W. Clay, Yorkshire Archaeological Society Record Series (YASRS) 48 (1912), p. 127.

then but had made an earlier visit or received information from a friend. It is likely that the Robin Hood legend would have interested Leland in view of its popularity at Henry VIII's court of which he was a member,[22] and the popularity of printed copies of the *Gest*. His entry suggests a physical grave at Kirklees was already linked to Robin Hood before the Dissolution.

From the late sixteenth to the eighteenth century there are literary and antiquarian references to the grave at Kirklees, which must have kept the connection in the public consciousness and probably encouraged early tourism to the grave site. The first reference available to a wider audience, Grafton's chronicle, states that Robin was buried at Kirklees at the 'high way side', at the behest of the Prioress and that the names of 'Robert Hood, William of Goldesborough and others were graven' and 'at eyther ende of the sayde Tombe was erected a crosse of stone, which is to be seen there at this present'.[23] In the first half of the seventeenth century there were several references to Robin Hood's grave, whilst Lives of the hero related the story of his death. Munday's *The Death of Robert, Earl of Huntington*, 1598, brought the story to a large new audience.[24] His version of the death, however, is that Robin dies in the King and Queen's presence in Sherwood, after being poisoned by a prior who hopes to inherit his earldom of Huntington. Robin commands his followers to take his body to Wakefield for burial, 'underneath the abbey wall' (805) and there is no reference to Kirklees. Yet at one point the recently poisoned hero enters with 'a cuppe, a towell' (518), perhaps for bleeding to counteract the poison,[25] but they are probably table ware. The Sloane *Life of Robin Hood*, about 1600, states,

> Therefore, to be eased of his payne by letting bloud, he repaired to the priores of Kyrkesly, which some say was his aunt, a woman very skilful in physique and surgery. Who, perceiving him to be Robin Hood, and waying howe fel an enemy he was to religious persons, toke reveng of him for her owne howse and al others by letting him bleed to death, and then buryed him under a greate stone by the hy wayes side. It is also seyd that one Sir Roger of Dancastre, bearing grudge to Robyn for some injury, incited the priores (with whome he was very familiar) in such maner to dispatch him. And then al his company was soone dispersed. The place of Little Johns burial is to this tyme celebrated for the yielding of excellent whetstones.[26]

22 Jeffrey L. Singman, *Robin Hood: The shaping of the legend* (Westport, Conn., 1998), p. 69.   23 Richard Grafton, *A chronicle at large*, 2nd ed. (London, 1569), 85.   24 Anthony Munday, *The death of Robert Earl of Huntingdon*, Malone Society reprint (London, 1965). 25 Meagher's suggestion, see *RHOOT*, p. 436.   26 BL MS Sloane 780, f. 48v. *RRH*, pp 286–7. An edition of the Sloane Life, and other early Lives is being prepared by Thomas Hahn, from whose text this comes.

The last sentence refers presumably to Hathersage, Derbyshire, renowned for the production of millstones and whetstones, and site of John's alleged grave. Dobson and Taylor thought this Sloane information derived from a lost source, from the last quarter of the sixteenth century, pre-dating Munday's additions to the legend.[27] By 1607, the fifth edition of Camden's *Britannia* mentioned Kirklees as Robin Hood's burial place.[28] John Saville, part of the Saville family who had briefly owned Kirklees, provided Camden with this information in a 1589 letter.[29] Philemon Holland's English translation in 1610 brought this to the attention of a much wider audience.[30]

Roger Dodsworth (1585–1664), an impressive early antiquarian, compiled elements for a history of Yorkshire by copying muniments from all available repositories. He visited John Armytage III of Kirklees in January 1618, transcribing the Kirklees foundation charter and other early documents for the Priory and neighbouring manors of Clifton and Hartshead.[31] Dodsworth writes of a local legend in which Robert Locksley from Bradfield in Hallamshire came to Clifton upon Calder where he met Little John.[32] The strength of this local legend is indicated by its reappearance 130 years later in the notes of Joseph Ismay, who could not have had access to Dodsworth's notes: 'Little John was an ancestor of ye Naylors of Clifton'.[33] Dodsworth noted a doggerel rhyme: 'Clifton standes on Calder bancke / and Harteshead on a hill / Kirkeleyes standes within the dale / and many comes ther still',[34] which both Ismay and Hunter felt was part of a lost Robin Hood ballad.[35] It would be dangerous to take this rhyme literally, though it might record the number of visitors to the grave by 1618, as a result of the grave's growing fame and location adjacent to the old road to Clifton. Another early reference occurs in Drayton's *Poly-Olbion*, 1622, in the twenty-eighth song.[36] Ten years later, Parker gives for the first time the alleged epitaph.[37]

---

27 *RRH*, p. 286.   28 William Camden, *Britannia*, 5th ed. (London, 1607), pp 564–5. 29 Letter dated 25/12/1589, BL MS Cotton Julius C.v. f 34, published in *Gullielmi Camdeni, et Illustrium Virorum ad G. Camdenum: EPISTOLAE cum Appendice Varii Argumenti*, ed. Thomas Smith (London, 1691), cited in Ritson, vol. 1, p. xlv.   30 William Camden, *Britannia: Written first in Latine by W. Camden*, trans. Philemon Holland (London, 1610), p. 693.   31 Bodleian Library, MS Dodsworth 118, f 147v.   32 Bodleian Library, MS Dodsworth 160, 64v, quoted in Joseph Hunter, 'The great hero of the ancient minstrelsy of England, Robin Hood', *Critical and Historical Tracts* 4 (London, 1852) 69; Holt, p. 44, says, 'these miscellaneous jottings scarcely suggest that Dodsworth was convinced'.   33 Joseph Ismay, Notebook, 1747–61(?), *Eminent men in Cumberland, Kirklees nunnery*, p. 41. I am indebted to Leslie Oldroyd, and the late Judge Richard Nevin, for allowing me access to transcribe and photograph the Ismay papers, now to be found at WYAS, YAS, Leeds, MS 1625.   34 British Library, Harleian MS 797, f 34v, copied from Bodleian Library, MS Dodsworth 118, f 147.   35 Hunter, 'Great Hero', p. 51.   36 Michael Drayton, *Poly-Olbion*, in *Works*, ed. J. William Hebel (Oxford, 1933), vol. 4, p. 547.   37 *RHOOT*, p. 625. See Appendix.

Robert Earle of Huntinton
Lies under this little stone.
No archer was like him so good:
His wildnesse named him Robbin Hood.
Full thirteen yeares, and something more,
These Northerne parts he vexed sore.
Such out-lawes as he and his men
May England never know agen.
Decembris quarto die, 1198: anno regni
Ricardii Primi 9

Kirklees Robin Hood connections retained their interest through the seventeenth century and beyond. The Pontefract antiquarian Dr Nathaniel Johnston assembled material for a history of Yorkshire and was physician to the wife of Sir John Armitage IV of Kirklees,[38] visiting the Hall in 1669, when he or his brother Henry drew the armorial devices.[39] He allegedly also drew the grave, which would be in keeping with his normal practice of recording monumental and armorial inscriptions. His original drawing is, however, probably lost amongst papers lent out for copying,[40] which means that the provenance of the version published as Johnston's in the *Yorkshire Archaeological Journal*, 1902, and widely reproduced since, needs careful consideration.

The epitaph, which has nothing to do with the writing round the grave-stone mentioned by Grafton in 1569 and recorded by Johnston, is also mentioned by Thomas Gale, Dean of York 1697–1702. The antiquarian Ralph Thoresby quotes an epitaph, in his 1715 *Ducatus Leodiensis*,[41] followed by Gent's *History of York*, 1730.[42] Given its remarkable similarity to the 'epitaph' in Parker's *True Tale of Robin Hood*, Parker seems a likely provenance for Gale and Thoresby's epitaph. As the Appendix shows, there appear to be two broad forms of the epitaph, either both stemming from Parker's, which seems likely, or from some earlier lost source. We can observe through time the mutation of the epitaph, as if through a game of Chinese whispers stretching over the century, from the first publication of Parker's *True Tale* to the epitaph's erection at Kirklees.

38 Bodleian Library, MS Top. Yorks. c18, f 177, from 'Your assured Friend John Armytage', 1 January, 1668.   39 Bodleian Library, MS Top. Yorks. c13, f 161v, dated July 1669.   40 E. W. Crossley, 'The MSS of Nathaniel Johnston, MD of Pontefract', *YAJ*, 22 (1936) 435–8.   41 Ralph Thoresby, *Ducatus Leodiensis*, (London, 1715), 120; appendix, in 2nd edition, ed. T.D. Whitaker (Leeds, 1816), p. 576.   42 Thomas Gent, *The antient and modern history of the famous city of York*, (York and London, 1730), p. 234.

The role of the Armytage family

At what point the Armytage family took an interest in the grave or the legend is not clear, but take an interest they certainly did! The first evidence of interest occurred in 1706 when Samuel Armytage had the ground underneath Robin Hood's tomb dug during estate works that also resulted in the discovery of the tomb of Prioress Elizabeth de Staynton.[43] These works and their findings were recorded and discussed by antiquarians of the time, which helps us to date the first enclosure of the tomb and identify the source of the spurious epitaph. John Watson, preparing notes for his *History of Halifax*, was guided around the estate by the agent Mr Ramsden, and his notes, dated 1758, include the following:

> At some distance from this [Castle Field, Kirklees Park], in an inclos'd Plantation is Robin Hood's tomb, as it is call'd; which is nothing but a very rude stone note quite two yards long, & narrow in proportion; it has the figure of a cross, cut in a manner not common upon it; but no inscription, nor does there appear ever to have been any letters upon it, notwithstanding Mr Thoresby has pub-lish'd a pretended one found amongst the papers of Dr Gale Dean of York. See Thoresby's Topog. p 576. It will indeed admit of some doubt whether this noted robber was buried under this stone or not. Tradition is the only proof for it. That some one had been deposited there is plain, because the father of the present Sir George Armitage caus'd the ground under it to be dug up and some bones were found. It is probable that they would scarcely have put this mark upon Robin's tomb considering the character he bore.
>
> The old Religious house is almost all destroy'd. Some lead pipes were lately dug up near it & some stones found in the same place with the visible marks of fire upon them. Elizabeth Stainton's tomb which is here has lately been repair'd & there are also two other tomb stones which are antique but have nothing on them but crosses. See Thoresby p 91 & 576.
>
> NB Mr Ramsden of Kirklees said that the bones mention'd above were found in the burying ground near the Religious House, not under Robin Hood's Tomb for when they dug for about a yard deep under this last place, it appear'd that the ground had never been cast up before.[44]

Watson's notes cast doubt on whether anyone was buried at the gravesite and whether any writing was had previously been present on the slab. Ninety

43 *Remarks and collections of Thomas Hearne*, ed. C.E. Doble, 11 vols (Oxford, 1885–92), vol. 3, p. 409.   **44** York Minster Archives, MS Add 203/2, 72.

years had elapsed since Johnston's drawing: not enough time for legible inscriptions to be eroded without trace, but perhaps chippings from the stone by tourists had already damaged it.

It became *de rigeur*, when writing a 'Life' of Robin Hood to finish with his death and a reference to the grave at Kirklees. In addition to the 'Lives', travel was becoming more popular in England, and a number of 'Travels' through Britain published in the seventeenth and eighteenth centuries mentioned Robin Hood sites as tourist attractions. Many quoted or mis-quoted the Parker/Gale epitaph, implying it was of ancient provenance. There is a brief description of Robin Hood's death at the Priory in James Brome's 1694 *Travels*.[45] Tom Thumb in 1746 misquoted the epitaph and rewrote it in modern (eighteenth-century) English,[46] and Ely Hargrove in 1792 quoted the epitaph and referred to Elizabeth de Staynton's tomb and supposed relationship to Robin.[47] In 1712, Richard Richardson wrote to the antiquarian Thomas Hearne, describing the de Staynton gravestone and quoting its inscription.[48] Hearne included the de Staynton tomb in his edition of Leland's *Itinerary*.[49] In 1715, Richardson, writing to Thoresby, referred to both Elizabeth de Staynton and Robin Hood's gravestones, adding, 'the inscription upon Robin Hood's grave was never legible in my time; and is now totally defaced; insomuch that neither the language nor character is to be distinguished; only you may perceive it was written about the verge of the stone. I have heard Dr Armitage [later Sir Samuel Armytage] say, (who was most part of his time at Kirklees,) that he could read upon it '* * * *Hic jacet Robertus Hood, filius secundus Comitis de Huntingdon, * * *;' but I must own, tho' he was a person of merit, I gave little credit to this report'.[50] Richardson gives support to the notion that Johnston could have made out writing: clearly some evidence of it remained in the early eighteenth century. Armytage's fanciful version of this inscription reveals the importance the family attached to the Robin Hood associations with their estate.

45 James Brome, *Travels over England, Scotland and Wales giving a true and exact description of the chiefest Cities* (London, 1694), pp 70, 75.   **46** Tom Thumb (Roger Dodsley), *The travels of Tom Thumb over England and Wales* (London, 1746), p. 105.   **47** Ely Hargrove, *Anecdotes of archery from the earliest ages to the year 1791 Including an account of the most famous archer of ancient and modern times* [...] *Robert Fitz-Ooth Earl of Huntingdon, Robin Hood* (York, 1792), pp 24–5, perhaps a source for Hunter's hypothesis.   **48** Doble, *Remarks and collections*, p. 409.   **49** Thomas Hearne, 'Account of several antiquities in and about the University of Oxford', in Leland's *Itinerary*, 9 vols (Oxford, 1710–12), vol. 2, p. 2, pl. 28.   **50** *Extracts from the literary and scientific correspondence of Richard Richardson, MD, FRS*, ed. D. Turner (Yarmouth, 1835), p. 119; also in *Letters of eminent men addressed to Ralph Thoresby*, ed. Joseph Hunter, 2 vols (London, 1832), vol. 2, pp 310–11.

The epitaph and enclosure of the grave stone

Watson's 1758 comment, 'in an inclos'd Plantation is Robin Hood's tomb', indicates that in the eighteenth century, not the nineteenth as Walker believed, the grave was enclosed. The epitaph was also added in the eighteenth century:

> Hear Underneath dis laitl Stean
> Laz Robert earl of Huntingtun
> Ne'er arcir ver as hie sa geud
> An pipl kauld im robin heud
> Sick utlawz az hi an iz men
> Vil England nivr si agen
> Obiit 24 kal: Dekembris 1247

It is in bogus medieval English with an equally spurious date. The enclosure in the mid eighteenth century and the provenance of the epitaph were in fact documented by Joseph Ismay, who was vicar of Mirfield between 1739 and 1778. The Armytages owned the advowson of Mirfield. Sir Samuel Armytage appointed Joseph Ismay, first as a chaplain/tutor for his children, later transferring him to Mirfield. Ismay wrote copious notes and in correspondence with other antiquarians about Kirklees included references to Robin Hood, culled from published texts including Parker and Thoresby (indicating that either the Armytages or he owned these volumes). According to Ismay, by the mid-eighteenth century the tomb had become threatened by its own popularity: 'ye sepulchral Monument of Robin Hood near Kirklees, which has been lately impaled in ye form of a Standing Hearse in order to preserve the stone from the rude hands of the curious traveller who frequently carried off a small Fragment of ye stone, and thereby diminished it's (sic) pristine Beauty'.[51] The enclosure suggests both care and awareness of tourism on the part of the Armitages. Ismay says that 'The curious antiquarian Mr Thoresby informs us, that amongst the papers of the learned Dr Gale Dean of York was found this Epitaph of Robin Hood', adding, 'I could never discover any vestigial of that kind upon ye stone'.[52] He also refers to four wooden statues portraying 'Robin Hood, Little John, Will Stukely and Midge ye Miller's son standing in the Hall at Kirklees'.[53] These statues appear, with illustration, as

---

51 Ismay, notebook, 14 April, 1752, probably finished in 1756/7. Also in a letter to Richard Frank, 17 November, 1757.   52 Ismay, *Eminent men*, 36–9, probably completed 1761.   53 Ibid., 18, 41; *RRH*, p. 19, n.3, citing Thomas Allen, *A new and complete history of the county of York* (London, 1831), vol. 6, p. 295, which says that the figure of Robin 'formerly stood at one side of the entrance into the old hall' and 'over the Kitchen Door is placed a large image of wood, forester like dress'd in a green Livery, representing the renowned Archer Little John'.

'Three 17th century carved oak figures of warriors and a later similar lime wood figure', in the brochure for the sale of the contents of Kirklees Hall.[54]

The Robin Hood legend did not appeal to this active cleric, but through his contact with Richard Frank (1698–1762), a Pontefract antiquarian who owned Johnston's papers, we get his description and drawings of the grave.[55] By his own admission, his drawing is a 'rough sketch'.[56] Judging from his drawings of Elizabeth de Stainton's tomb, Ismay's drawings are accurate if amateurish. He drew Robin Hood's gravestone in 1754 and 1759.[57]

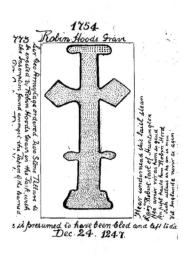

If we examine three published drawings of the grave, in Richard Gough's 1785 English edition of Camden's *Britannia*, a second version in his *Sepulchral Monuments* (1786–96), and Hearne's edition of Leland's *Itinerary*, we see variations. Comparison therefore suggests that Ismay, working directly from the actual gravestone, may be a more reliable source than his published sources for the design and appearance of the stone.[58]

As mentioned above, Nathaniel Johnston visited Kirklees in 1669, and from his papers we know that he and his brother Henry were meticulous artists. In the 1669 Johnston drawing, it is clearly a common three-step Calvary, typical of those found across England. Ismay's drawings, particularly of 1754, suggest the remains of a Calvary step, eroded by weathering.

---

54 Philips Auctioneers, Leeds, *Kirklees Hall sale brochure 1987*, 29, lot 247. 55 Ismay, letter to Richard Frank at Pontefract, 17 November 1757. 56 Ibid., 13. 57 Ismay, *Eminent men*, p. 43: 1752 drawing; Ismay, *Armytage of Kirklees*, notes probably written in 1755: 1754 drawing. 58 There is a version of the *Britannia* drawing, done by Ethel Walker, in J.W. Walker's *True history*. She eliminated the broad cross feature in the original and enhanced what she thought the floriated head would have looked like. Another image, which first appeared in Hearne's edition of Leland's *Itinerary*, appeared in Samuel J. Chadwick, 'Kirklees Priory', *YAJ*, 16 (1902), 320, facing 322.

There is also a similarity between the two slightly splayed cross arms. The foot of the Ismay shaft is not a well-defined Calvary steps design shown in the Johnston drawing, and the head is not a floriated cross. Peter Ryder's studies of south Yorkshire grave covers show the style of the Ismay design resembles other extant slabs around the south of the county.[59] Given the simplicity in design and the fact that the slab was clearly an average-sized cross slab, it suggests a thirteenth century, rather than mid fourteenth-century execution when compared with the forms and styles in Ryder's *Medieval Cross Slab Grave Covers.*[60] The Ismay and Johnston drawings show the lower terminal displaced downwards to form a *knop* or ring on the cross shaft. The only surviving slab in West Yorkshire that bears any resemblance is found in St Michael's, Thornhill, which Ryder dates to late thirteenth or early fourteenth century.[61]

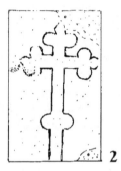

St Michael's Thornhill

The alleged text around the perimeter, first mentioned by Grafton, is an unusual feature. Possibly Johnston added the text in his drawing to make it fit to Grafton's words, but Johnston's drawings of other monuments that have survived shows he was not prone to adding detail

The extant grave drawing, however, is *not* by Johnston, but a copy by Stukeley, and Stukeley may have added Grafton's text. Given Stukeley's treatment of the Robin Hood material, and the fact that the texts surviving on slabs up to the period of the Dissolution are in Latin not the vernacular, and that of the surviving examples of text running round the perimeter, very few in West Yorkshire pre-date the mid fifteenth century, the weight of evidence tends to come down in favour of him adding Grafton's text. However,

59 Peter F. Ryder, 'The cross slab grave cover in South Yorkshire', MA dissertation, University of Sheffield, 1980; *Medieval cross slab grave covers in West Yorkshire*, West Yorkshire Archaeology Handbooks, West Yorkshire Archaeology Service (Wakefield, 1991). 60 pp 49–60.   61 Ibid., p. 44, fig. 2 and notes. See also pp 7, 13, 28, 32, 39, 43, 47–8,

Grafton did not mention a 'Thomas', and it would be more in keeping for a Stukeley's addition to have alluded to Robin's fanciful nobility, be it as Robert Locksley Earl of Huntingdon, or Stukeley's own invention for Robin Hood: Robert Fitzooth.[62]

The widely-reproduced drawing of Robin Hood's Grave, attributed to Johnston, published in the *Yorkshire Archaeological Journal* in 1902 and subsequently appearing in nearly every Robin Hood history, was not by Johnston but a copy from Stukeley's drawing, made by the wife of the Reverend Harris Fleming St John, whose family owned the Stukeley papers.[63] According to notes attached to a letter dated 5 December 1900 from St John to Sir George Armytage,[64] Stukeley records, 'The gravestone yet remains near the park at Kirksley Abby Yorkshr. but the Inscription scarce legible. It is drawn out in the next page as by Dr Johnstone in his Yorkshire Antiquitys. I suppose the above writt Epitaph was upon the cross-mentioned to be at the head of the grave at the highway side. Tis overshadow'd with Trees'.[65] Stukeley transcribes a version of the epitaph from Thoresby, derived from Gale.

The extant drawing is therefore a copy of Johnston's drawing of the grave and Stukeley put it into its landscape context: the background trees are colour washed in brown and added into the original imagery, although this does not show up in the black and white printed version. Whether the inscription around the slab is genuine is debatable, but its lack of specificity to the legend goes some way to supporting its authenticity.

The 'Prospect of Kirkleys' drawing, in the same article in the *YAJ*, had earlier appeared in the second edition of Stukeley's *Itinerarium Curiosum*, where it was also attributed to Johnston.[66] The original drawing at the Bodleian has no such attribution.[67] Neither Stukeley or Johnston could have seen all the elements present in the drawing, since the turreted buildings in the location of the old priory were not standing even in Johnston's day, and must be a conjectural reconstruction.[68] The quality of landscape drawing

---

but, see slabs at Pontefract (39) and Thorp Arch (45) with such texts, datable to fourteenth century. **62** See Appendix for drawing. **63** WYAS, Calderdale KMB 887/2, private letter to Sir George Armytage, 5 December 1900, explains St John will not loan out the Stukeley manuscripts, but his wife will copy the grave drawing. WYAS Calderdale, KMB 887/9 is the drawing, as reproduced in the *YAJ*; see also Stuart Piggott, *William Stukeley, an eighteenth-century antiquary* (rev. ed. London, 1985), p. 168; Janet D. Martin claims the grave and 'prospect' drawings reappeared in the 19th century, perhaps after the image of it was published in the *YAJ*, 'The antiquarian collections of Nathaniel Johnston (1629–1705)', B.Litt. dissertation, Oxford University (1956), p. 87. **64** WYAS Calderdale KMB 887/2. **65** WYAS Calderdale KMB 887/1, 887/2, copied from a manuscript of Dr Stukeley's from 1720. The information reflects Grafton. **66** William Stukeley, *Itinerarium curiosum* (London, 1776), I. 1, Pl. 99. **67** Bodleian Library, MS Top. Gen. b53 f 79v. **68** Sir G.J. Armytage, *Account of the excavations of Kirklees Priory*, Proceedings of the Society of Antiquaries, second series (London, 1906), vol. 21, p. 1, p. 182. Sir George made a full inventory of all the masons' marks in Kirklees Hall and (allowing for Stukeley copying a Johnston original) is similar to a known Johnston landscape of Pontefract.[69] The representation of Kirklees Hall could not have been made without sight of the actual building. It clearly shows the northern Jacobean 'E' gable, accurate eastern elevations, the unusual turret and Bradley Wood. The building between the Hall and the Priory site could have been drawn by Johnston, but it may have been a recent building.[70] These core elements, and those of the Low Hall buildings (now Home Farm) are too accurate to have been drawn without first hand reference. Careful examination of the original Bodleian drawing shows a very different pen-stroke for the alleged priory buildings. They are an afterthought to the orig-inal, a 'fantastic' reconstruction that is pure Stukeley. Stukeley travelled in Yorkshire in 1740 and 1747,[71] and the drawing of Robin Hood's Well on the back of the same folio as the grave drawing could not have been Johnston's, as its Vanbrugh canopy was not erected until 1710.[72] In the first edition of his book on Stukeley, Piggott attributes the drawings of Robin Hood's Grave, Well, and the Prospect of Kirklees to Stukeley without question.[73]

Stephen Knight reproduces Stukeley's 'Johnston' drawing of the grave stating that it is from Gough,[74] but a different drawing appears in Gough's *Sepulchral Monuments*:[75]

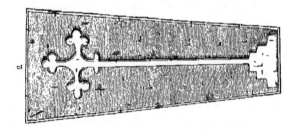

This changes the cross sections, by ending them with *fleur de lys*, some-thing not apparent in the drawings of the people known to have seen the grave, and gives no border text. Stukeley's friend Richard Gough acquired

remaining buildings of Home Farm, the modern name of the Priory Site. The same marks were found at both sites confirming that stonework from the Priory buildings was used for the new hall. Some reproduced Chadwick, 'Kirklees', facing p. 335.   69 WYAS Leeds, BF 6.   70 Royal Commission for Historic Monuments 49301, 4/134, building 9, malt-house, which dates the building on stylistic grounds to the late 17th century.   71 *The family memoirs of the Rev. William Stukeley M.D.*, ed. W.C. Lukis, Surtees Society, 3 vols (Durham, 1882, 1882, 1887), vol. 1, p. lxxiii; vol. 2, p. lxxvi, vol. 3, p. lxxx, p. 377.   72 Howard Colvin, *A biographical dictionary of British architects, 1600–1840* (London, 1978), p. 853.   73 Stuart Piggott, *William Stukeley*, 1st ed. (London, 1950), pp 189, 215 and 218.   74 *A complete study*, p. 20.   75 Richard Gough, *Sepulchral monuments* (London, 1786), vol. 1, part i, p. cviii and Plate 1 figure ii.

some of his manuscripts after 1766 and perhaps saw the surviving drawing.[76] His drawing of the de Staynton tomb, compared with Ismay's, puts the words in the wrong place.[77] Gough misdated the discovery of Stainton's tomb (May 1744: local evidence shows it was 1706).[78] Gough cannot be relied upon for accuracy; Ismay, in contrast, seems to have been a careful copyist.

Stukeley was a very important and influential historian. By 1738, Piggott says that 'he was already established as the outstanding British antiquary of his time', and that from 1710 – 25, 'he was actively engaged in the field work which can now be recognized as the main scientific achievement of his archaeological career [...] After his death in 1756 we have to wait until the nineteenth century before we find men taking up the tradition of archaeological field work where he left it'.[79] His relationship with the Robin Hood legend is however, problematical. His interest in part, lay in his early childhood fantasy that he was a descendant of either Will Stukely, one of Robin Hood's men in the *Gest,* or the Elizabethan 'Bold Stutly'.[80] His *Paleographia Brittanica* offered an invented identity and genealogy for Robin Hood as Robert Fitzooth pretended Earl of Huntingdon, *ob.* 1274. This 1274 date appears to have been arrived at by inverting the last two digits of the 1247 in the epitaph.[81] By the time that this appeared, during the latter part of his life, even his admirers knew that his ideas 'were becoming increasingly fantastic'.[82] Hearne was critical of Stukeley at a much earlier date in his career: 'a very fanciful man, and the things he hath published are built upon fancy [...] He hath published a draught [drawing] of Waltham Cross, all fancy, yet the Cross is standing, and Mr Bridges hath published a true draught of it'.[83] This criticism, however, may say more about Hearne's own personal and political bias than it does about Stukeley's accuracy at the time.[84] It would be wise, however, when considering the attribution of the 'Johnston' drawing, to bear in mind these two sides of the Stukeley legacy.

The Armytage family and estate development

Since October 1565, the Armytage family has owned the Kirklees estate. The grave is older, perhaps dating back to the thirteenth century; the legend of Robin's death at Kirklees goes back to the *Gest,* and specific mention of the grave goes back to 1534. For over four centuries the Armytage family has owned this Robin Hood legacy, the protector and defender of the monument, a relationship that has often yielded family pride yet also been intrusive and

76 Piggott, *Stukeley,* p. 168.   **77** Gough, *Sepulchral monuments,* cix, Plate 4, figure v; Ismay, *Eminent men,* p. 34.   **78** Gough, *Sepulchral monuments,* vol. 2, part I, p. ccxlvii. **79** Piggott, *Stukeley,* pp 13, 15, 32.   **80** Piggott *Stukeley,* p. 28.   **81** William Stukeley, *Paleographia Britannica* (Stamford, 1746), p. 115, no. 2; repr. Knight, *A complete study,* p. 18.   **82** Piggott, *Stukeley,* p. 15.   **83** Lukis, *Family memoirs,* p. 169, extract from Hearne's Diary, 9/10/1722.   **84** Lukis, *Family memoirs,* p. 169, n.22.

difficult. Its popularity as a tourist site followed major publications of the ballads. Has the Robin Hood legacy rubbed off onto the Armytage family at times? Could the Armytage family have produced the legendary gravestone for their own benefit?

Between the dissolution of Kirklees in 1539 and John Armytage's purchase in 1565, the Priory buildings and site were subject to the property speculation of the post-Dissolution land market, changing hands six times. One early owner, John Saville, we have seen, was concerned with the estate's historical associations. Saville, from a well-established family that had joined the nobility, was a scholar, with the time to read and write about matters of historical interest. His family no longer had the same needs as the early Armytages, merchants who made good out of the Tudor property and mercantile boom.

John Armytage of Farnley Tyas, yeoman, had bought the mansion house or manor of Kyrklees with appurtenances on 26 October 1565 from Robert and Alice Pylkington, who had built the Tudor mansion house with stone from priory buildings.[85] From this point onwards, it is impossible to separate the history of the tomb from the rise of the Armytage family. It seems that they were not initially interested in Kirklees because of the Robin Hood association, but this did become of interest to later generations of the family, by which time the gravestone had already become a widely reported curio and so it was almost certainly not a fabrication of the Armytage family. The Armytage family of Huddersfield were in succession husbandmen, clothiers, yeomen and eventually merchants.[86] John I sent his son John to Trinity College, Cambridge in 1563–4,[87] thereafter transferring to the Middle Temple in London.[88] This indicates his ambition and wealth. John I was not to enjoy the benefits of this new estate and local prestige for long; he was murdered on 21 February 1574 by rebel 'kernes' in Northern Ireland in horrifying circumstances.

Muniments from John II's time, show that this was the period of the largest number of land acquisitions, consolidating the core estate. He became 'landed gentry', earning money by estate management, money-lending, legal work and mercantile activity, becoming a Justice of the Peace for the West Riding, and dying in 1606.[89] In his lifetime the Sloane *Life of Robin Hood* was copied, although there is no evidence to show that it was disseminated.[90] Because of

85 West Yorkshire Archive Service (WYAS): Calderdale, KM288.   86 The early history of the family is complex and will be presented in David Hepworth, '*The rise of the Armytage family of South Crosland*,' *YAJ*, forthcoming.   87 John Venn and J.A. Venn, *Alumni Cantabrigienses* (Cambridge, 1922), part 1, I. 39.   88 Sir Henry F. Macgeagh and A.H.C. Sturgess, *Register of admissions to the Honourable Society of the Middle Temple* (London, 1949), I. 31.   89 WYAS, Calderdale, KMB868.   90 British Library Sloane MS 780; *RRH* states that it was published with inaccuracies by W.J. Thoms in 1858 and J.M. Gutch 1847. According to recent unpublished work, by Thomas Hahn, Thoms made his own transcript, copied with all inaccuracies and omissions by Gutch. I am grateful to Professor Hahn for access to this material.

his business and legal interests in London, John could have known and possibly seen Munday's Robin Hood plays. Judging from the landscape shown in a 1757 estate survey, before the 'arcadian' reworking of the estate, it appears that he and his heirs kept the park in its Jacobean style.[91] Careful measurements from all the existing estate surveys, up to the current Ordnance Survey map, show that the position of the grave remains constant, despite the extensive landscaping, suggesting they felt that it was appropriate to maintain the site, as part of the national and their own heritage. Eighteenth-century landscape designers such as Capability Brown and Repton included classical follies or statuary into newly reworked estates: Kirklees apparently did not need such embellishments because of the presence of the grave of the nation's legendary hero.

John III inherited the estate in 1607, living until 1650. He met Roger Dodsworth and possibly gave him the version of the Robin Hood story, which has all the overtones of a localized legend, mentioning Little John in Clifton on Calder: the village that the Armytage family was quickly purchasing. Shortly after John III inherited the estate, the 1607 revision of Camden's *Britannia* appeared, now including mention of Robin's grave, from details supplied by John Saville. Was the Little John story developed by the Armytage family for their children (and they were, after all, a family of Johns), adding colour to the grave on their estate? Even before the advent of early tourism, the popularity of Robin Hood ballads must have added a degree of pride in the grave, for the children if not the parents. During John III's lifetime, Parker published his *True Tale of Robin Hood*, 1632. Perhaps this, with the English version of Camden's *Britannia*, fostered an antiquarian and embryonic tourist interest in the Kirklees site, though there is no record, and John III was personally and financially burdened by the Civil War; it is unlikely that in turbulent times many people would have sought out the grave as a visiting place.[92] He was buried at Hartshead on 16 July 1650, outliving his son, Francis who died in the Siege of York in 1644.[93] Around now, one member of the family must have commissioned the sculpting of the four statues, said to be Robin Hood, Little John, Will Stukely and Midge the Miller's son.

It is during the life of Sir John IV that the documented history of the grave becomes traceable. He succeeded to the estate in 1650, became Sheriff of Yorkshire in 1669, the year in which Johnston visited Kirklees.[94] Kirklees suffered badly during the Civil War and Sir John used his position as Sheriff to fight religious dissenters and former Parliamentarians, and surviving local

91 WYAS, Calderdale, KMA1215/1 estate plans dated 1757: before and after plans of landscape works drawn by Francis Richardson; WYAS Calderdale KMA 1213, a copy of a much older estate plan, shows medieval field layout with field names which coincide with those given in the priory's Dissolution papers, as well as key buildings, but not the grave or other minor features. 92 WYAS Calderdale, KMB 862. 93 R. Skaife, 'Register of burials in York Minster', *YATJ*, 1 (1870), 235. 94 Bodleian Library, Top. Yorks. 13 f 161v.

diaries tell that they 'had a great enemy in Sir John'. He met an unusual death, falling from his horse twice as he returned home from a drinking party at Nunbrook on the edge of the estate, in April 1677. Records state 'A second time he fell, just by Robin Hood's grave; his man lifted in vain [...] went back to Nunbrook for help, but found him dead'.[95] Needless to say, the dissenters traded on this story for many years to come, claiming it as God's justice.

Sir John V, who succeeded in 1694, was a friend of Dr Richard Richardson, the antiquarian who gave information about the estate to Thomas Hearne, Ralph Thoresby and many other early eighteenth-century antiquarians. This was the beginning of the grave coming into the public's eye. His brother, George, who died in 1736 unmarried, succeeded him; he was disliked and squandered money, ignoring the estate. Sir John V made a distant relative, Samuel Armytage of Kerresforth Hill, near Barnsley his successor. Samuel took an active interest in the grave, digging under the stone, as shown in the Richardson letter to Ralph Thoresby, quoted above, and judging from Ismay's notes, having the grave enclosed. His successor, John VI, was killed in action against the French during the Seven Years War. *The Gentleman's Magazine* for 1758 refers to his conduct and death, and there were a number of poems written about him, including 'Kirk-Leas', a eulogy to both the estate and Sir John, in the *Cambridge Chronicle* of Saturday, 5 February 1762.[96] 'Kirk-Leas' contains verses covering the presence of Robin Hood's grave on the estate and a footnote about Robin Hood's bow, allegedly lost in the confusion surrounding Sir John's death. Ismay referred to the bow in his letter to Richard Frank. By the mid eighteenth century the family were clearly greatly interested in the legend, caring for the grave and claiming to have Robin Hood memorabilia.

Sir John VI began plans to modernize the estate and in 1755 spent money on the grave, presumably because of damage by souvenir hunting tourists, or locals, or estate workmen.[97] His son, Sir George II, began a radical scheme of improving the house, parkland and estate, and his successor, Sir George III, in 1773 ordered works which included the erection of the epitaph, as well as new walls, the present pillars, upright and top railings.[98] Thereafter no substantial works were undertaken on the grave until 1904–7, when Sir George John Armytage spent £77 9s. 6d. on work around the Nuns' Graves, a further £8 15s. 8d. on priory excavations and £39 9s. 1d. on work restoring Robin Hood's Room in the 'Gatehouse'.

95 Joseph Hunter, *The rise of the old dissent exemplified in the life of Oliver Heywood, 1630–1702* (London, 1842), pp 152, 282.   96 Richard Griffith, 'Kirk-Leas: a descriptive poem', 1760, published London, 1802.   97 WYAS Calderdale, KMB 868, note dated 19/2/1755.   98 Ismay 1773, says the work was completed by 26 October. The vouchers for this work are found under the above dates in WYAS Calderdale KMA 732/28, with the cashbook entry appearing in KMA 741, under 6 April. See also WYAS Calderdale, KMA 732/40, voucher dated 6 August 1785.

The Wakefield and Huddersfield Armytage families

The extended Armytage family included local branches and there is evidence that they too prided themselves on the family's connections to the Robin Hood legend. A branch of the family, living in a property called 'The Lodge' at Outwood, Wakefield in the seventeenth century, came from Thomas Armytage of Morley, probably a brother of John I of Kirklees. The will of Sir John V of Kirklees, 1732, names the Outwood branch as heirs in the remainder to the Kirklees estate, failing heirs to Samuel Armytage who actually inherited.[99]

Hunter suggested that the original Robin Hood was Robert Hood who, with his wife Matilda, appears in Wakefield Court Rolls during the late thirteenth and early fourteenth centuries. As scholars have noted, there was a field name, *Robinhoodstreteclose*, recorded 1650, and *Robin Hood Hill*, 1657, within Outwood in the Stanley graveship of Wakefield,[1] suggesting local interest in the legend and its Wakefield associations, and perhaps even residual stories stemming from the offspring of John and Raghnild Hood of 1202, at Bottom Boat in Stanley.[2] There is also, within the muniments of the Outwood Armytage family, a transaction, 1628–9, of a surrender of 'two closes called Robinhood Street Closes containing 4 acres... near Wakefield Outwoodside in the graveship of Stanley'.[3] We also, however, find the field-name, 'Roberdrode,' 1348; 'Robert Royd,' 1597;[4] and 'Robbinroyd,' 1699.[5] 'Royd', from Old English *rod*, ' clearing', is a common place-name element in Lancashire and the West Riding: the sense is 'Robert's clearing'. The earliest names, then, are recording a *Robert*, as the owner of the land, not *Robin Hood*, and it looks as if the *Robin Hood* names followed from such naming and from the outlaw's fame or the Hood family and one of its members. Michael Evans shows how plain *Robert / Robin* place-names could change to *Robin Hood* names (see below, 186). The 'Robert Rode' name in particular may have added an auditory prompt to change to Robin Hood names.

---

99 A copy of the will is found at WYAS, Calderdale, KMB 862. **1** A.H. Smith, *The place-names of the West Riding of Yorkshire*, 6 vols, Part 2, *The wapentakes of Osgoldcross and Agbrigg*, EPNS (Cambridge, 1961–86), p. 158, citing WYAS, YAS, MD225/1/376, m. 3d; Holt, p. 51; *RRH*, p. 309. There is a transaction, 1628–9, of a surrender of 'two closes called Robinhood Street Closes containing 4 acres [...] near Wakefield Outwoodside in the graveship of Stanley'. **2** *Pedes Finium Ebor. Regnante Johanne AD MCXCIX–AD MCCXIV*, Surtees Society, vol. 94 (Durham, 1897 for 1894), p. 23. These muniments are housed in Lincolnshire County Archives, under Hotchkin. Hereafter LCA Hotchkin. **3** LCA Hotchkin 1/7/2, 9 January 1628/9. **4** LCA Hotchkin 1/7/1, admission, 9 September 1597. **5** Smith, *Place-names of the West Riding*, II. 162; WYAS, YAS, MD225/1/74, m. 6r, translated and calendared in *The court rolls of the manor of Wakefield from September 1348 to September 1350*, ed. Helen M. Jewell, Yorkshire Archaeological Society, Wakefield Court Roll Series, Second Series, (Leeds, 1981), vol. 2, p. 32. A bond of 1632 confirms that 'Robert Roide' was also known as 'Robyn Roide', LCA Hotchkin 1/7/5; 1/7/6.

This Wakefield land, however, had associations with the Armytage family. Transactions in 1631 show that the land included 'The Lodge house', which became the Armytage family home.[6] William Armytage, grandson of Thomas Armytage of Morley, was in residence in the Lodge and purchased Robin Hood Street Closes from Thomas Fleming on 21 April 1662.[7] It should be noted from the location of The Lodge on Jeffrey's 1771 map, it is east of Wakefield centre and near Bichill, and also near to Newton – both areas associated with the fourteenth-century Hood family of Wakefield. Family interest and local Wakefield associations could both have played a part in the development of the 'Robert' and 'Robin Hood' names.

This may seem coincidence but, if we next consider the branch of the Armytage family that remained near to their home village of Armytage Bridge, we find another coincidence. The first recorded Armytage ('Adam dell Hermitage'), in South Crosland near Huddersfield, is dated to 1340.[8] By the early seventeenth century again, Richard Armitage acquired a property called Dudmanstone, just to the east of Armitage Bridge.[9] Intriguingly, Robin Hood Hill and House (as well as the later Robin Hood Tunnel) are within what was their landholding, though the point at which these names originated is not known.[10]

6 LCA Hotchkin 1/7/3 dated 19 February 1630/1; LCA Hotchkin 1/7/4 dated 4 November 1631, when it refers to 'The Lodge house' in an endorsement.   7 LCA Hotchkin 1/7/11–12.   8 WYAS, Kirklees, KX163, p. 6, transcript of PRO, DL43, Bundle 10, No. 5, a rental for the Honour of Pontefract, including the Manor of Almondbury, under which South Crosland and Armitage Bridge fell. Adam dell Hermitage holds the Hermitage, one of thirty-seven free tenants listed.   9 Sometimes spelled Deadmanstone, within what is now Berry Brow. According to Smith, *Place-names of the West Riding*, p. 259, first recorded in 1434, WYAS, Kirklees, DD/WBD/47.   10 *RRH*, p. 309.

With three different branches of the family having Robin Hood names associated with their landholdings, it is tempting to say that the legend permeated the main branches of the family. There may also be connections with the Hood family of Wakefield.

The possible identity of Robin Hood at Kirklees

Is it possible to know which Robert or Robin Hood was buried at Kirklees? Many have assumed it was the fourteenth-century Wakefield Robin Hood.[11] Hunter believed he was related to Prioress Elizabeth de Staynton, and because of the ballad evidence identified her as his murderess. Was this pure conjecture, subsequently promulgated by more recent writers?[12] What has gone unnoticed is a more definite connection between the fourteenth-century Wakefield Robert Hood and Kirklees priory; that link was Robert and Matilda Hood's neighbour at Bichill in Wakefield, Thomas Alayn, who also held a corrody at Kirklees.[13] The Hood family are extensively recorded in Wakefield from 1202, with all subsequent members appearing to originate in the Graveship or area of Stanley. In 1316, 'Robert Hode and Matilda his wife give 2/- for leave to take one piece of the Lord's waste on Bichill between the booths of Philip Damyson and Thomas Alayn of the length of 30 ft & breadth of 16ft to hold to the aforesaid Robert & Matilda & their heirs, rendering therefore yearly 6d at the three terms &c'.[14] This shows that Robert Hood and Thomas Alayn were at least business neighbours. The previous entry in the court rolls shows Thomas Alayn and his wife purchased their plot on Bichill at the same time. Mid fourteenth-century records show that by 1357/8 Robert Hood no longer held the property: 'William Hallestede and Alice his wife surrendered a tenement in Wakefield formerly in the tenure of Robert Hode, lying on Bichill'.[15] By Trinity Term Thomas Alayn was also no longer in possession, perhaps having taken up his corrody: 'In 10th Edward III (1336–7), Thomas Aleyn of Wakefield and Margaret his wife and their heirs in fee simple were granted 1 messuage and 4.5 bovates of bond land in Horbury, within the manor of

11 Hunter, 'The great hero'; Walker, *True History*; John Bellamy, *Robin Hood: an historical enquiry* (Bloomington, 1985); Graham Phillips and Martin Keatman, *Robin Hood: the man behind the myth* (London, 1995); Barbara Green, *The outlaw Robin Hood: his Yorkshire legend* (Huddersfield, 1991); 'The mystery of Robin Hood's grave', Ottakar's Local History Series, compiled by Nik Taylor (Stroud, 2001), 39–45; Brian Lewis, *Robin Hood: a Yorkshireman; the case for the Wentbridge Robin Hood* (Pontefract), Harold Speak and Jean Forrester, *Robin Hood of Wakefield* (Ossett, 1970), to name the most prominent and recent. 12 Hunter, 'The great hero', pp 51–66. 13 British Library, Harleian 4630, f 272a, from Saville of Thornhill papers. Confirmed by reference made by Johnston, WYAS Leeds, BF13, 268, stating that John Saville of Methley held the original in the mid 17th century. 14 YASRS, vol. 78, *Court rolls of the manor of Wakefield (1315–1317)*, ed. John Lister (Leeds 1930) vol. 4, p. 109. Original is Leeds University, Brotherton Library MS 295/30640, m 14d. 15 WYAS YAS, MD 225/1/83/1, m 1, Court roll of the manor of Wakefield, 1357–8, translation by Walker, 'True History', 126.

Wakefield and were accustomed to pay 27/– held of John de Warenne late Earl of Surrey'.[16] By 1357, this same entry shows that the lands were held by William de Hallestede and were paying 38s. 9d., along with other lands in Horbury formerly granted to the Alayns. William Hallestede became owner of the lands of both the Hoods and the Alayns. Could this suggest inter-marriage?

The dates of Robert Hood or Thomas Alayn's deaths are not known. It could be that Thomas and Robert were buried together, as the name 'Thomas' also appeared on the gravestone, according to Stukeley's picture.

The identity of the prioress at this time is also not known, perhaps Margaret Saville, who became prioress in 1350,[17] and granted the corrody to Thomas Alayn; not Elizabeth De Staynton. Elizabeth and her sister entered Kirklees in 1347 when both were less than twelve.[18] It is unlikely that she could have been prioress much before the mid 1360s, by which time Robert Hood and Thomas Alayn had been inactive in Wakefield for some years and were probably dead. She definitely was prioress before 1373, because on the back of a charter dated 47 Edward III (1373/4) granting licence under the statute of Mortmain to acquire lands, transcribed by John Watson, the following was written: '*Orate pro Elizabetha de Staynton quondam priorissa de Kirklese quia in tempore illius ista carta fuit adquista*' (Pray for Elizabeth de Staynton, formerly prioress of Kirklees because in her time this charter was acquired), so she was prioress when this application was made in 1371/2.

It is possible therefore, that both Robert Hood and Thomas Alayn ended their lives at Kirklees. Robert Hood may also have had a corrody there, or was perhaps visiting Thomas Alayn, when he died. It is likely therefore, that Robin Hood's grave at Kirklees is of the fourteenth century Wakefield Robert/Robin Hood promoted by Hunter and Walker. Whether he was anything like the Robin Hood of the ballads and whether he met his end in the manner described in the ballads is unlikely. This Robert Hood and many of his family members, both antecedents and descendants, exist in the record, particularly the Wakefield court rolls, yet none ever seem to have been outlaws. His entry, in death, into legend was probably the result of conflation made by the author of a lost ballad using extensive local knowledge. Perhaps the existence of the grave preceded the legend of the famous outlaw's death at Kirklees.

We have seen above, however, that the style of the grave might be late-thirteenth, rather than fourteenth-century. If so, could the man buried there be Holt's early thirteenth-century 'Hobbehod', a tenant of the Archbishop of York and outlawed by 1226?[19] It is possible, and there was a William Goldsborough living at that time; however, further information about this must remain for a future paper.

16 Coram Rege, Trinity 32 Edward III, m 35 (1358/9).   17 BIHR Register, 10 Archbishop Zouche, f 48r, appointed 10 May 1350.   18 Joseph Hunter, *South Yorkshire* (London, 1828–31) vol. 2, pp 384–5.   19 Holt, p. 54.

Framing Robin Hood: temporality and textuality in Anthony Munday's Huntington plays

LIZ OAKLEY-BROWN

In the early modern period the figure of Robin Hood is constructed as both the subject of history and fiction. The fifteenth-century Scottish historians Andrew of Wyntoun and Walter Bower, for instance, placed Robin Hood in the reign of Edward I and Henry III respectively.[1] John Major's *Historia Majoris Britanniae* (1521) fashioned Robin Hood in the reign of King John, whilst the second edition of William Camden's *Britannia* (*c.*1587) mentions the outlaw. Richard Grafton's *Chronicle at Large* (1568) was the first text to suggest he was of noble rank before being outlawed.[2] Raphael Holinshed's compendium *The Chronicles of Englande, Scotlande and Irelande* (1577) and John Stow's *Summary of English Chronicles* (1592) also include accounts of Robin Hood's exploits.[3] And from the earliest surviving ballad *Robin Hood and the Monk* (*c.*1450) onwards, poets and playwrights regularly employed Robin Hood in a variety of textual guises.[4] As part of the Robin Hood tradition, Anthony Munday's plays, *The Downfall of Robert, Earl of Huntington* and *The Death of Robert, Earl of Huntington* (*c.*1598), occupy a noteworthy position in their particular adaptation of material from both the historical and the fictional texts.[5] From a modern critical perspective, the figure of Robin

---

1 Andrew of Wyntoun, *The Orygynale Chronicle*, ed. D. Laing (Edinburgh, 1903–14); Walter Bower, Continuation of Fordun's *Scotichronicon*, ed. Thomas Hearne (Oxford, 1722). 2 Grafton says he was 'discended of a nobel parentage: or rather beyng of base stocke and linage, was for his manhode and chivalry advaunced to the noble dignite of an Erle,' but was outlawed for debt, *RHOOT*, p. 28. His earldom is not named. 3 John Major, *Historia Majoris Britanniae tam Angliae quam Scotiae*, (Paris, 1521); William Camden, *Britannia*, ed. and trans. R. Gough, 3 vols (London, 1809); John Stow, *Summary of English chronicles* (London, 1592); Richard Grafton, *A chronicle at large and mere history of the affayres of England; and kings of the same* (London, 1568–69); Raphael Holinshed, *The chronicles of England, Scotland and Irelande*, 3 vols (London, 1577); see Jeffrey L. Singman, *Robin Hood: The shaping of the legend* (Westport, Conn., 1998), p. 106. 4 For a discussion of 'The chroniclers' Robin', see *RHOOT*, pp 21–9. 5 Tracey Hill, *Anthony Munday and civic culture: history, power and representation in early modern London, 1580–1633* (Manchester, 2004) was published after this essay was written. I am grateful to Tracey Hill for helpful comments on this essay. Knight, *A complete study*, p. 122, states that Munday 'was commissioned by Henslowe for £5 to produce a Robin Hood in February 1598; soon after Henry Chettle and Munday shared £5 for the second part and then Chettle 10/– for mending the first'. There is some debate regarding the authorship of these plays, and many critics, including Malcolm A. Nelson, have attempted to establish which author wrote which parts and there is no clear answer regarding which author wrote which part: see Nelson, *The Robin Hood tradition in the English Renaissance*,

Hood that appears in the chronicles is no more 'real' than the character that appears in other literary, and more overtly, fictional, forms.[6] As Michel de Certeau has written 'history is not an epistemological criticism. It remains always a narrative'.[7] In this essay it is my intention to discuss ways in which Munday's sixteenth-century plays already explore the problematic subject that is Robin Hood. I will argue that *The Downfall* and *The Death* not only draw attention to issues of representation, but they are texts which also disrupt the opposition between history and fiction, leaving the textual politics of history itself open to question.

Because of their dependence on chronicle sources, *The Downfall* and *The Death* have been described by Richard Helgerson as history plays.[8] They also have the high rhetorical style that marks Elizabethan tragedy and history plays. Robin's story, his banishment and the treacheries and deceptions that accompany it, are played out in the context of court and government. His adventures as an outlaw in the forest are framed by this context: beginning with his the earl at dinner, his betrothal feast, in the presence of the queen, and ending with a scene where (in Robin's woodland camp) the king's court and government are restored to their rightful state just as the earl is restored to proper recognition by the king. Within the Robin Hood tradition, Munday's plays are distinctive in their presentation of the Robin Hood narrative. The figure of Robin Hood had previously appeared on the London stage in George Peele's *The Famous Chronicle of Edward I* (1593), in the anonymous *George a Greene* (1593), and in the lost *Pleasant Pastoral Commedie of Robin Hood and Little John* (1594).[9] These plays offer, as Jeffery L. Singman states, 'an unprecedented interpretation of Robin Hood – a historically-oriented biography of a hero whose legend had hitherto been dominated by episodic narratives and folk-plays'.[10] This historicizing of the hero on the stage comes just before the development of a series of lives of Robin Hood, beginning with the Sloane Life. Rather than providing a simple account of Robin Hood's life, however, the audience of Munday's plays is to be presented with a more complex biography of the gentrified Robert, Earl of Huntington.[11] In fact, the death of Robin Hood, as presented by Munday,

Elizabethan and Renaissance Studies, Salzburg Studies in English Literature (Salzburg, 1974), pp 124–9. **6** See *RHOOT*, pp 4–5. **7** *The writing of history*, trans. Tom Conley (New York, 1975), p. 43. **8** 'Writing empire and nation', in *The Cambridge companion to English literature*, ed. Arthur F. Kinney (Cambridge, 2000), p. 320. In particular, Munday uses Grafton's *Chronicle at large*. See Singman, 'Munday's unruly earl,' in *Playing Robin Hood: the legend in performance*, ed. Lois Potter (Newark, Delaware, 1998), pp 63–76, for a comparison of Grafton's text with Munday's plays. **9** Singman, 'Munday's unruly earl', p. 63. **10** Ibid. **11** The history of Prince John's treacherous seizing of Richard I's throne comes into Munday's play, and after that into the Robin Hood tradition, from Holinshed's *Chronicle*; the story of the Bruces also comes into Munday's drama, in the *Death*, from Holinshed's *Chronicle*: see Celeste Turner, *Anthony Mundy: an Elizabethan man of letters* (Berkeley, 1928), pp 117–18.

illustrates the very different depiction of the hero offered by these texts. Robin Hood's death had already been enacted in the late medieval ballad, the *Gest of Robin Hood*, but in that work Robin dies an outlaw.[12] In contrast, Munday, at the point of death, reinstates Robin as Robert, Earl of Huntington. This distinction between the two subject positions occupied by Robin and Robert is made clear at the outset of *The Downfall*: 'This youth', Skelton tells the audience,

> Is our Earle Robert, or your Robin Hoode.   (86, 88)

The action of the plays pivots around this binarism of 'our Earle Robert' and 'your Robin Hoode', initiating a code of social difference that is inscribed throughout both *The Death* and *The Downfall*.[13]

Indeed, it has been suggested that the plays are more concerned with the story of the Earl than that of Robin Hood, to such an extent that the figure of the outlaw almost disappears, for 'we are never quite allowed to forget that we are watching an earl playing at being an outlaw'.[14] Even though there are texts predating these plays that suggest that Robin Hood was a noble, as Malcolm Nelson states, 'it is nonetheless astonishing to hear him named as the Earl of Huntington' at the start of *The Downfall*.[15] Munday's audience would, he argues, have been used to Robin Hood as 'a ballad hero and the leader of May games ... Few of them could have been aware that a generation earlier a chronicler had suggested he had been a member of the nobility, or that a minor poet had called him a county'.[16] Essentially, for the future tradition, it was Munday who created the Earl of Huntington identity for

---

12 Anthony Munday, *The Downfall of Robert, Earl of Huntington*, ed. John Carney Meagher, The Malone Society Reprints (London, 1965); and *The Death of Robert, Earl of Huntington*, ed. John Carney Meagher, The Malone Society Reprints (London, 1967). All quotations are from these editions. Richard hails Robin, shortly before his death, as 'Earle Robert', but agrees that in future he shall be called Robin Hood, *Death*, 394–420; Singman, 'Munday's unruly earl', p. 70.   13 Scenes at court and greenwood scenes alternate; Skelton calls the play both 'noble Roberts wrong' and 'Robins Tragedie', 2226–9. See Knight, *A complete study*, p. 124 for a further discussion of this distinction.   14 Nelson, *Robin Hood tradition*, p. 160. Nelson argues that *The Pleasant Pastoral Commedie of Robin Hood and Little John* (1594) had presented a traditional yeoman-outlaw Robin Hood in the context of May games and the morris dance, whereas *The Downfall* and *Death* mark a departure from this tradition: Skelton fears the absence of such homely elements may displease Henry VIII but Eltham insists that the King and he have decided that this play will present a more elevated theme, the hero's 'honorable life, in merry Sherewod', pp 115–16.   15 Nelson, *Robin Hood tradition*, pp 130–1; Nelson suggests Munday got the idea from Holinshed's reference in his *Chronicles of Scotland* to David of Scotland who became Earl of Huntingdon in Richard I's reign.   16 Ibid., pp 119–20. The chronicler is Grafton, the poet is William Warner, author of *Albion's England* ('county' here = 'earl': Robin rules a band of 'yomandrye' in the woods, robbing the rich to help the poor, in the woods).

Robin. In part, the fashioning of Robin Hood as the Earl of Huntington is determined by the generic demands of the tragedy that Munday is attempting to construct.[17] There are, however, contemporary political imperatives that deem this aristocratic revision appropriate:

> The impact of the Elizabethan period's powerful monarchy is evident in the text as the viewpoint accepts royal authority and fears most forcefully those arch-enemies of the hierarchy, the untrustworthy confidante or employee.[18]

In contrast to the earlier notions of Robin Hood as benevolent thief, a depiction realized even in Grafton's historicising account, Munday's Earl is suddenly branded an outlaw merely because he owes money to his uncle, Gilbert Hood, the prior of York.[19] Furthermore, in Munday's version of Robin Hood it is not the authority of the sheriff of Nottingham, corrupt clerics, or the king that constitute his enemies, as more readily found in the tradition; rather, the threat to the earl's social position comes from the more localized hostility of family, frustrated lovers, and a sycophantic but unfaithful steward.[20] As Robin announces in *The Downfall*: 'I am outlawed by the Prior of Yorke, / My traiterous uncle' (329–30).

Bevington has accounted for the gentrification of Robin Hood rather differently. In 1598, Munday was commissioned by Philip Henslowe to produce a Robin Hood play.[21] With reference to this particular context, Bevington argues that

> Perhaps the Admiral's men's most ambitious efforts to give sympathetic expression to the Puritan viewpoint are to be found in their popular Robin Hood series ... the name of Huntington had compelling topical associations for the English elect; the third Earl of Huntington had been, as a candidate for succession to the throne

---

17 Nelson comments 'the death of an outlaw, no matter how noble, was not a fit subject for tragedy, which Munday was attempting', *Robin Hood tradition*, p. 131.   18 Knight, *A complete study*, p. 123.   19 *Downfall*, 145–212. His position is therefore altered to one more like that of Sir Richard of the Lee in the *Gest*. He has also been too generous to supposed friends who now turn against him: 'fawning sycophants, / That while the sunshine of my greatnesse dur'd, / Reveld out all my day for your delights, / And now you see the blacke night of my woe', 336–9. The underlying cause is the malice of the Prior and Warman, the false steward, plus the lusts of Prince John and Queen Elinor, trying to part Robert and Matilda. A web of destructive treachery spreads through court and government, as in *King Lear*. Nelson, *Robin Hood tradition*, pp 140–1, observes that Munday mingles invention with 'material cribbed and twisted from history' to make this Robin Hood tale a high political drama at times of 'vital change in the rule of the kingdom and ... possible civil war'.   20 Knight, *A complete study*, p. 123, observes that literature of the period had established these as agents of aristocratic downfall; see also Singman, 'Munday's unruly earl', p. 64.   21 Knight, *A complete study*, p. 122.

> during the 1560s, the hope of many ardent Protestants fearful of
> Elizabeth's untimely death, and his brothers had served the Puritan
> cause in Parliament throughout the reign.[22]

This seeming intertextual link to the plays' historical context, however, really
serves as a means for Bevington to place Munday's plays within a historical
frame that appears to uphold the politics of English Puritanism. Commenting
on the 'evident simplicity' of Bevington's thesis, Stephen Knight refutes this
method of historicization, stating that this 'work is…no more than a literary
historical equivalent of asking just who was the real Robin Hood'.[23] Arguably,
it is the unproblematic reading of history represented in Bevington's argument that Munday's plays, unwittingly, challenge.

   The gentrification of Munday's Robin Hood is further assisted in the
characterization of other roles in the plays, in particular Prince John and his
mother, Queen Elinor. His outlawing takes place in a context of high treason and political scheming at the royal court. The Prince is presented as an
autocratic usurper of the crown, who deals with opposition by threatening
exile. Elinor is figured as a scheming Queen Mother who, resenting Ely's
regency, with 'ambitious John […] rais'd many mutinies' (75–6).[24]
Significantly, Munday's use of certain details concerning these historical characters has caused debate. For instance, legend rumoured that Eleanor of
Aquitaine had Rosamond, Henry II's mistress, murdered: an act alluded to
in *The Downfall* (659–69).[25] In the notes which accompany their edition of
The Downfall, Knight and Ohlgren comment that, as Prince John speaks to
Queen Elinor of 'the curse of Rosamond' which 'rests on [her] head' (661),
Munday, is having 'fun' with 'history.'[26] Somewhat more forcefully, Nelson
announces that

> A much more serious and surprising perversion of history lies in the
> use of members of the royal family as unlawful lovers of the play's
> hero and heroine.[27]

In contrast to a more regal depiction, Prince John in Munday's version simply
becomes Robin Hood's rival for the love of Maid Marian. And in a similar

22 David Bevington, *Tudor drama and politics* (Cambridge, Mass., 1968), p. 295. 23
Knight, *A complete study*, p. 131. 24 Munday probably took this characterization of
Queen Elinor from Shakespeare's history play, *King John*: Turner, *Mundy*, p. 117. 25
For a hypothesis that Munday may have associated Marion with Rosamund, as two vic-
tims of a jealous Queen Elinor, through the literary connection between Daniel's *Fair
Rosamund* and Drayton's *Matilda the faire and chaste daughter of Lord R. Fitzwater* (1594),
which imitated it, see Nelson, *Robin Hood tradition*, pp 133–4 and 139. 26 See also
Knight, *A complete study*, p. 131. It could be argued that Munday is blackening his vil-
lainous Queen Mother's character, as a woman driven to heinous crimes by sexual rejec-
tion and jealousy; John rails melodramatically against her 'sharpe furie, and infernall rage
[…] cankers hate', 641, 662. 27 Nelson, *Robin Hood tradition*, p. 82.

manner, Eleanor of Aquitaine becomes a woman motivated purely by her lust for Robin.[28] Munday's plays, therefore, take figures from history and refashions them according to his purpose, elevating both the focal hero and the type of genre, setting and plot is which his outlawry is now constructed.

Whether this strategy is viewed as playfulness or 'perversion', what is clear is that Munday's texts interrogate the politics of history itself. For these plays not only manipulate historical characters, they also play with notions of historicity. Rather than foregrounding history as a linear narrative, the plays manufacture a version of reality that hinges on a mise-en-abîme of temporal frames: the plays are set within the court of Henry VIII, the plot concerned with the time of Richard I, while Munday's texts themselves are the products of Elizabethan England.[29]

It seems significant that *The Downfall* and *The Death* were produced in a period that was becoming increasingly conscious of the subject of history. Indeed, Munday's own interest in historical narrative is witnessed in his editions of *A Brief Chronicle of the Success of Times from the Creation of the World, to this Instant* (1611) and an edition of John Stow's *Survey of London* (1618). Graham Holderness has argued that during the late sixteenth and early seventeenth century, '"modern" history was being created', citing Camden's *Britannia* (1586), Stow's *Survey of London* (1598) and John Selden's *History of Tithes* (1618) as examples of 'landmarks in the growth of the new historiography'.[30] Humanist discourses which were breaking with the 'providential concept of history', motivated instead by the interrelation of classical culture with their own period, and influenced by the new historical thought of Machiavelli, Jean Bodin and Francis Bacon, all assisted in constructing an intellectual environment in which the criteria of historical narrative were being debated and challenged.[31] Some writers of the late sixteenth century, particularly poets, voiced dissension regarding the role of the historians and the ways in which they were 'bound by detail'.[32] Most famously, Philip Sidney stated that the historian, 'being captivated to the truth of a foolish world, is many times a terror from well-doing and an encouragement to unbridled wickedness'.[33] Nevertheless, 'history' was deemed significant enough for the Society of Antiquaries to be founded during the years 1584–86.[34] Munday's Robin Hood plays thus negotiate the

28 In melodramatic soliloquies, 644–58, 659–69, they declare their double-dyed deceits and malice; John defines his own state as 'revengefull murderous hate', 677.   29 There is an analogous set of plays: the frame play, the dumb-show and the play within a play.   30 Graham Holderness, *Shakespeare's history* (Dublin, 1985), p. 27. Mundy also produced another edition of Stow's *Survey* which was posthumously published in 1633. I would like to thank Tracey Hill for this astute observation.   31 Paul Avis, *Foundations of modern historical thought from Machiavelli to Vico* (London, 1986), p. 24.   32 F.J. Levy, *Tudor historical thought* (San Marino, 1967), p. 235.   33 Sir Philip Sidney, *Defence of Poetry*, ed. J.A. Van Dorsten (London, 1966), pp 37–8.   34 Avis, *Foundations*, p. 25. As Avis observes, however, the Society disappeared under the disapproval of James I.

complex subject of producing history in the early modern period, exploring, as John Skelton in *The Downfall* declares, 'the ground wheron our historie is laied' (39).

In most of the fictional texts that preceded the Huntington plays, Robin Hood had been a 'consummately unofficial character'.[35] Part of Munday's orthodox political project, however, is to present Robin Hood as more of an official figure and the plays construct a character that is part of the establishment rather than one that is in opposition to it.[36] Scenes in the greenwood alternate with political scenes that would not be out of place in a history plays. Treacherous royal villain and villainess weave their webs of deceit, hate, and lust, making honest courtiers seem traitors and evil politicians seem virtuous: the Earl's outlawing is only one element in the web of deceit and overturning of true order created by Prince John's usurpation and rectified by King Richard's return. In the concluding scene, trumpets enter the greenwood glade, with a procession of state surrounding the King, into which the leading merry men are now incorporated (Little John with a massive gold chain of ranks) just after Robin has rapidly arranged everyone in the greenwood in proper hierarchical order, admonishing them, 'Lords, yeomen, maids, in decent order stand' (2696).

With reference to the action of the plays taking place in the reign of Henry VIII, Singman states that the 'historicization' of Robin Hood helped to make him 'fundamentally less threatening by embalming him in the past.'[37] 'In the later sixteenth and early seventeenth century', in Holderness' view, 'the writing of history was approaching the point where the past would become [...] a lost world of experience as alien as the most distant foreign country.'[38] Elizabethans, however, were still taught that history was a providential experience, and were encouraged to read historical biography as mirrors of their own lives, as in William Baldwin's *Mirror for Magistrates* (*c.*1559). Instead of historical narratives being perceived as redundant repositories, a knowledge of history was still relevant to the present. The 'Downfall' and 'Death' of the Earl of Huntington are shaped, to some extent, to fit with such a pattern of the tragic fall of a man from high estate.[39] Moreover, the fact that these plays are set in the court of Henry VIII, a keen participant in Robin Hood games and, more significantly, father of Munday's current monarch, has political resonance for audiences of the 1590s.[40] If, as Knight and Ohlgren suggest, Henry VIII is 'the ultimate validator' of *The Downfall*, then Skelton, the one-time Orator Regius, Poet Laureate and tutor to Henry

35 Singman, 'Munday's unruly earl', p. 69.   36 See Knight, *A complete study*, p. 124. 37 Singman, *Robin Hood*, p. 131.   38 Holderness, *Shakespeare's history*, p. 27.   39 They have become 'matters tragicall', as Skelton says, announcing the *The Death* to follow, at the close of *The Downfall*, 2788.   40 As part of the May games celebrations, Henry VIII liked to dress up as Robin Hood: David Wiles, *The early plays of Robin Hood* (Cambridge, 1981), p. 45.

VIII, is the means through which the political use of language is to be displayed.[41] In terms of exploring the construction of narrative, the opening of the play is crucial, for it is here that the processes of textual production are made visible. Scene I, for instance, takes place in Skelton's study:

> Eltham: Howe, maister Skelton? What, at studie hard?
>   [Opens the doore
> Skelton: Welcome and wisht for, honest sir.
>   I have sent twice, and either time
>   He mist that went to seeke you.
> Eltham: So full well hee might.
>   These two howers it pleas'd his Majesty
>   To use my service in survaying mappes
>   Sent over from the good King Ferdinand,
>   That to the Indies, at Sebastians sute,
>   Hath lately sent a Spanish Colonie.
> Skelton: Then twill trouble you, after your great affairs,
>   To take the paine that I intended to intreat you to
>   About rehearsall of your promis'd play.   (1–13)

The invocation by Eltham of the colonialist project of 'good King Ferdinand' recalls the history of the relationship between England and Spain that had reached a climax in 1597 when England, France and the Dutch Republic made a Triple alliance against Spain.[42] The reference to Sebastian, King of Portugal, however, provides the play with another fissure in the representation of historical fact. According to John C. Meagher:

> Since [Ferdinand] died in 1516 and [Sebastian] was born in 1557, the business of negotiations is plainly the fanciful invention of the dramatist, designed merely to provide the equally fictitious Sir John Eltham with great affairs.[43]

On the one hand, it is possible to view this temporal collapse as a form of poetice licence, but it is also plausible to read this extract as evidence of the plays' awareness of the textuality of 'history.' For *The Downfall* and *The Death* continually rehearse the effects and affects of language as they perform a rather different history, the domestic narrative of Robin Hood, which is to become Eltham and Skelton's supposed respite from the wider socio-political arena (the 'great affairs', involving maps, kings, and colonial expeditions).

---

41 *RHOOT*, p. 298.   42 Philip Edwards, *The making of the modern English state, 1460–1660* (Basingstoke, 2001), p. 248.   43 *RHOOT*, p. 386.

With reference to Munday's intervention in the Robin Hood tradition, Singman observes that:

> Munday undertakes to authorize his version of Robin Hood through a complex and comprehensive intertextuality that interweaves the diverse strands of the tradition with one another and with other textual traditions current in late sixteenth-century England. Munday is the first author to attempt to gather the chaotic diversity of the Robin Hood tradition into a single text, embracing the entire corpus of both the narrative and dramatic traditions.[44]

The mastery of texts is an evident concern at the outset of the Huntington plays, and is undoubtedly represented in the figure of Skelton. As the Induction draws to a close, a dumb show of the entire play is presented. The dumb show is then repeated, this time with Skelton explaining the action. This somewhat excessive recapitulation really serves to construct Skelton as author and explicator:

> For many talk of Robin Hood that never shot in his bowe,
> But Skelton writes of Robin Hood what he doth truly knowe.
>
> (116–17)[45]

Here, Skelton is seen to legitimize his version of Robin Hood through self-authority and self-promotion, an action that he will perform throughout the plays. Even though Skelton takes the part of Friar Tuck, on several occasions he steps out of character and appears as Skelton. In scene vi, 843–5, for instance, as Friar Tuck is performing a diatribe against the vanity of the world, Skelton becomes so engrossed in rhetoric that he breaks out of character.[46] His fifty-line ensuing speech (in Skeltonics) is only brought to a halt by Little John/Eltham crying 'Stoppe, master Skelton' (890). At a later stage, the action is once again interrupted as Skelton and Eltham discuss the nature of *The Downfall* and the Robin Hood tradition:

> Lit. John: Skelton, a worde or two beside [about] the play.
> Frier: Now, Sir John Eltam, what ist you would say?
> Lit. John: Me thinks I see no jeasts of Robin Hoode,

44 Singman, 'Munday's unruly earl', p. 65.   45 A later speech, 2237–47, also expresses Skelton's control over the presentation of 'the history al, / And tale tragical'.   46 The speech condemns 'Age barbarous, times impious, men vitious'. It talks of 'The Rimes and the laies / Of Poets Laureate, / Whose verse did decorate / And their lines lustrate / Both Prince and Potentate', 845, 848–53, and a contrast between good and bad writing is interwoven with one between good and bad society. The Friar/Skelton apologises: 'Gods pittie [...] I had forgotte myself', 891–2.

> No merry morices of Frier Tuck,
> No pleasant skippings up and downe the wodde,
> No hunting songs, no coursing of the bucke.
> Pray God this Play of ours may have good lucke,
> And the Kings Majestie mislike it not.

Frier: And if he doe, what can we doe to that?
> I promist him a Play of Robin Hoode,
> His honourable life, in merry Sherewod;
> His Majestie himselfe survaid the plat,
> And bad me boldly write it, it was good,
> For merry jeasts, they have bene showne before [...]

> Our play expresses noble Roberts wrong.

                                            (2208–21, 2226)

The novelty of Skelton's, and, of course, Munday's, play is brought to the attention of the audience. Once more, as in the Induction, Skelton emphasizes the difference between the previous 'merry jeasts' of Robin Hood and this more sombre text which 'expresses noble Roberts wrong.' Nevertheless, Skelton is also presented as an author whose status is dependent on the reception of this revision of the play. In the address to the audience that ends the Induction Skelton announces that:

> [...] if ye once frowne,
> Poore Skelton goes downe,
> His labour and cost,
> He thinketh all lost,
> In tumbling of bookes
> Of Mary goe lookes.
> The Sheriffe with staves,
> With catchpoles and knaves,
> Are comming, I see,
> High time tis for mee
> To leave off my babble
> And fond ribble rabble.   (128–39)

The 'bureaucratic regulation of the stage' by the Master of the Revels, who sought to censor a play before performance and an ecclesiastical licencer, who checked the text prior to publication, is a testimony to the political strictures in operation during the 1590s.[47] Through Skelton, here presented as an author writing clearly at the behest of the king (who 'survaid the plat' beforehand), and one who alludes to the threat of physical violence in the above

---

47 Janet Clare, *Art made tongue-tied by authority: Elizabethan and Jacobean dramatic censorship,* 2nd ed. (Manchester, 1999), p. 29.

quotation, Munday's plays explicitly show the audience ways in which meaning in language is manipulated, controlled and held in place by ideological
constraints.[48]

In general, Munday's plays have been viewed by recent critics as texts
that are mindful of their socio-political frame:

> In accordance with this socially conservative reconstruction of this
> myth, Munday's own career was that of a semi-official agent of the
> state. His activities hovered between fact-finding missions and out-
> right espionage, and his literary work was consistently close to the
> interests of the powerful and the wealthy.[49]

While Munday's rendition of the Robin Hood myth may well be in overt
accordance with orthodox ideologies of the period, *The Downfall* and *The
Death* also negotiate the precarious political circumstances to which Munday
was personally subject. Eager to advance his studies and to secure a wealthy
literary patron, at the age of about seventeen, Munday travelled to the English
College in Rome with a 'desire to see strange countries, as also affection to
learn the languages'.[50] Whilst the actual circumstances of his trip to Rome
are unknown, it would seem that his travels were facilitated by Catholic hospitality and financial assistance. From *c*.1588–*c*.1612 Munday was officially
employed as a government messenger, at one time working for the Queen's
executioner and chief interrogator Richard Topcliffe, and gave evidence
against those with whom he studied at the College in Rome.[51] At times, however, Munday was mistrusted by both Catholics *and* Protestants, and it is
possible to read Francis Mere's description of Munday as one of the period's
'best plotters' as being tinged with a hint of irony.[52] Nevertheless, the nature
of his government work meant that Munday inhabited the interstices of the
Protestant/Catholic divide, moving between the ideological boundaries that
determine political and cultural difference.

Significantly, if Munday oscillated between these political borders, his
work as a translator suggests an awareness of textual *différance*:

> [...] translation practices the difference between signified and signi-
> fier. But if this difference is never pure, no more so is translation,
> and for the notion of translation we would have to substitute a notion
> of *transformation*: a regulated transformation of one language by

---

48 Skelton employed the figure of Robin Hood in 'Why Come Ye Nat to Courte?' (*c*.1522)
in his satirical description of Cardinal Wolsey. See further Greg Walker, *John Skelton and
the Politics of the 1530s* (Cambbridge, 1988), p. 125. Skelton is told that the King will
expect to see the 'other matters tragicall', following on from the plot of *The Downfall*
(2785–9).   49 *RHOOT*, p. 298.   50 Introduction in *Anthony Munday: the English Roman
Life*, ed. Philip Ayres (Oxford, 1980), p. xiv.   51 Ibid., p. xvi.   52 Turner, *Anthony
Munday*, pp 85, 123.

another, of one text by another. We will never have, and in fact never have had, to do with some 'transport' of pure signifieds from one language to another, or within one and the same language, that the signifying instrument would leave virgin and untouched.[53]

Translation, as Derrida suggests above, is a dynamic process which emphasizes the impossibility of equivalence, a process which moves meaning unproblematically from source to target language, whether that equivalence is sought inter- or intralingually.[54] Munday's translations, such as *Palmerin of England* (*c.*1581), *The Famous, Pleasant, and Variable Historie, of Palladine of England* (1588) and *Gerileon of England* (1592), are all witness to his interest in recasting European romance narratives into texts displaying a domestic, and an importantly, nationalistic impetus.[55] Throughout Munday's various careers, it is evident that language and ideology are closely bound together, and issues concerning textual and cultural politics are particularly resonant in the way in which he translates the myth of Robin Hood for the late sixteenth-century stage: a perceptiveness that is still acute when he reproduced the myth for the seventeenth-century in the civic pageant *Metropolis Coronata, The Triumphs of Ancient Drapery or Rich Cloathing in England* (1615). Here Robert/Robin pays tribute to the aldermen who rule the city of London.

Apart from constructing the aristocratic lineage of Robin Hood, in keeping with a conservative process of gentrification, Munday also erases most of the physical activity that is a feature of the greenwood in earlier outlaw texts. Little John is said, in a stage-direction, to enter one scene fighting the Sheriff and his men (*Downfall*, 430); Robin draws his sword and frightens the Sheriff into running away at another point (999). Otherwise, the only serious violence is committed by the villains: Prince John, who strikes Ely's messenger (674), stabs Lacy (720), fights Fitzwater (1210–22), Scathlock and Friar Tuck (2577–89), and the Prior, who has Warman murdered (*Death*, 210). As Knight comments,

> almost all the exciting action of the myth has gone because judged too vulgar; the only fight that occurs is between Prince John and the friar [...] the forest is never seen as a world of freedom and possible resistance, just as a site of aristocratic shame.[56]

53 Jacques Derrida, *Positions*, trans. Alan Bass (London, 1987), p. 20.   54 See *Translation and nation: towards a cultural politics of Englishness*, ed. Roger Ellis and Liz Oakley-Brown (Clevedon, 1981) for a discussion concerning the cultural politics of translation in the early modern period.   55 The nationalistic imperative of Munday's translative strategy is evident in Drayton's commendatory verse prefixed to *Primaleon II* (1596): 'If in opinion wit, / Primaleons sweet Invention well deserve: / Then he (no lesse) which hath translated it, / Which doth his sense, his forme, his phrase observe,/ And in true methid of his mome-borne stile,/ (Following the fashion of a French conceate) / Hath brought him heere into this famous Ile, / Where but a Stranger, now hath made his seate. / He lives a Prince, and coming in this sore, / Shall to his Country of your fame report.' (Cited in Turner, *Anthony Munday*, p. 115.)   56 *RHOOT*, p. 298.

It is possible, however, to read this suppression of action as a strategy that goes beyond the question of aesthetics. Whilst the plays overtly remove physical violence from the figure of Robin Hood, the audience of the Huntington plays is presented with the violence of language in Robin's very first appearance in *The Downfall*. When Robin speaks emotionally to Little John of his newly outlawed status he declares:

> What shall I heare thee say?
> Alreadie hast thou saide too much to heare.
> Alreadie hast thou stabd mee with thy tongue,
> And the wide wound with words will not be clos'd.   (178–81)

A precedent is thus established for these plays, as language – rather than physical action – is shown to violate the body: an aspect of Munday's texts that is not altogether surprising. As products of post-Reformation England, *The Downfall* and the *The Death* record the political shift from a visual to an increasingly textual culture. Apart from the opening scene in Skelton's study, it is significant that Matilda's chaste and pious image following Robin's death is suggested by her entrance 'in mourning vaile, reading on a booke' (961).[57]

The processes and politics of textual production and consumption are thus inscribed in these plays. Athough Munday's Huntington plays are overtly orthodox in their presentation of Robin Hood as the Earl of Huntington, as I have tried to suggest in this essay, there are inherent tensions in the plays that interrogate textual and cultural politics. Most noticeably, the complex temporal structure that frames these plays draws attention to ways in which history itself is constructed. Within that structure, the plays, primarily concerned with a conservative representation of Robin Hood, rather more interestingly seek to historicize the more usually subordinate subject of Maid Marian. In the medieval tradition, Robin had no female partner. By the late sixteenth century, however, Marian had been 'incorporated' into the tradition and so Munday's use of the figure has contemporary relevance.[58] Early on in *The Downfall*, as he introduces her as a 'Scene of grief' (194), Robin gives a summary of Marian's life:

> [...] Then Marian list to mee.
> This day thou wert a maide, and now a spowse,
> Anone (poore soule) a widdowe thou must bee: (207–9)

These lines make plain the fact that Marian's history is to mirror his own. Indeed, the second play, entitled *The Death of Robert, Earl of Huntington with*

---

57 This line was brought to my attention in Eve Rachel Sanders, *Gender and literacy on stage in the Early Modern period* (Cambridge, 1998), p. 89.   58 Singman, *Robin Hood*, p. 131.

the Lamentable Tragedie of chaste Matilda, his faire maid Marion, is more concerned with the woman's narrative. As the Earl is dead by line 863, the rest
of the play is about Matilda's escape from the amorous clutches of King John,
and her own death.[59] It has been argued by Singman that Munday finds the
figure of Marian at odds with the political agenda that he has constructed
throughout the two plays:

> We know few details about Marian's role in the legend before
> Munday, but her appearance in the play of *Robin Hood and the Friar*,
> where she effectively becomes the Friar's concubine, shows her as a
> decidedly sexualized figure. In many instances, perhaps most, Marian
> was played by a man, but this would only help bring suppressed
> questions of gender and sexuality to the surface. Such questions were
> consistent with the traditionalist and syncretic world of Robin Hood
> games, but are problematic from the perspective of official Tudor
> culture. Munday feels he must include her, but he is troubled by the
> sexual issues she raises [...] Not only does Munday's anxious treat-
> ment of the sexual issues highlight the awkward questions he tries
> to silence, but his suppression of her sexuality severs her from the
> figure of Maid Marian as she was known to his audience, creating a
> severe disjuncture between text and its cultural context.[60]

Here Singman certainly raises questions concerning gender and genre, and
he suggests that the sexualized aspect of Marian, permissible in the tradition
of the Robin Hood games, may prove troublesome in a text that aspires to
be tragedy. With regard to the way in which Munday has sought to refashion Robin Hood as the gentrified Robert, it is not surprising that similar ideological strategies of containment are at work in his treatment of Marian.
And yet, upon closer examination of the text, it is not at all obvious that
Munday really suppresses issues of sexual and textual politics. For instance,
in the induction to *The Downfall* it is brought to the audience's attention that
Marian is to be played by a man, as Skelton declares:

> Faith little Tracy you are somewhat forward:
> What, our Maid Marian leaping like a lad?
> If you remember, Robin is your love:
> Sir Thomas Mantle yonder, not Sir John.   (29–32)

Instead of trying anxiously to suppress the image of the sexualized form of
Marian from the Robin Hood games, Skelton *reminds* the audience that this
is a dramatic representation that has its origins in that earlier depiction.

59 Knight, *A complete study*, pp 128–9. As Knight discusses, a testimony to the actual
focus of this play, Robert Davenport reworked the *The Death* as *King John and Matilda*
(1655). 60 Singman, 'Munday's unruly earl', p. 72.

Indeed, 'little Tracy' is figured as a flirtatious creature, 'somewhat forward.' Persuasively Nelson presents the hypothesis that, in the sixteenth-century May games, Robin often took the part of the riotous ('lewd swaggering' 62) Lord of Misrule, while Friar Tuck became a 'lecherous trull-chaser' (61), and Marian was the trull, comically lascivious and overtly a man dressed as a woman (49, 62).[61] Apart from Marian's depiction in the May games, there are other textual precedents for the portrayal of Marian in the late sixteenth century. A text that Munday seems to have used, Michael Drayton's *Matilda the faire and chaste daughter of Lord R. Fitzwater* (1594), provided a model for his character of the chaste, dignified and tragic Marian in both *The Downfall* and *The Death*.[62] With the figure of Maid Marian, then, as elsewhere, Munday constructs a character that is more intertextually complex than the one that Singman proposes. Ultimately, Munday's text is actually drawing attention to the socio-political context of gender construction.

Throughout both plays, Marian's identity is wholly constructed through her association with men. Robin, as discussed above, has already made it plain that her life is inextricably bound with his. This point is reiterated later in the play through the figure of Prince John as he discusses Matilda's flight into exile with Robin: he says to her father,

> Living with him, she lives in vitious state,
> For Huntington is excommunicate.
> And till his debts be paid, by Romes decree,
> It is agreed, absolv'd he can not be.
> And that can never be. So never wife,
> But in a loath'd adult'rous beggers life,
> Must faire Matilda live? ...
>
> Cal her from him; bring her to Englands court,
> Where, like faire Phoebe, she may sit as Queene,
>
> (1190–6, 1199–200)

In both *The Downfall* and *The Death*, Marian/Matilda circulates as an object of exchange, from her father, Fitzwalter, to the Earl Robert/Robin Hood, and to John. At the end of *The Death* her father speaks of his desire for her to remain 'spotlesse' (2208), but she has already functioned like a blank page throughout both plays, her identity being continuously rewritten by the men who surround her. This is most noticeable in the way that she is named, especially by Robin: 'Matilda', he states as they begin an outlawed existence in the forest, 'shall be my Maid Marian' (1021). Eventually, as his own demise

---

61 Nelson, *Robin Hood tradition*, pp 49, 61–2. Skelton, about to play Friar Tuck, is therefore reminding Munday's audience of the traditional May game/morris scenario where the friar and the Marian dance seem to have danced lasciviously together. 62 Knight, *A complete study*, p. 128.

approaches, thus leaving Marian's status in doubt, Robin solves the problem
by re-naming her, this time in the form of the strange composite term 'Marilda'
(762). But this is the last time that Marian will be seen. In the remaining por-
tion of *The Death* the audience watch as Matilda attempts to construct an independent identity. Without Robin, however, her existence is in jeopardy and
the play ends with 'Matilda martyred for her chastity' (3048). In terms of most
modern criticism, too, once Robin dies, Matilda/Marian/Marilda, dies with
him. According to Knight, for instance, 'the rest of *The Death* is irrelevant to
the Robin Hood tradition'.[63] However, as part of a literary tradition thoroughly
inscribed with issues of masculine power and authority, through their representation of Matilda/Marian in *The Downfall* and *The Death*, the Huntington
plays throw into relief the very androcentric nature of that tradition.

In conclusion to his own discussion of the Huntington plays, Singman
states:

> Munday is in the position of a Renaissance architect faced with the
> challenge of turning a medieval castle into a stately home: the fun-
> damental structures are hostile to the desired aesthetic, and in the
> end, all he can do is give it a new façade. The resulting edifice is full
> of disjunctures.[64]

Munday's plays, however, are not solid structures; they are, in Barthesian
terms, *texts*: spaces 'where no language has a hold over any other, where languages circulate'.[65] As texts that are seemingly self-reflexive about their own
status, both *The Downfall* and *The Death* present the fixity of meaning in
language as a dynamic and, somewhat, precarious process. Through the figure
of Skelton, Munday shows his audience how attempts are made to control
the ludic dimension of language. And elsewhere, the plays emphasise the
problems of textuality:

> When I was taught, true dealing kept the schoole:
> Deeds were sworne partners with protesting words.
> We said and did, these say and never meane.   *(Downfall, 39–41)*

Moreover, in the complex historical frame in which they seek to place the
ever-elusive figure of Robin Hood, what Munday's Huntington plays really
perform is the problematic nature of representation in these 'crouching hyp-
ocrite dissembling times' (1051).[66]

---

63 Ibid., p. 129.   64 Singman, 'Munday's unruly earl', p. 71.   65 Roland Barthes, *Image,
music, text*, trans. Stephen Heath (London, 1977), p. 164.   66 'The Robin Hood materials are inherently fugitive. Just as the hero himself eludes the oppressions of the sheriff,
abbot and king, so his story is transmitted in a range of elusive forms', Knight, *A complete study*, p. xv.

'Meere English flocks': Ben Jonson's *The Sad Shepherd* and the Robin Hood tradition

STEPHEN KNIGHT

The Robin Hood tradition has always been popular in the sense of being highly successful with audiences, but it is also popular in a more searching sense, apparently resisting elevation to the high literary canon. Major writers have either refused to enter the greenwood of the Robin Hood tradition or have done so without much commitment or success. Chaucer has sometimes been thought to refer to the forest hero when he makes Pandarus speak of the 'haselwode, ther joly Robyn pleyde', but this is probably a reference to the French pastoral lover Robin, of 'Robin et Marion'.[1] In the same period Langland does speak of 'rymes of Robin Hood' but slightingly, in the context of Sloth.[2] Shakespeare heads away from Sherwood when, shortly after the Admiral's Men had success with their Robin Hood repertoire in 1598–1600, he places his noble outlaws in an English version of upmarket pastoral Italy; the prologue of *The Two Noble Kinsmen*, quite probably by Shakespeare himself, is directly slighting, speaking of an enemy who 'blasts my bays and my fam'd works makes lighter / Than Robin Hood'.[3]

Other authors of note were involved to a limited extent in re-writing, or appropriating, the outlaw tradition. Scott in the 'Locksley' chapters of *Ivanhoe*, Keats in his verse letter 'Robin Hood', Peacock in the least known of his novellas, *Maid Marian*, Tennyson in his late and somewhat languid verse-play *The Foresters*, all offered an engagement of sorts with Robin Hood tradition, but made no major impact on the national literature or the outlaw tradition.

Ben Jonson also made a contribution to the Robin Hood tradition, but it was literally incomplete: like the outlaw play by Richard Brinsley Sheridan and another by Robert and Caroline Southey, *The Sad Shepherd* is unfinished. Some have thought that this was Jonson's second engagement with the Robin Hood story. In his conversations with Drummond of Hawthornden, in 1619, Jonson spoke of 'The May Lord', his lost masque-like piece, which

---

1 Geoffrey Chaucer, *Troilus and Criseyde*, V.1174, *The Riverside Chaucer*, ed. L.D. Benson (Oxford, 1988), p. 575. 2 In *Piers Plowman: The B Text*, ed, G. Kane and E.T. Donaldson (London, 1975), Passus V, p. 331, l. 395. 3 *The Two Noble Kinsmen*, ed. G.R. Proudfoot (London, 1970), p. 4, ll. 20–21. On the Admiral's Men's Robin Hood productions, and Shakespeare's *As You Like It*, see Knight, *A complete study*, pp 131–34; A.H. Thorndike, 'The relation of *As You Like* to Robin Hood plays', *JEGP* 4 (1902) 59–69; Richard Wilson, '"Like the old Robin Hood": *As You Like It* and the enclosure riots', *Shakespeare Quarterly* 43:1 (1992) 1–19.

evidently has some resemblance to the later unfinished forest play.[4] He told Drummond it was a pastoral with clowns, claiming this as rare; that it had noble ladies playing parts, including the Countess of Rutland; had an old witch and a rustic woman; and that he himself played a wise figure called Alkin. The nature, status and even date of *The Sad Shepherd* have been to some degree entangled with 'The May Lord'. In their edition of the plays and masques, C.H. Herford and Percy and Evelyn Simpson report that a 'Mr Fleay' suggested that the two were the same, though he had no explanation of why the surviving text was not published until after Jonson's death, or where the rest of it had gone.[5] Herford and Simpson, rather more credibly, suggested that *The Sad Shepherd* was a reworked and fully literary version of the masque-like 'The May Lord': as Jonson did not mention Robin Hood in his fairly full account of 'The May Lord' it would seem that adding him and his entourage, including Marian, was a major part of the reworking. That *The Sad Shepherd* is late in Jonson's writing career is clearly indicated by the Prologue's emphatic opening-line reference to the author as 'He that hath feasted you these forty years'.[6] As Jonson apparently first wrote for the public in 1597 and died in 1637 this suggests the play is very late; most commentators think it was interrupted by the author's death – an opinion to be questioned later in this essay.

The Sad Shepherd certainly bears a general resemblance to Jonson's reported description of 'The May Lord', apart from the apparent addition of Robin Hood. It combines high style poetry and robust rustic comedy where 'The May Lord' was 'a pastoral with clowns'; both include a witch; a link with the aristocratic Rutland household in the masque is paralleled in Robin Hood's visitors from the Vale of Belvoir, focused on the Earl of Rutland's seat at Belvoir Castle; most persuasive of all in linking the two, *The Sad Shepherd* has a character called 'Alken the sage': in naming the comparable figure in 'The May Lord' Alkin, Drummond may well have mistaken the precise nature of Jonson's pronunciation and also the implication that this sage is all-knowing. Robin Hood is described as 'chiefe Wood-man, Master of the Feast', Marian is 'His Lady, the Mistris', Friar Tuck is their 'chaplaine and Steward', Much is '*Robin-Hood*s Bailifee, or Acater'.[7] Although 'The May Lord', as a pastoral entertainment, would not have had the literary expanse and range of reference evident in *The Sad Shepherd,* Anne Barton's view that there is no real connection between the two texts seems unlikely in the light of these apparent links.[8] It is more probable, as Herford and Simpson suggest, that in his last years Jonson, seeking to create something in the pastoral mode that had become, as Barton stresses, newly pop-

4 See C.H. Herford and Percy and Evelyn Simpson (eds), *Ben Jonson* (Oxford, 1941), vol. 2, p. 216.   5 *Ben Jonson*, vol. 2, pp 216–17.   6 *Ben Jonson*, Prologue, VII. 9, l. 1. 7 'The Persons of the Play,' *Ben Jonson*, II. 7.   8 *Ben Jonson, dramatist* (Cambridge, 1984), pp 341–2.

ular at court, reworked his earlier piece.[9] He did this in part by drawing on new sources but principally by adding Robin Hood to his earlier entertainment, and locating popular English outlaw within the classical and quasi-tragic story of a lost pastoral love, as indicated by the title.[10]

'Meere English flocks'

What English sources there might have been for the amplification of a masque into *The Sad Shepherd* is the main interest of this essay; Jonson makes it clear early in his Prologue that he is thinking consciously of combining in *The Sad Shepherd* specific English sources with a classical pattern:

> And though he now present you with such wooll,
> As from meere English Flocks his Muse can pull,
> He hopes when it is made up into Cloath;
> Not the most curious head here will be loath   *sophisticated head*
> To weare a Hood of it; it being a Fleece,
> To match, or those of Sicily, or Greece.[11]   *either those*

'Mere' had the sense 'pure', 'unmixed', but was also used, as the OED puts it, particularly 'of a people and their language'.[12] It also, during the sixteenth and seventeenth centuries, had the sense 'autonomous', 'self-sufficient'.[13] Jonson is announcing his proud confidence in the quality of a text woven out of purely national materials, which will be able to match the pastoral (shepherds') songs of classical tradition. The robust metaphor asserts the value of English primary production in both wool products and poetry, the richness of English literary sources and traditions for the production of pastoral poetry. The 'Hood' clearly signals that the Robin Hood tradition is central to this native resource. Herford and Simpson recognize the native material: 'the Robin Hood legend offers a far richer and more fruitful source than all the rudimentary stories of Theocritus taken together'.[14] But their eye is nevertheless primarily on the classical model: they give no reference to these notional native sources and offer no argument for their involvement in the actual making of *The Sad Shepherd*, saying only that Anthony Munday's 'handling is too perfunctory to require notice'.[15] This is far too casual a dismissal: whatever might be Munday's faults, he is hardly perfunctory, and there are clear links between his play and *The Sad Shepherd*, as will be argued below.

---

9 *Ben Jonson*, vol. 2, pp 214–15; on the new popularity of the form in the 1630s see Barton, *Ben Jonson, dramatist*, pp 340–1, and David Riggs, *Ben Jonson: a life* (Cambridge, Mass., 1989), p. 343. 10 *The Tale of a Tub* underwent a very similar process: most editors agree that a version existed very early in his career, before 1600, and reworked significantly in 1633. 11 *Ben Jonson*, vol. 7, p. 9, ll. 11–14. 12 *OED, mere* A. adj. 1.c. 13 *mere* A. adj, 2. 14 *Ben Jonson*, vol. 2, p. 224. 15 *Ben Jonson*, vol. 2, p. 224.

Jonson's use of the Robin Hood references in Michael Drayton's *Poly-Olbion*, was recognized by Herford and Simpson, but only in terms of the brief list of local rivers given in I.v.51–4.[16] The origin of the play, according to Herford and Simpson, is partly to be found in a displacement of some Shakespearean material from *The Winter's Tale* and *As You Like It*,[17] and some possible links with Spenser, but they see the main sources as being classical, mostly from Theocritus.[18] Their Introduction is general on this point, but specific classical connections are indicated in their notes to the text.[19] Anne Barton develops more fully the Spenser connection, showing how the story of Aeglamour and his lost love Florimell in Books III and IV of *The Faerie Queene* is a basis for Jonson's love plot and that the witch and her clumsy son may well be drawn from the same source – a connection known to Herford and Simpson, but not seen by them as having much significance.[20] Barton also notes a possible source for Clarion in *The Sheapherdes Calendar* and she stresses, in part to relate the text to the 1630s, a possible link with John Fletcher's *The Faithful Shepherdess* (first produced in 1609 but restaged successfully in 1634), itself a major instance of the renewed interest in the pastoral at court in that period.[21] Unlike Herford and Simpson, Barton insists on primarily English sources for *The Sad Shepherd*, yet she makes no mention, even a negative one, of the English Robin Hood materials.

While there is some valid element in the way these scholars cite classical and high-canon English sources, there is also in their account a striking lack of consideration of what Jonson might have drawn from the English Robin Hood materials that were, in his own lifetime, going through one of their most varied and thriving periods. These must be the subject of his Prologue reference to 'meere English flockes'.

Michael Drayton

In establishing the members of Jonson's English flock, it is appropriate first to look at an English Robin Hood text which was in Jonson's library and which has previously been identified by scholars as influencing him, though in too limited a way.[22] As Herford and Simpson recognize, when they call Drayton Jonson's 'nearest English precursor' (*Ben Jonson*, 1. 230), *Poly-Olbion*

---

16 Herford and Simpson discuss Jonson's river passage in *Ben Jonson*, vol. 2, p. 225, in the general context of his English sources, but only give the Drayton reference in their notes, vol. 10, p. 370. 17 *Ben Jonson*, vol. 2, pp 221–2. 18 See *Ben Jonson*, vol. 2, p. 233. 19 See *Ben Jonson*, vol. 2, pp 222–4 and pp 228–9 for general statements, and vol. 20, pp 361–3 for a discussion of the 'Amie' scenes (II.iv and II.vi.77–116) as derived from Theocritus, and vol. 10, p. 375, for the tracing of Lorel in II.ii to Theocritus. A brief connection with Virgil is made in vol. 10, p. 365 (I.i.5–6) and to Lucian (II.iv.5) in vol. 10, p. 382. 20 See *Ben Jonson*, vol. 10, p. 233. 21 See Barton, *Ben Jonson, dramatist*, pp 347–8. 22 *Ben Jonson*, vol. 11, p. 597.

was an immediate source, including as it does in its twenty-sixth song, dealing with the Leicestershire, Rutland and Nottinghamshire area, an account of Robin Hood which Jonson must have known because he derives from this part of the text his list of river names that flow into the Trent. Aeglamour, one of the shepherds visiting Sherwood from the Vale of Belvoir, mourns what he believes to be the death of his love the nymph Earine, and speaks of the natural lamentation for her as rivers broke their banks:

> Doe not I know
> How the Vale wither'd the same day, how Dove,
> Deane, Eye, and Erwash, Idell, Snite, and Soare
> Each broke his Vrne [...].   (I.v.51–4)

Drayton mentions each of these rivers, though not in such a condensed sequence: Jonson remembers and reworks rather than lifts material. Similarly his reference to 'the drowned lands of Lincolneshire' (II.viii.26) probably derives from the long sequence of inundations described in Drayton's twenty-sixth Song.

But there are other contacts between *The Sad Shepherd* and *Poly-Olbion* Song 26, not hitherto noticed. One of the things Jonson seems to have remembered most vividly from *Poly-Olbion* is its bird's eye view – or, literally, flying muse's eye view – of the countryside. In *The Sad Shepherd* it seems as if the Vale of Belvoir is next to Sherwood and so it is natural for the noble shepherds to call over to Robin's domain: the castle painted on the 'Landt-shape' described at the start of the play as in the background of the action must be Belvoir. Geographically this is not the case at all: there is a good twenty miles between the two districts; but not in Drayton's flowing imagination, and certainly not on the map which prefaced the song, in which Belvoir and Sherwood seem in easy strolling distance. The map also shows a nymph in the waters of the Trent. She is of course the water-sprite which each river both possesses and is symbolized by, but it seems likely that her depiction suggested to Jonson the idea of an allegedly drowned nymph, Aeglamour's love, Earine.[23] This map is populated by personified figures: the water-sprite has on one side a forester representing Sherwood Forest and a reaper with a sickle and corn representing the Vale of Belvoir.

It also appears that Jonson has borrowed Drayton's list of Robin's supporters: both texts share Little John, Scarlock, Much, Tuck and – the revealing touch – George a Greene. This last character, also known as the Pinder of Wakefield, is nowhere else listed among Robin's followers at the time. He is no more than a friendly rival to Robin in the play *George a Greene*

---

23 For a discussion of the issue and the *Poly-Olbion* illustration, see Knight, *A complete study*, pp 138–9.

(possibly by Robert Greene and written by about 1592), while in the ballad 'The Jolly Pinder of Wakefield', known by the later sixteenth century, he fights Robin and finally only says he may in the future join his band. George was certainly added to Jonson's *dramatis personae* from Drayton.

It was obviously also from Drayton that Jonson took the idea of Marian as a serious hunter. In some of his finest lines Drayton describes her:

> [...] his loved Marian
> Was ever constant knowne, which wheresoer she came
> Was soveraigne of the Woods, chiefe Lady of the Game:
> Her Clothes tuck'd to the knee, and daintie braided haire,
> With Bows and Quiver arm'd, she wandred here and there,
> Amongst the Forrests wild; Diana never knew
> Such pleasures, nor such Harts as Mariana slew.   (26.352–8)

This concept of Marian as Diana is clearly behind her imposing entrance in full hunting mode in *The Sad Shepherd*, I.6. She is, also as in Drayton, Robin Hood's love and equal in action: Drayton called her Robin's 'Mistress deare' (352) and Jonson uses the same conception of her and the same term emphatically in the first line of two scenes: Robin greets her as 'My Marian, and my mistress!' (I.vi.1), and repeats this with 'O are you here, my Mistresse?' (II.v.1).

A clear verbal borrowing from Drayton occurs in the word 'dimble', which is emphasized in the scene setting ('The Witches' Dimble', 25) and used in a later scene (II.viii.15); it also appears in several stage directions which are presumably authorial. This is a genuine East Midlands word, meaning 'dingle', used by Drayton in 26.134 and 28.352 (curiously, Herford and Simpson only cite the second usage, a plural and well away from the area of *Poly-Olbion*, songs 25 and 26, which, we have just seen, Jonson clearly read carefully).[24] The rare dialect word is cited from these two literary sources for three out of its four entries in the *Oxford English Dictionary*, and it must be a deliberate borrowing by Jonson to give linguistic English regional colour.[25]

But while these instances show that Jonson certainly knew Drayton's work and used it for his general setting in *The Sad Shepherd*, as a guide to the supporting Sherwood characters, and for some incidental details, there are also major differences between his text and Drayton's. Jonson does not present Robin as an outlaw, as Drayton does, but merely as a gentleman happening to live in the forest – Maudlin twice calls him an 'outlaw' in her anger

---

24 See *Ben Jonson*, vol. 10, p. 364, under 'The Scene', l. 30.   25 *OED*, *dimble*: there is one earlier reference from 1589 (also two entries from Shropshire and Leicestershire dialect dictionaries). For further comments on localization see J. Sanders, 'Jonson, *The Sad Shepherd* and the North Midlands', *Ben Jonson Journal*, 6 (1999) 49–68. Jonson, like Drayton, calls *dimble* gloomy: 'gloomy dimbles', 'dimbles hid from day', Drayton; 'a gloomy dimble', Jonson.

(III.4.47 and III.5.3), as if she is slandering him. This motif is not developed in the action, and, though it could conceivably have been an element in the missing acts, it is unlikely that the outlaw element would have been ignored early on if it were to be of any importance later. Also Jonson does not offer any of the 'pranks', robberies or escapes that Drayton synopsizes as the typical activities of his outlawed hero. Nor does Jonson refer to the material found briefly in Song 28 when, in referring to Kirklees in Yorkshire, which Drayton calls Kirkby, Drayton mentions Robin's traditional death and burial there (67–70), though the hero's death was no doubt outside the planned action of Jonson's play (as it is in most Robin Hood texts).

Jonson and Munday

The ideas, both general and specific, which Jonson drew from Drayton were evidently (in spite of Herford and Simpson's opinions to the contrary) amplified in the context of a different, non-criminal and more lordly conception of Robin Hood, one which is found in another English source, Anthony Munday's *The Downfall of Robert, Earle of Huntington*. This, with its partner play *The Death* of the same hero (1598–9), marks an important stage in the development of the Robin Hood tradition in that for the first time in the history of the myth Robin appears fully formed as a distressed gentleman. Outlined in Grafton's *Chronicle at Large* in 1569,[26] glancingly referred to in Warner's *Albions England* (1589, to be discussed below), this idea of Robin as a nobleman who is exiled by bad King John, and therefore whose resistance to authority becomes a defence of true aristocratic authority, is filled out in narrative by Munday in a way that was to imprint its image in various ways on much that was to follow in the outlaw myth. It changed Robin Hood, in mainstream English tradition thereafter, from the yeoman outlaw of the extant medieval ballads to a dispossessed aristocrat, temporarily joining outlaws in the wood before defeating his enemies and regaining his estate.

Clear evidence that Jonson knew Munday comes in their shared use of the two characters Scathlock and Scarlet as brothers and sons of a widow, not as a single character with varying names, as is usual in the tradition. Jonson has, as with Marian, added to Munday their interest in hunting (not in the brothers' case, unlike Marian, derived from Drayton) and the precise nature of the names and the relationship must confirm Munday as Jonson's source here.

Also derived from Munday is Robin's gentlemanly spirit; Jonson does not use a noble title for the hero, and does not suggest he has an aristocratic life outside the forest, but he clearly shares Munday's gentrified concept of Robin, as is realized in the relatively servile position of his companions. In the early

26 See *RHOOT*, pp 27–9.

ballads Robin was at best *primus inter pares*, and sometimes less than that; he was elevated in the *Gest* to be an unquestioned leader, but was still essentially a yeoman like the other outlaws (famously any attempt to impose rank, symbolized by Robin's asking a comrade to carry his bow, is fiercely resisted by his band).[27] Drayton follows the same pattern, but Munday imagines a more lordly context. Little John first appears busying himself with moving his master to the forest, acting as a steward rather than a comrade in arms, and this is exactly their relation in *The Sad Shepherd*, where John is Robin's 'bow bearer' in the *dramatis personae*. Robin in Munday is a generous lord, in every way like the figure of *The Sad Shepherd* as 'bounteous Robin Hood, our gentle master' (I.iii.49). The context of performance was aristocratically appropriate: Cave comments that 'Jonson clearly envisaged performance at court'.[28]

Another major link between Munday and Jonson is found in the context of Marian. While Jonson's treatment is obviously influenced by Drayton, and Munday has no sense of her as a huntress (the main focus in both Drayton and Jonson), it seems clear that one particular idea Jonson uses in his treatment of the relationship of Robin and Marian derives from Munday, as it appears nowhere in Drayton or anywhere else. In *The Downfall*, as Robin and Marian plan to leave the court after his betrayal by his enemies, Queen Eleanor the queen mother, driven by her passion for Robin Hood, persuades Marian to exchange clothes with her, ostensibly so Marian will be safer. In fact the queen plans to escape with Robin herself, but Robin, warned by Marian, is not taken in and dismisses this 'foul Marian' with her 'bewitching eyes' as a 'sorceress'.[29] It is true that, as Herford and Simpson point out,[30] Spenser has previously offered a witch-like impersonation of the heroine, in the case of Duessa as the false Una of Book I and the witch-created false Florimell in Book III. But these notional sources link most clearly with the impersonation of Aeglamour's lost love Earine by Maudlin's daughter Douce. The way in which Jonson's witch Maudlin shapes herself as a false Marian clearly develops from Munday's sequence.

Jonson also derives from Munday an idea about the amatory nature of the relationship of Robin and Marian. In *The Sad Shepherd* they are seen by Lionel and Clarion as 'The turtles of the wood', 'A billing pair' (I.5.108–09), and straight afterwards they share a lively, even erotic love-scene:

> *Rob.*   My *Marian*, and my Mistris! *Mar.* My lov'd Robin!
> *Mel.*   The Moone's at ful, the happy paire are met!
> *Mar.*   How hath this morning paid me, for my rising!
>   First, with my sports; but most with meeting you!
>   I did not halfe so well reward my hounds,

---

27 The most notable example occurs in *Robin Hood and the Monk*.   28 Richard Cave, *Ben Jonson* (Basingstoke, 1991), p. 145.   29 *RHOOT*, pp 320–1, ll. 601, 602, 616.   30 *Ben Jonson*, vol. 2, p. 233.

As she hath me today: although I gave them
All the sweet morsels, Calle, Tongue, Eares and Dowcets!
Rob.   What? And the inch-pin? *Mar.* Yes. *Rob.* Your sports then
pleas'd you?
Mar.   You are a wanton. *Rob.* One I doe confesse
I wanted till you came, but now I have you,
I'le grow to your embraces, till two soules
Distilled into kisses, through our lips
Doe make one spirit of love. *Mar.* O *Robin !*   (I.vi.1–13)

Clearly 'inch-pin', part of an animal's innards, also has a sexual double meaning, and the play on 'wanton' and 'wanted', and 'grow', develops this register. As Richard Cave notes, the printed text indicates that the performance
must be insistently amatory: 'Asterisks within the dialogue in *The Sad
Shepherd* at I.vi.33–6 indicate precisely where Robin is to kiss Marian'.[31]

This interaction is, it seems, a more vigorous version of the mutually
affectionate, even innocent, end of the celebration of forest life in Scene ix
in *The Downfall*:

Marian.   Marian hath all, sweete Robert, having thee,
And guesses thee as rich, in having mee.
Robin.   I am indeede,
For having thee, what comfort can I neede?
Marian.   Goe in, goe in.
To part such true love, Robin it were sinne.   (1382–7)

There may be a more general inspiration: it might well be that the late burst
of lyric power in *The Sad Shepherd* – to some commentators surprising for
both its lateness and its power – also in fact derived from the inspired hints
of Munday.[32] Jonson makes Robin welcome the Belvoir visitors to the wood
in a passage of finely sensuous pastoral:

Welcome, bright Clarion and sweet Mellifleur,
The courteous Lionel, faire Amie; all
My friends and neighbours, to the Jolly Bower
Of Robin-hood, and to the greene-wood Walkes:
Now that the shearing of your sheepe is done,
And the wash'd Flocks are lighted of their wooll,
The smoother Ewes are ready to receive
The mounting rams againe; and both doe feed,

31 Richard Cave, 'Script and performance' in Richard Cave, Elizabeth Schafer and Brian
Woolland (eds), *Ben Jonson and theatre: performance, practice and theory* (London, 1999),
23–37, see p. 25.   32 See *Ben Jonson*, vol. 2, p. 215; Barton, *Ben Jonson, dramatist*, p.
340.

As either promist to increase your breed
At eaning time; and bring you lusty twins.
Why should, or you, or wee so much forget
The season in our selves: as not to make
Vse of our youth, and spirits, to awake
The nimble Horne-pipe, and the Timburine,
And mixe our Songs and Dances in the Wood,
And each of us cut down a Triumph-bough ?
Such are the Rites, the youthful Iune allows.   (I.4.1–16)

Fluent and muscular as Jonson's passage is, and redolent of his mature style, it looks very much as if it is written to match and outdo Munday's sequence of high colour on the quality of the forest life, a passage also of exactly sixteen lines:

Marian, thou seest though courtly pleasurs want,
Yet country sport in Sherewodde is not scant.
For the soule-ravishing delicious sound
Of instrumental musique, we have found
The winged quiristers, with divers notes,
Sent from their quaint recording prettie throats,
On every branch that compasseth our bower,
Without commaund, contenting us each hower.
For Arras hangings, and rich Tapestrie,
We have sweete natures best inbroithery.
For thy steel glasse, wherein thou wontst to looke,
Thy christall eyes, gaze in a christall brooke.
At court, a flower or two did decke thy head:
Now with whole garlands it is circled.
For what in wealth we want, we have in flowers ,
And what wee loose in halles, we finde in bowers.   (1366–81)

The imagery of the passage is not borrowed by Jonson, but the idea of a richly sensuous set-piece is, and at least one related idea is shared, as Jonson picks up the theme of Munday's line 1379 when Karol speaks of:

[...] Marian and the gentle Robin-hood
Who are the Crowne, and Ghirland of the Wood.   (III.2.8–9)

Two minor motifs from *The Downfall* also appear to resurface in *The Sad Shepherd*. Herford and Simpson feel confident that Lorel, son of Maudlin the witch, is descended from the clumsy witch's son in Book III of *The Faerie Queene*, who threatens Florimell, with perhaps an element of 'the sullen shep-

herd' from Fletcher's *The Faithful Shepherdess*.[33] There are clear connections
with both figures, but it is curious that Friar Tuck in Munday's *The Downfall*
follows a path of action very like that of Lorel in Jonson's plot, as he initially promises to betray Robin to his enemies (1405–15) for the sake of getting a girl. The phrase 'lozel Friar' (812) is used of him, which might have
suggested the link with the figure that Jonson, like Fletcher, called Lorel:
according to the Oxford English Dictionary, 'lozel' is a variant of 'lorel' (with
the senses 'worthless person' or 'good-for-nothing').

A further link with Munday's work, apparently tenuous but one perhaps
harder to dismiss as accidental, is the fact that the witch Maudlin, while
appearing to thank Robin for his generosity, goes into a spinning dance while
singing what seem like Skeltonic couplets:

> Looke out, looke out, gay folke about,
> And see mee spin; the ring I'm in
> Of mirth, & glee, with thanks for fee
> The heart puts on, for th' Venison
> My Lady sent, which shall be spent
> In draughts of Wine, to fume up fine
> Into the braine, and downe againe
> Fall in a Swoune, upo' the growne.   (II.vi.14.21)

This is strongly reminiscent of several scenes in *The Downfall*. In lines 845–89
the Friar seems to slide into Skeltonics, and he says finally 'I had forgott
myselfe' (892); in 1583–1606 the Friar confides to Robin that he is pretend-
ing to betray him and the Skeltonics seem to provide some sense of verac-
ity. Tuck speaks to Robin in the same style later (2146–54), and finally, after
Sir John Eltham (playing Little John) complains about his lapses into 'ribble-
rabble rimes' (2235), he produces them in an ironic apology, speaking in his
own voice as Skelton (2242–7).

Some of these connections are no doubt not fully conscious, the re-cre-
ations of a less than fully remembered source; others are more evident bor-
rowings. Together they indicate clearly that just as *Poly-Olbion* provided a
positioning context and some ideas for Jonson's development of his Robin
Hood play, so Munday's *Downfall* offered substantial motifs and building
blocks of the plot and treatment that Jonson was developing.

The Sad Shepherd *and a* Gest of Robyn Hode

But there remain elements of *The Sad Shepherd* not based on Munday nor
drawn from Drayton. There is another major source for Jonson's ideas and

---

33 *Ben Jonson*, vol. 2, pp 229–30; Barton, *Ben Jonson, dramatist*, pp 342, 347.

motifs: the early sixteenth century *Gest of Robin Hood*. Printed at least eight
times by 1600, this major text, generically best seen as a ballad-epic, influenced many accounts of the hero in drama, ballads and prose, ranging from
pure fiction to quasi-biography. There is no trace in Jonson – or indeed his
contemporaries – of the three long ballads which appear to predate the *Gest*,
but were not available in printed form to Jonson, *Robin Hood and the Monk*,
Robin Hood and the Potter and *Robin Hood and Guy of Gisborne*.[34]

The *Gest* has a number of contacts with *The Sad Shepherd*. The forest
feast is a major structural element in both texts. It is a concern in Jonson's
first lengthy scene when Marian goes hunting for the purpose of providing
for a feast in I.ii, and she reports her success to Robin in I.iv. Clearly the
munificent feast over which Robin will preside is designed as framing the
whole play. The feast is deferred, however, when the evil Maudlin appro-
priates the venison by impersonating Marian, and causes unfestal confusion
among the characters. It is clear that Jonson planned to make everything
return to harmony the end of the play: 'Reuben the Hermit' is to act as the
dramatis personae indicates, calling him 'The Reconciler'. The sad shepherd
will regain his love, the Maudlin's misdoings will be resolved – and probably she will be reconciled to Robin and Marian. There can be little doubt
that the frustrated feast of the early scenes will return in triumph as the site
of reconciliation and the emblem of social harmony: this is a pattern found
recurrently in the *Gest* and not in the other sources.

There are other links between the two texts. At the start of the *Gest*, as
Robin is waiting in somewhat Arthurian fashion for a guest to appear and
justify his first harmonious feast, he makes a statement of the principles of
forest outlawry:

> '[...] loke ye do no husbonde harme,
> That tilleth with his ploughe.
>
> No more ye shall no gode yeman
> That walketh by grene wood shawe,
> Ne no knyght ne no squyer
> That wol be a gode felawe.
>
> These bisshopes and these archebisshoppes,
> Ye shall them bete and bynde:

---

34 These three early ballads, surviving only in manuscript anthologies (one of which, the
Percy manuscript, could not have been available to Jonson as it was not copied until c.
1650) did not impact on the seventeenth century broadside tradition at all, with the par-
tial exception of a version of *Robin Hood and the Potter*, entitled *Robin Hood and the
Butcher*, which was quite popular as a broadside. *Robin Hood and the Monk* was so little
known it did not even appear in Joseph Ritson's great collection of outlaw ballads in 1795.

The hye sherif of Notyngham
Hym holde ye in your mynde.'[35]

This is inherently similar in both its tone and its place in the text to a passage in Act I Scene iv of *The Sad Shepherd*. After Robin welcomes his visitors to the forest for festive pleasures and after Clarion and Tuck speak of 'the sourer sort Of shepherds', Puritans who with 'covetise and rage' annoy the present, as much as did bishops and archbishops in the past, for the Robin of the *Gest*, the forest lord imagines a world of order like that implied in the *Gest*:

> '[...] when on the Plaines
> The Wood-men met the Damsells, and the Swaines
> The Neat'ards, Plow-men, and the Pipers loud,
> And each did dance, some to the Kit or Crowd,
> Some to the Bag-pipe; some the Tabret mov'd,
> And all did either love, or were belov'd.' (I.iv.42–7)

Somewhat festive and even eroticized as this is, in keeping with the pastoral genre Jonson is using, it is still the same kind of underlying evaluative analysis of a good society that is placed in Robin's mouth at the start of the *Gest*.

There are other relations with the *Gest*, or at least its opening. In the *Gest* the 'uncouth [unknown] gest' who arrives and so permits Robin to eat is a poor but clearly genteel knight. Oppressed by St Mary's Abbey, York, he is lent money by the outlaws to save his son and his lands, and is even equipped by them for his newly secure life, including having a powerful squire in Little John.[36] In *The Sad Shepherd* Robin similarly begins the story by welcoming to his forest a severely distressed but still genteel figure: Aeglamour, having lost his love Earine; the direction the unfinished plot is taking makes it clear that under the aegis of the lord of the forest the distressed gentleman's situation will return to emotional prosperity, as happens in the *Gest*. At the end of each text a new figure acts to resolve all the troubles: this is the King in the *Gest*, and in *The Sad Shepherd* it is – or is to be – Reuben the Hermit. As the play is unfinished it is not clear if he has any further links with the king, but it may well be that the hermit was to remove his holy gown and reveal himself as some kind of aristocratic authority, as does the king in the denouement of the *Gest* in casting off his disguise as an abbot.

Another suggestive connection between the two texts is that Jonson names his troublesome witch Maudlin as coming from Papplewick, a real village in Sherwood Forest, then and now. Identifying a real village has a Drayton-like specificity, but the witch's name appears to relate to the *Gest*. At the end of

---

35 *RHOOT*, p. 92, ll. 51–60. 36 See *Gest*, ll. 277–324, *RHOOT*, pp 98–100.

the *Gest*, when Robin is persuading King Edward to let him return to the forest he says that he yearns to worship at the chapel he has established deep in the forest dedicated to Mary Magdalene. The essential identity of the names Magdalene and Maudlin makes the choice curious in Jonson's time: a name that is implicitly medieval, Catholic and morally dubious might well seem eminently borrowable for a woman who is a sorceress and general menace to the genteel folk of the forest, residents and visitors alike; but it also seems likely that under the influence of Reuben the Hermit, Maudlin was going to be reconciled to Robin, just as her namesake turned from sinner to faithful follower of Christ.[37]

A number of motifs in *The Sad Shepherd*, of different extent and pervasiveness, seem likely to have been borrowed from *The Gest of Robin Hood*. But there are also two major differences between the outlaw leader of the *Gest* and Jonson's forest lord. Firstly, the Robin of *The Sad Shepherd* undertakes no real physical action, especially not of an outlaw sort, while the *Gest* is rich in fights, tricks and busy action. And secondly the *Gest* lacks that central figure in *The Sad Shepherd*, Maid Marian. Both languidity and lady relate directly to the gentrification which Jonson follows: although he does not name Robin as a lord, the character is clearly lordly. Drayton's image is elevated via Munday, with some confirming features from the *Gest*.

Inconclusion

But that is not a complete roll-call of the 'meere English flockes' that influenced Jonson. One little-regarded source may have offered a feature of considerable importance if the play had been finished. William Warner's *Albions England* (1589) is a lengthy verse survey of the country, its culture and its institutions, a kind of *Poly-Olbion* without its emphasis on myths and locations. It speaks of Robin Hood in Chapter 27 as a 'malcontent' with men living in 'pleasant caves and bowers/ Oft saying to his merry men, what juster life than ours'.[38] This sounds rather more political than Jonson's festal forest hero and his leisurely bowers, but there is a more compatible moment in the earlier reference to Robin in Chapter 25, when Warner provides a lengthy sequence of good advice from a hermit who preaches abstinence. He ends with an account of the festivities of the year, including the 'May / When Roben hood, litell Iohn, Ffrier Tucke, and Marian deftly play'.[39] No source has been suggested for Jonson's Reuben the Hermit. It seems highly

---

37 It is not clear why she comes from Papplewick, a Sherwood village not named in Drayton or any of the other surviving Robin Hood texts. It is conceivable that Jonson chose the name to play on the word 'pap', a feature often dealt with in witch descriptions, while 'wick,' primarily meaning 'village' (from Old Norse *vik*), resembles an early form of the word 'witch' itself (Anglo-Saxon *wicce*). 38 See William Warner, *Albions England* (London, 1589), p. 132. 39 Warner, *Albions England*, p. 121.

possible that this important but, in the circumstances, enigmatic figure is derived from Warner as an addition to the other material that Jonson found in the English Robin Hood tradition.

A Robin Hood text that needs to be noted, though it apparently did not influence Jonson at all, is Martin Parker's *True Tale of Robin Hood* (1632). This lengthy ballad-epic, using the verse form and narrative range of the *Gest*, has many motifs and episodes found in the ballads (Robin's nobility, robberies, conflicts with church and king) as well as contemporary features like a special hate for Catholic priests – Parker claims Robin even castrated some of them – and an uneasy ending which states there is nowadays no room for such unruly figures. None of this comes through in Jonson: Parker's brief mention of Robin's hospitality, the only contact between the two texts, is too well embedded in the other texts, especially the *Gest*, and the general Robin Hood tradition, for it to need to be an influence.[40] But perhaps Parker gave Jonson a different kind of stimulus. Appearing in 1632 or possibly late 1631, his *True Tale* was a considerable success, going into a reprint within a year.[41] If Barton is right, as seems probable, and Jonson was working on *The Sad Shepherd* in the mid 1630s,[42] then he must have known of Parker's text and it may well be he decided that, in order to match Fletcher's pastoral success in the 1634 revival, he could dignify this humble but popular English material with his own talent and his classical elegance; he could do something much better than Parker's clumsy effort, on the basis of combining together with the 'May Lord' idea the English Robin Hood traditions and classical, pastoral elevation.[43]

As has been argued here, much of his material was indeed shorn from 'meere English flockes' that were found grazing in English books. They did not provide the whole of *The Sad Shepherd*; indeed it is clear from this analysis that some of the strongest links with the English Robin Hood materials come early in the unfinished play while Jonson's later scenes grow more and more pastoral-classical. Perhaps that pattern in itself indicates a force that shaped the play – or finally unshaped it. As is evident in Munday, and painfully clear in the dull Robin Hood ballad operas of the eighteenth century, the gentrified tradition not only gave up the robustly radical concept of Robin Hood the social bandit, a hard-handed righter of wrongs, seizer of money, and a ready killer of oppressors: it also gave up the highly entertaining tricksterish and carnivalesque stories, both bloodthirsty and bloody-

40 See Martin Parker, *The True Tale of Robin Hood*, in *RHOOT*, pp 602–25, ll. 188–9. 41 See *RHOOT*, p. 602.   42 See *Ben Jonson, dramatist*, pp 340–2.   43 Helen Cooper, *Pastoral: Medieval into Renaissance* (Ipswich and Totowa, NJ, 1977), pp 180–1, argues that 'pastoral' had been quite widely understood as referring as much to native May games as ancient Arcadian poetic idylls by the Elizabethans, observing that Jonson's *Sad Shepherd* 'shows how the association was acknowledged by even the rigorous scholar' (see further 195).

minded, that embodied the native hero in ballad and simple plays. Narratively
and dramatically impoverished as a result, the gentrified tradition had little
artistic vigour, and Jonson's play suffers theatrically for it. While it is true
that the notion of Robin as a passive figure, waiting in his bower for visitors
and a feast, is consistent with what we know of the early play-games, where
Robin presided in a bower over village festivities (which, of course, included
martial contests, prominent among them archery and wrestling matches), in
terms of five-act drama, unlike court masque or village ritual, this is a dam-
agingly inactive model to pursue.[44] It could be that this passivity points to
an underlying similarity between *The Sad Shepherd* and the traditional Robin
Hood play-game, with Robin Hood as presiding May Lord.

Noting the narratively impoverished nature of the gentrified tradition
gives rise to a final speculation. It may well be that it was not Jonson's death,
as scholars morbidly assume, that brought *The Sad Shepherd* to its sudden
end. It may have been Jonson's realization that he had taken on an artistic
combination that was just not going to work. Like the shepherds from
Belvoir, he did not really belong in Sherwood. The saddest thing about the
play is that having vigorously espoused the pastoralization of Englishness
Jonson was ultimately neither native enough nor classical enough for success,
dramatic or ideological. What Spenser managed in *The Sheapherdes Calendar*,
Jonson did not achieve because he did not retain the inherent strength of the
native language or its political thrust. The popular tradition did not work in
high-canon mode. By Englishing the pastoral Jonson also pastoralized the
English Robin Hood, abandoning the popular (in both senses) plot material
that gave it such robust narrative health. Jonson's 'meere English flockes'
prove too hybrid to be productive, and it is quite possible that the author
realized this was going nowhere and recognized that, like other gentrifiers of
the English outlaw tradition, he had become lost in an over-genteel forest of
his own making.

44 I owe this observation to John Marshall, in his response to this essay given as a con-
ference paper. For a discussion of the play-games see Knight, *A complete study*, pp 98–115;
Jeffrey L. Singman, *Robin Hood: the shaping of the legend* (Westport, Conn., 1998), see
Chap. 2, 'Robin Hoodes Daye', pp 61–103; Alexandra F. Johnston, 'The Robin Hood of
the records' in *Playing Robin Hood: the legend as performance in five centuries*, ed. Lois
Potter (Newark, Delaware, 1998), pp 27–44.

The noble peasant

LINDA TROOST

In the mid 1780s, just as Britain was recovering from a war with its colonies and with France, after the government had changed three times in two years, and after indirect taxation had increased dramatically on a host of consumables to pay the government's escalating bills, there was a small boom in Robin Hood and outlaw drama in London. In 1783 Francis Waldron published a continuation of Ben Jonson's *Sad Shepherd*: *The Sad Shepherd; or A Tale of Robin Hood*. In June of that year, Philip Astley presented a version of *Robin Hood* at the Royal Circus and Equestrian Philharmonic Academy. The following April, Covent Garden had great success with a comic opera called *Robin Hood; or Sherwood Forest*. A few months later, the only London theatre open in the summer, the Haymarket, presented a work in the same tradition: *The Noble Peasant*, with music by William Shield, a rising composer who had also scored *Robin Hood* for Covent Garden.[1]

The Noble Peasant, by struggling actor, playwright, novelist and confessed radical Thomas Holcroft, avoids going over the same ground as the Covent Garden comic opera but keeps many Hoodian conventions: disguise, mockery of fat friars, archery, the greenwood, outlawry, and traces of a ballad source. The plot, set in the late ninth century during the Danish raids on Saxon England, is complicated. The main story involves Earl Walter and his much-desired daughter named Edwitha. As the opera opens, Anlaff the Dane has tried to carry her off but has been defeated in battle and his brother killed. The Earl wants to marry his daughter to Earl Egbert so that he will have a strong ally in future raids, but Edwitha has fallen in love with a peasant named Leonard. Fortunately, Leonard turns out to be Leoline, Prince of the Britons, who defeats Anlaff in a final battle and wins the hand of the fair maiden.

The secondary plot involves the outlaws with whom Leonard has allied himself while in disguise: Adam Bell, Clym o' the Clough, and William of Cloudesley, characters from the popular non-Robin-Hood outlaw ballad printed in the sixteenth century and dating back to the fifteenth.[2] The outlaws have

1 Thomas Holcroft, *The Noble Peasant. a comic opera in three acts* (London, 1784); all quotations are from this edition; William Shield, *The Noble Peasant. a comic opera set to music by William Shield* (London, 1784). Holcroft had originally intended *The Noble Peasant* for Sadler's Wells Theatre: *Memoirs of Thomas Holcroft*, in *The complete works of William Hazlitt*, ed. P.P. Howe, 21 vols (London, 1932), vol. 3, p. 87. 2 A fragment of a printed copy dates from 1536 (London, John Byddell); the first full version that survives dates from the 1560s, published by Copland; see *RHOOT*, pp 235–68. In *Robin Hood's birth, breeding, valour and marriage* (1662?), Adam Bell is mentioned as having shot

gone in disguise to the assistance of Earl Walter in his battle with Anlaff and helped save the day. In fact, Leonard had personally killed Anlaff's brother. Adam Bell then disguises himself as a friar, goes to Earl Walter's court to see what they are saying about the 'peasants' who helped save the day, and, if matters look promising, to ask Earl Walter to intercede on their behalf with the King. When 'Friar' Adam arrives, he finds that Earl Egbert is taking credit for killing Anlaff's brother, so Adam spreads the word that he has just shriven a peasant who claimed to have killed the Dane. Earl Walter, however, believes Earl Egbert's story: 'A Peasant! 'Tis some mistake' (24).

When Anlaff returns for vengeance, Adam Bell once again calls the outlaws to the aid of the Earl, but Anlaff asks for single combat with the man who killed his brother. Earl Egbert is terrified at this news and hides under a pile of armour. Leonard finds him and insists on borrowing Earl Egbert's armor to meet Anlaff in his stead. After a dramatic on-stage fight sequence, Leonard disarms Anlaff and is declared the winner of Edwitha's hand. He explains that he came in disguise to court Edwitha, 'not as a Prince, who could confer, but as a Suppliant who besought [her] favour' (66) and her heart. The outlaws are brought back into the fold by becoming Leonard's soldiers, and Adam Bell proposes marriage to Edwitha's maid Alice, whom he has been courting for some time. Earl Egbert does not appear for the finale, having sneaked away sometime during Act 3.

The comic opera was a moderate success, running for ten performances, which meant that Holcroft profited from all three of his allotted benefit nights (nights three, six, and nine).[3] Only two mainpieces had longer runs that summer: one written by the manager George Colman, and one by Colman's son. William Hazlitt, who completed Holcroft's memoirs, describes the opening night as follows:

> The evening it was acted, Mr. Holcroft had placed himself behind the scenes, as authors generally do, to watch the progress of the piece, or be of occasional assistance. At the end however of the first act, the effect produced on the audience seemed so discouraging, and disapprobation began to manifest itself so strongly, that Mr. Holcroft could no longer stand it. He left the theatre, quite hopeless of success, and went and walked for an hour in St James's Park. He had

against Robin's father, and Gamwell, possibly from another outlaw tradition, also appears, illustrating the tendency for the Robin Hood tradition to appropriate characters from other traditions, a notable example being Maid Marion. It was well known in the late medieval period and popular in the sixteenth and seventeenth centuries. Its appearance in Percy's *Reliques of English poetry*, 1765, would have brought it to readers' attention in the years before Holcroft's opera.   3 The performances were 2, 4, 7, 9, 11, 12, 16, 31 August and 3, 15 September; see Charles Beecher Hogan, *The London stage, 1660–1800*, 5 vols (Carbondale, 1968), vol. 5, 1776–1800.

by this time so far mastered the agitation of his spirits that he returned to the Haymarket, tolerably resigned to his fate. He got in just at the conclusion of the third act, and was most agreeably surprised, when he heard the house resounding with applause, and saw himself surrounded by the actors and others, who came to congratulate him on the complete success of the piece. – It however only ran [ten] nights.[4] It was then stopped by Mr. Colman, in consequence of a disagreement with the author, whom he had without reason suspected of writing some paragraphs in the Morning Herald against [one of Colman's works]. Mr. Holcroft soon after vindicated himself so fully from this charge, that Mr. Colman was satisfied.[4]

The reviews were generally favourable, with the Shakespearean echoes appreciated (*Monthly Review*, p. 440) and the scenery found to be 'remarkably well executed' (*Town and Country Magazine*, p. 395).[5] The fact that *The Noble Peasant* was a comic opera caused some consternation. *The English Review*, for example, observed that

It will be readily seen that this story is full of wildness and improbability; but we ought by no means to forget that the piece . . . is a comic opera. This is a species of composition, that bids defiance to the severest laws of criticism, and in which the refinements of the highest comedy, and the accurate discriminations of character, would in reality be much misplaced (279–80).[6]

The *European Magazine* understood the genre better:

this drama, like all other Operas, depends chiefly on the music, which is indeed excellent, and affords a fresh instance of the skill and judgement of Mr. Shield, both in compilation and composition. . . . There is, however, on the whole, too much music, and some of the airs, though not void of merit, had better be omitted.[7]

As the opera has twenty-three songs, an average number for a three-act mainpiece, this final comment is rather odd.

Holcroft and Shield had known each other since the mid 1770s, when both had worked in theatres in Durham and Scarborough. They even took a walking tour together in 1777, during which they made the acquaintance of the 25-year-old Joseph Ritson.[8] He became a particular friend of Shield's, collaborating with him on a folk-song collection in 1784 and travelling with

---

4 Hazlitt, *Memoirs*, p. 109; Hazlitt erroneously wrote 'eleven'.   5 Reviews: *Monthly Review*, 71 (1784), 440–8; *Town and Country Magazine*, 16 (1784), 395–6.   6 *English Review*, 4 (1784), 279–81.   7 *European Magazine*, 5 (1784), 87.   8 Hazlitt, *Memoirs*, p. 79.

him in France during 1792. I suspect that Shield's and Holcroft's interest in outlaw ballads was inspired by Ritson, who would publish his famous collection of Robin Hood ballads in 1795.

The music in *The Noble Peasant* is an atypical William Shield score. Usually, he blends original compositions with folksongs; in his score for *Robin Hood*, for example, he used several popular English, Irish, and Scottish airs. In *The Noble Peasant*, however, almost all the music is original. There is only one popular air: an 'ancient glee' from Thomas Ravenscroft's *Deuteromelia* of 1609, a collection of old English songs.[9] The words have been changed to suit the characters:

> We three Archers be,
> Rangers that rove through the North Country,
> Lovers of ven'son and liberty,
> That value not honours or money.   (58)

The text of the opera is also not quite what one might have expected. A comic opera featuring Adam Bell and his cohorts would surely end with the famous scene in which William of Cloudesley shoots an arrow through an apple placed on his son's head, but that scene never appears. In fact, the opera outlaws are much younger than their ballad counterparts and still unmarried. Tinkering with traditional stories annoyed at least one reviewer: 'Most of the dramatic writers of these days seem to consider old stories as fit only to be told in a new way. Thus we have the title of a received tradition frequently prefixed to a piece, replete with incidents that bear not any analogy to those our forefathers have handed down to us, as the essential parts of the ancient fable.'[10] Of course, part of the tradition had always been to create new stories with the old characters. But there are plenty of traditional Hoodian elements in this work. Adam Bell leads a gang of forest-centered merry men who eat the king's deer and sing four-part glees and songs like this:

> We are Archers so stout and so good,
> With hearts unacquainted with fear;
> We live in the merry green wood,
> And feed on the King's fallow deer.
> We feed on the King's fallow deer
> In spite of the Sheriff and law;
> We ne'er from the Poor draw a tear,
> But keep Monks and fat Abbots in awe

9 Thomas Ravenscroft, *Deuteromelia: or The second part of Musicks melodie* (1609), repr. in E.H. Fellowes (ed.), *English madrigal verse*, rev. and enlarged ed., Frederick W. Sternfeld and David Greer (eds), 3rd ed. (Oxford, 1967), pp 219–34. Facsimile of music at http://www.pbm.com/~lindahl/ravenscroft/deuteromelia/deut_08small.gif.   10 Review of *Robin Hood* in *The Critical Review*, 58 (1784), 396.

Chorus
And so merry, so merry live we,
  With hearts light as air,
  We are strangers to care,
All under the green wood tree.

For Archery England is fam'd,
Expert are her sons at the bow;
Their broad arrows often have tam'd
The rude insults and vaunts of the Foe.
But England itself can't excel,
For valour and good archery,
Bold Clym o' the Clough, Adam Bell,
And William of Cloudeslee. (9)

They also rob the rich: 'Why truly, my boys, there are dangerous complaints gone abroad against us; your fat Monks, and your lean Usurers, have taken exception at us Forresters, and called us Free-booters – for which reason the King's pardon would be a good thing' (8). Adam Bell calls his men together with a bugle horn, and, most important, he dons disguises. He is not, how-ever, a gentrified figure as Stephen Knight notes Robin Hood was generally in the eighteenth century; the role of gentrified outlaw is taken rather by Leonard, the noble peasant who has joined Adam Bell's merry band.[11] By splitting the outlaw character thus in two, Holcroft can have it both ways: he can bring one figure, Leonard, into line with authority,[12] yet keep an anti-authoritarian outlaw in Adam Bell. Perhaps it was the fact that the Inglewood outlaws Adam Bell, William of Cloudesley and Clym of the Clough were yeomen and had not undergone gentrification (as Robin Hood had, into an earl) that attracted the radical Holcroft to them, even though they were, by his era, little known, in contrast to Robin Hood.

Some of the most interesting sections in the opera are the jibes against figures of authority who do not measure up. The historian Paul Langford notes that in late eighteenth-century England, attacks on 'blue-blooded delin-quents' and the House of Lords tended to increase in times of political 'tur-bulence', and this comic opera is part of that pattern.[13] Earl Egbert, a char-acter modeled on Shakespeare's Sir John Falstaff, bears the brunt of it. He does little in the initial battle, leaving the work to be done by Adam Bell and his outlaws. After Leonard slays the Dane, the noble lord is 'nimble at run-ning away with the slain Alric's arms' (6) and then gets his dwarf to cor-roborate his testimony that he heroically killed Alric. The next day, when

---

11 Knight, *A complete study*, p. 134.   12 Ibid., p. 143.   13 Paul Langford, *A polite and commercial people: England, 1727–1783* (Oxford, 1989), p. 590.

the other men go hunting in the Cheviot Hills, Earl Egbert stays home to woo Edwitha. As they walk in the woods, he claims that he is protecting her, but when a cry of 'The wolf! The wolf!' (35) is heard, he panics: 'O Lord! – which way shall I run? – what will become of me? . . . I'm a dead man' (35). He runs behind some trees and misses a chance to save Edwitha from the attack. Once again, it is Leonard the peasant who does the deed the earl should have done: kill the wolf. Earl Walter's Fool taunts Earl Egbert by singing a song about another knight very like him. The song is a parody of the ballad 'Sir Eglamore', which first appears in Samuel Rowland's 1615 poem *The Melancholie Knight* and acquired a tune by the 1650s.[14]

> Sir Eglamore, that valiant knight
>   Fa la, lanky down dilly
> He took up his sword and he went to fight
>   Fa la, lanky down dilly
> And as he rode o'er Hill and Dale
> All Armed with a coat of Mail
>   Fa la, la, la, la, la, lanky down dilly
>
> There leap'd a Dragon out of her Den
> That had slain God knows how many men
> But when she saw Sir Eglamore
> Oh that you had but heard her roar!

In the rest of the ballad, Sir Eglamore stabs the dragon and it runs away with his sword, for which he is sorry but resigned: 'But riding away, he cries, "I forsake it, / He that will fetch it, let him take it"'. Shield composes a new traditional-style melody for this ballad but keeps the same structure, rhythm, and syllabic setting. Holcroft's words, however, are very different, the anti-heroic twist turning Sir Eglamore into a prototype of the Duke of Plaza Toro:

> Sir Eglamore was a valiant knight,
> He call'd for his sword, and went forth to fight,
> He went forth to fight, as I've heard say,
> And when he came there he ran away.
>
> A hungry wolf did tow'rd him leap,
> But he'd rather have met with a score of sheep;

---

14 Samuel Rowland, *The Melancholic Knight* (London, 1618); the song appears in the 1650s in a two-part arrangement, in a three-part version in John Playford's *The Second Book of the Pleasant Musical Companion* (London, 1686), and in Thomas D'Urfey's *Wit and Mirth: or, Pills to purge melancholy* (London, 1719); Greg Lindahl, 'Early Child Ballads: Sidebar 6: "Sir Eglamour"', http://www.pbm.com/~lindahl/ballads/early_child/sidebar6.html.

Then he ran so fast that his sword did drop,
And he scorn'd to turn back to pick it up.

Then there came whistling down the plain
A surly, sturdy, dauntless swain:
Mean while the knight ran up a tree,
That if they should fight, he the combat might see.

Oh then began a bloody fray,
As the knight durst not fight, he resolv'd to pray;
But had you beheld Sir Eglamore,
When as he heard the savage roar!

This Peasant did his ribs so roast,
That Mr. Wolf gave up the ghost:
So when the knight saw the Monster Dead,
His courage return'd, and he cut off his head.   (44)

The fool's ballad recapitulates what has just happened on stage: Leonard has killed the wolf and Earl Egbert will try to take credit for it. In this subversive play, the aristocrat proves the worthless one and the peasant the noble hero, the sort of anti-authoritarian image dear to Holcroft's democratic heart.

The outlaw tales gave Holcroft a way to express radical views without running foul of England's Licensing Act of 1737, which screened all plays to be performed for unacceptable political content. For instance, the following stanza for the Fool's analogy song 'The World is a Fair' was not performed, although it appears in the published libretto (which was not subject to the Licensing Act):

Here puppet-show Patriots their booths have erected,
To tell how the rights of mankind they've protected;
When in hopes to be brib'd, Sir, each man with his fellow,
Of brib'ry and slav'ry will bluster and bellow.
Then it is that you see these Whirligigs, Roundabouts, Ups and
    Down, Ins and Outs,
Scrambling for fal-lals, drums, trumpets, globes, sceptres, and
    crowns,
Swords, maces, and woolsacks, and scarlet furr'd gowns.
Such wonders, wonders, and wonders' are enough to make a blind
    man stare!
Oh! don't you think it is a wonderful Fair!   (20)

This stanza is very much in the line of John Bunyan's description of Vanity Fair in *Pilgrim's Progress*, with its thick irony and attacks on the trappings of rank, power, and political authority (for example, the king's sceptre and the

Lord Chancellor's woolsack). The *English Review* was not pleased with the verses of this song that *were* performed (though they were much milder), considering them as suffering from 'grossness' and violating the 'laws of taste and elegance'.[15] No doubt it was the degree of political satire that made the song distasteful.

With a setting in the Golden Age of Saxon England, a time when the English people had greater liberty than they had under the Norman yoke (or at least so thought the eighteenth-century Englishman),[16] Holcroft had the safety of chronological distance for expressing his views. The outlaw material also gave him a traditional way to express his anti-authoritarian sentiments, and, although Robin Hood was off limits anyway to Holcroft, since Covent Garden had the lock on the character, he had equally good material in Adam Bell, Clym of the Clough, and William of Cloudesley. These Robin Hoods of the North could be recast as noble Saxons who, despite their outlaw status, were greater lovers of humanity and England than some members of the aristocracy.

Holcroft could also show that the Saxons were liberal enough to recognize the shallowness of the class system. Leonard has no trouble consorting with the outlaws. Edwitha loses her heart to a peasant. Fortunately, her beloved turns out to be of noble rank, but Holcroft does make clear that rank alone is nothing. Instead, nobility depends on personal conduct. Leonard is the noblest in deeds; therefore, he becomes the noblest in rank. One might think that Holcroft has betrayed his radical principles by making Leonard a prince in disguise, but by concealing this fact from both Edwitha and the audience, Holcroft makes us all acknowledge that a peasant can be as noble – perhaps even more noble – than a person born to a higher rank, like Earl Egbert. Deeds make the man, even if that man is an outlaw, and the finest Englishwoman knows to judge a man on them and not on superficial qualities. The real peasants, Adam Bell, Clym o' the Clough, and William of Cloudesley, the 'lovers of ven'son and liberty', have their worth recognized at the end of the opera and are rewarded. These are the type of men that Britain needs to defend its liberty, and they do not have to be noblemen to be worthy of praise.

Holcroft believed that literary works had to have a 'moral tendency'[17] and that court government was the 'source of all social evil in his time'.[18] As he saw it, 'man's inherent goodness had simply been warped by corrupt aristocratic values'[19] and his job was to reveal this truth to the world. The demo-

15 *English Review*, 281 and 280.   **16** Gary Kelly, 'Thomas Holcroft', *British reform writers, 1789–1832*, ed. Gary Kelly and Edd Applegate, *Dictionary of literary biography*, 158 (Detroit, 1996), pp 148–57, p. 152; Knight, *A complete study*, p. 156.   **17** Quoted in Jerry Beasley, 'Thomas Holcroft', *British novelists, 1660–1800*, Part 1 A–L, ed. Martin Battestin, *Dictionary of literary biography*, 39 (Detroit, 1985), pp 265–74, p. 269.   **18** Kelly, 'Thomas Holcroft', p. 151.   **19** Sid Sondergard, 'Thomas Holcroft', *Restoration and eighteenth-cen-*

cratic sentiments expressed in *The Noble Peasant* are mild compared with what he wrote in later works, especially in his novels, and with what his friends William Godwin, William Blake, and Mary Wollstonecraft, would write. His next play, brought out four months later at Covent Garden, was another work that shows the aristocracy in a bad light: a translation of Beaumarchais' current Paris hit, *The Marriage of Figaro*. A few years later, Holcroft joined the seditious Society for Constitutional Information, which led to his being one of the Twelve Reformers jailed for high treason against the government during the panic of 1794, when the government suspended *habeas corpus*. He was released without a trial two months later but never shook the stigma of Newgate, despite being guilty only of speaking his mind.[20] In the remaining years of his life, he had a few successes in the theatre and helped develop a new genre, the melodrama, but never regained his reputation.

tury dramatists, 3rd series, ed. Paula Backscheider, *Dictionary of literary biography*, 90 (Detroit, 1989), pp 181–97, p. 196. **20** Hazlitt, *Memoirs*, pp 141–54.

Robin Hood, the prioress of Kirklees, and Charlotte Brontë

HELEN PHILLIPS

Robin Hood is mentioned just twice in *Shirley*. Yet the two references, to Robin Hood in volume II, chapter I, and the Earl of Huntingdon in volume III, chapter VI, are intriguingly positioned and form part of the novel's use of intertextuality to make provocative contributions to the creation of meaning. Intertextuality both supports and challenges surface meanings. In *Shirley* it increases the dialogic tensions of a politically complex novel. *Shirley*'s literary allusions include the Bible, French literature, and Shakespeare – specifically *Coriolanus*. Intertextuality is used to explore themes of power, feminism, and myth-making. While these are also central overt themes of the text, if we probe their more covert expression through these areas of intertextual allusion what is revealed is a complex, interrogative structure (not unlike the social and psychological structures experienced in the novel), where matters of importance often run submerged and half-hidden, or interweave in a counter-pointing or conflicting way with a dominant narrative. The novel offers no single, unequivocal, political perspective on women's or workers' subjugation. That is one of its strengths, with potential to convey not just a recognition that the moral issues were not simple (which could be a conservative-tending outcome) but also that the discourses available prevented full and equal articulation of all the issues (a recognition with more radical implications). The text is notoriously equivocal over issues of power, such as Shirley's submissiveness after betrothal, the unemployed factory-worker's transformation into a gardener, the situation of factory children, or the imposition of industrialization over the older world of the Hollows and its fairies – itself almost a symbolic parallel to the regimentation of the children – and this evasiveness has an equivalent in the way the narrative reveals ambivalent gleams of radical themes within its subterranean resources of intertextual allusions. The Robin Hood allusions are part of this multiply-stranded exploration of power, submission and rebellion.

Besides the two brief specific Robin Hood allusions, *Shirley* uses more expansively certain elements in the tradition: the story of his murder by the prioress of Kirklees and the three-fold image of the outlaw as it had developed by the early nineteenth century, as an aristocrat, a radical fighting for the oppressed, and a figure of English rural folklore. Brontë uses these to explore the novel's three key political issues: feminism, political violence, and industrialization. They also play a role in her examination of the Church, an institution conceived, perhaps more we readily realize today, not just as one element in society but as central and pervasive across the social, political, and psychological worlds of the novel, and to the way authority, civil unrest, and gender conflict – and any hope for resolution of these – are constructed.[1]

Brontë's exploration of these issues is dialectic, acknowledging oppositions and cross-currents: neither wholly conservative nor radical. The diverse and contradictory elements which developed within the Robin Hood tradition over the centuries time, making him a figure who can embody equally conservative and radical ideals, provide a parallel discourse and parallel set of motifs, haunting – an apt word for her treatment of the theme – around the edges of the novel's modern action. The Robin Hood of Charlotte Brontë's lifetime encompassed both the conformist Robin Hood of Scott's *Ivanhoe*, lending loyal support to restoring legitimate authority, and the revolutionary Robin Hood of Ritson, Keats, and several now-forgotten novelists and poets during the Chartist years who were attracted to the topic.[2] The Robin Hood associations thus connect with the major themes in *Shirley* and they mirror profound dichotomies in authorial stance. It is not surprising, in view of this, that the brief allusions to Robin present him multiply as the outlaw, 'Robin Hood', as an earl, and as a sort of fairy.

On a literal, biographical level too, Charlotte Brontë had links with the tradition. She was familiar with two areas with Robin Hood connections: Hathersage in Derbyshire, alleged site of Little John's Grave, where Ellen Nussey's brother became vicar, and the Hartshead-Kirklees area, including Kirklees Priory, where, according to legend, Robin died and whose woods contain his reputed grave. Here her parents had lived; here she attended school; here her most important friends lived. Locations in these areas helped to create settings in *Jane Eyre, The Professor,* and *Shirley,* and the history of industrialization and of insurrection during the Luddite rebellions around Kirklees is reflected in *Shirley.*[3]

The novel's landscape contains in close proximity a rectory, mills around which gathers the threat of industrial strife, and an ancient manor house and nunnery with woodlands associated with Robin Hood and fairies. These three

---

1 The question of leadership, raised by chapter one, whose focus on curates has often puzzled readers, is conceived primarily as leadership in the Church and in society conceived as a Christian community. Robin Hood, though tangential to this strand in the novel, owed his post-medieval survival as national hero partly to the congeniality of his anticlericalism for protestant England.   2 See Knight, *A complete study*, pp 153–78.   3 See Juliet R.V. Barker, *The Brontës* (London, 1994); Asa Briggs, 'Private and social themes in *Shirley*', *Brontë Society Transactions* (1958); A.N. Jefferes, '*Shirley*: a Yorkshire novel', *Brontë Society Transactions* (1969); *Shirley*, ed. Andrew and Judith Hook (London, 1974); J.J. Stead, *The Shirley country*, Brontë Society Publications (Bradford, 1907); Mabel Ferrett, *The Brontës and the Spen valley* (Bakewell, 1978). *The Professor* opens with scenes from an industrial area; in *John Henry or The Moores*, an uncompleted fragment, Brontë tried rewriting it with sharper socio-economic observations, but abandoned this for *Shirley*.

sources of power and ideology – church, industrialization, and the older feudal, rural community – are explored literally and symbolically. In real life, a similar geographical and socio-economic triangle of church, industrialization and an ancient estate with Robin Hood and nunnery connections, existed in the area of Hartshead and Kirklees, and its surrounding mills, including Rawfolds Mill whose owner's attitude had provoked a serious Luddite attack in 1812.

While this background sufficiently accounts on the literal level for *Shirley*'s allusions to Robin Hood and the thinly fictionalized Kirklees Priory area, that is not all there is to say about their import in the novel. The first page famously declares that this will be a realist narrative, not offering 'anything like romance', lacking 'sentiment, and poetry, and reverie'; *Shirley* is one of the most serious of the 1840s novels dealing with social problems in the industrial age and age of revolutions; and its heroine is a girl whose sphere is restricted to prosaic, everyday domestic and parish duties. Yet the text also contains a number of overlapping symbolic structures. Alongside realist depiction of society and explicit political debate, it is often through symbolism, myth and fable that it explores modern problems of industrialized society, class conflict, and the position of women. The legends and associations of Robin Hood play a role in constructing these symbolic structures. Brontë uses, and creatively remakes and inverts, elements from the legend of his death at the nunnery, and she does this as part of the feminist arguments of her novel.

Although it is fascinating to read in *Shirley* a thinly disguised representation of people and places its author knew, we can also see the juxtaposed localities – wood, mill, manor houses, and nunnery – and the characters with their permutations on a set of contrasts (radical/conservative, continental/English; feudal/commercial, powerful/dependent, male/female, and various sectarian positions within Christianity) – as operating together to form the novel's symbolic patterns and set up its debates on issues of power in matters of sex, class and economics. Structures of ambiguity are characteristic of Brontë's mature writings and the polysemous figure of Robin Hood fits into her dialectic and problematizing approach to industrial and social change at the centre of this novel.

The Robin Hood legend associated with Kirklees appeared in the *Gest of Robyn Hode* and the ballad *Robin Hood's Death*.[4] This is, unusually, a Robin Hood story centred on a woman: Robin trusts the prioress of Kirklees, his kinswoman, to cure him, but she, unchastely involved with Roger of Doncaster, betrays him and bleeds him to death. He tells his faithful comrade, Little John, what has happened, and shoots the arrow to mark where his grave should be. In this first appearance of a major female character in the tradition, the female is a combination of standard misogynist themes: the powerful woman is malevolent, treacherous, unchaste, and destroys the hero.

4 In *RHOOT*, pp 80–168, 592–601.

'Yet he was begyled, iwys, / Through a wicked woman', summarizes the *Gest* (lines 1801–2).

In *Shirley* it is the male characters who cannot be relied on: Caroline's father and lover, her kinsman, both prove unable to care sufficiently for her well-being; she is brought to the point of death by Robert's ruthless faithlessness, his preference for his real love – his mill – over her, his betrayal of her trust with Shirley, and the deprivation of power from her, as a woman. These drain her of life (as Robert will be more literally drained of blood, like Robin Hood, by an assassin's attack). As in the ballad, death and debilitation are at the emotional centre of this narrative, but the novel – having exposed the deadly consequences for victims of oppression and powerlessness, women and workers – permits a benign preservation, just as it allows its convicted radical assassins to escape execution. Like Robin's comrade John, the protagonist's reliable comrades are same-sex: Shirley and Mrs Pryor, who saves her. Mrs Pryor is the female author's reclamation and inversion of the ballad's misogynist picture of the murderous prioress, the healer who killed.

Shirley in multiple ways examines woman: the relationships between women; women's strengths; their socio-economic predicament in the early nineteenth century; their role in the Church; and the problems raised for women in negotiating, in such a society, heterosexual passion, marriage, and the power structures of male-female interactions. Robin Hood was particularly in the early nineteenth century a figure associated with reform and radical demands for rights, and *Shirley* locates the outlaw in an 'antique British forest'[5] that itself carries symbolism both of the female and of a reinstatement of primeval human rights, as well as representing a natural world that is being subjugated by industrialization. Allusions to Robin and his forest form part of the powerful symbolic margins of the narrative whose central themes are radicalism versus authority in the spheres of gender as well as class power-relations. Robin symbolizes radicalism and *Shirley*'s radical questionings. A hitherto unnoticed source, a poem that Brontë probably knew, 'The Gala at Kirklees', 1848, by George Searle Phillips, a journalist writing for the *Leeds Mercury* (read by the Brontës) and *Leeds Times*, and Secretary of the Huddersfield Mechanics Institution, presents the romantic situation and associations of the Robin Hood grave, the nunnery, and surrounding woods. It links Robin to Chartism obliquely, just as *Shirley* does through its narrative of Luddism:

> Who, in his native hills in Loxley chace,
> With Simon Montford fought at Evesham.
> For the great Charter of the people's rights,
> In unsuccessful battle, and became

5 Charlotte Brontë, *Shirley*, ed. Herbert Rosengarten and Margaret Smith (Oxford, 1979), p. 237. All quotations are from this edition.

A wild wood rover, rather than abide
The whips and arrows of a tyrant's power.[6]

Phillips and Charlotte Brontë may both, from their close involvement with cultural life in the area, have known Richard Griffiths' 'Kirk-Leas' (also hitherto unnoticed by Brontë scholars): a poem dedicated to Sir George Armytage of Kirklees Priory and containing strikingly many motifs that appear in *Shirley*, including the ghost of Robin Hood, belief about fairies in the area, a nun wandering near the area of grave, a description of stormy tumult amid the Kirklees trees, and the theme of Nature's power.[7]

Robin Hood is part of the novel's use of folklore, fable, and the supernatural. Feminist issues appear in several important scenes and discussions on the realist level but also in fables and myths that disturb the novel's modern narrative. These myths and fable, like the banished fairies and ghostly Robin Hood, provide a glimmering of a past, often a primeval past, that we have lost, which includes a celebration of what woman's identity is and what it could be in a radically reformed world or one that returned to ancient rights and dignity. Myths of the wilderness and the primeval as symbolic locations for untainted states of human nature are central to the fables and they form part of its presentation of Robin Hood, who is associated with the woods and their fairies.

Brontë overturns the misogyny of the Kirklees legend of Robin Hood, reformulating the figure of the prioress for feminism. Her recently-dead sisters may have been models for Caroline and Shirley, and, in returning to the Huddersfield area and its Luddite history for the setting, she was also returning to an area and era associated with the mother she lost in childhood: here Maria Brontë had lived during the first years of marriage. She had died when Charlotte could scarcely remember her. *Shirley* has many allusions to ghosts, and it contains a lost mother who returns. Miss Wooler, an intellectually and emotionally nurturing and maternal figure for Charlotte had, of course, also run her schools in this area. Brontë gives the name Mrs Pryor to the mother-figure in Caroline's story, who plays the role both of, first, a substitute mother in her kindness and role as teacher, and then, through a fictional magic transformation, the actual rediscovered mother. Her name, 'Mrs Pryor', like Brontë's use of 'Robert' for her hero (who is both attractive and, in some things, a rogue), confirms the connections with Robin Hood in the novel's conception. The intertextual links are not just isolated verbal details but parts of the imaginative matrices out of which the work was created, and part of larger networks of associations running throughout the narrative.

---

6 George Searle Phillips, *The Gala at Kirklees* (Huddersfield, 1848). He published other writings about Kirklees and Robin Hood at various times in the 1840s, as well as in the *Leeds Mercury*.   7 *Kirk-Leas* (London, 1802).

'Mrs Pryor' recalls the Kirklees Priory, where Robin was killed by the prioress, but this name also links to a major feminist theme in the novel, the position of unmarried women: not now nuns but nineteenth-century women in a protestant society, an analogy found elsewhere in Charlotte Brontë's writings. And these are positive images. (It is perhaps relevant that she was writing just as the idea of Anglican sisterhoods was about to develop.) Though Brontë draws on Kirklees nunnery, its legend, and landscape, as an imaginative resource for several aspects of her novel, she remakes the meanings with feminist boldness. The motifs of the prioress, the death-bringing female healer, and the nunnery are transformed into a rediscovered, loving and healing mother, and into female sisterhood. Brontë erases Robin Hood's murder entirely from her allusions. Clearly aware of the ballad's negative female image, she presents his association with the priory and woodland positively: as a place where Robin was in *life*, rather than the place of his death and grave:

'Was it not one of Robin Hood's haunts?'
'Yes, and there are momentos of him still existing [...]'   (238)

'Haunts', with its ambiguous senses of a ghost and a living habitation, links with the novel's theme of the past and the supernatural hovering round the everyday world. In *Shirley* we are constantly aware of hauntings: the ancient woodland and wilderness lying on the edge of habitations; the night-time and moonlight bounding the world of day; the poor and their demands submerged, or lying on the edge of middle-class privilege and authority. In darkness, amid woods and moors, the rebellious poor waylay their class enemies and their wagon trains, like bandits. Several night scenes increase this sense of disruption lurking just on the edge of civil order.

'Momentos' in the quotation above avoids exclusive definition of the nature of the chief real-life monument at Kirklees, Robin Hood's grave. Its emphasis is positive, and its setting is both an idyllic wilderness and a nunnery, a place where unmarried women lived in community, with a life and purpose of their own, a state the novel explicitly demonstrates is lacking in early nineteenth-century England. Brontë names her Robin Hood wood 'Nunnwood'; the parish is 'Nunnely'; there are also the 'Priory' feudal manor house at Nunnely, and 'Nunnely Forest'. Fictional variants on 'Kirklees' (= `church meadows'), these names foreground the role of women, especially unmarried women in the church, and this is an important issue in *Shirley*.

Brontë's second allusion to Robin Hood, as the Earl of Huntington's ghost, like her phrase 'Robin Hood's haunts', increases his affinity with another structurally and symbolically important theme, that of supernatural beings, epitomized in the fairies who inhabited the woods now threatened by industrialization (and who intriguingly reappear to form the appropriately unresolved concluding passage of the novel). She thus mentions Robin in association first with nuns and secondly with fairies. Louis would prefer, rather than meeting Sir Philip, to encounter,

> the ghost of the Earl of Huntingdon [...] and the shadowy ring of his merry men, under the canopy of the thickest, blackest, oldest oak in Nunnely Forest. Yes, he would rather have appointed tryste with a phantom abbess, or mist-pale nun, among the wet and weedy relics of that sanctuary of theirs, mouldering in the core of the wood.   (589)

The merry men resemble wood fairies in a fairy ring. By the early nineteenth century, folklorists had for some time been seeing Robin Hood as part of the ancient folklore of rural Britain, along with fairies.[8] Among several striking allusions to fairies in the novel, Caroline appears like a fairy mistress or wood nymph in the moonlit woods to Martin Yorke as he reads his fairy-tale book, just after he visualizes a green-clad fairy queen (645–7). Shirley is a Peri (597). Robin and his merry men as fairies and ghosts symbolize the uncertainties and contradictions that typify Brontë's characters as well as the socioeconomic changes around them; such ghosts from the past represent rural Britain destroyed by the mills but supernatural beings also operate as submerged romantic alter egos of the otherwise rational, humdrum characters of Robert and Caroline (as of Martin Yorke). This novel shows its protagonists exercised by the dual claims of rationality and romance, in a way that is analogous to its political balancing-act. Brontë's characters slide between a literally delineated modern world and a realm of myth and symbolism. The second allusion to Robin Hood, as the ghost in the baronet's feudal woods, confirms the extent to which the subversive woodland robber in his multiple identities, polysemously ghost, elf, and earl, typifies the novel's ambiguity in attitudes to contemporary radicalism. Brontë encompasses sympathy with, and apprehension at, radical violence. Her writing itself shows this and also she makes Robert undergo a change of perception about the justifications for rebellion. Passages like her evasive ones dealing with factory children (chapter 5), charity (Book 2, chapter 3), or Shirley's readiness to cross into masculine territory (Book 2, chapter 1, chapter 2) show courage in raising issues and equivocation in pronouncing on them. Eagleton (1976) castigated her characterization of workers: she vacillates 'between panicky contempt and paternalistic condescension', with workers remaining caricatures, because the novel is preoccupied with splits in the ruling class, between feudal and commercial wealth.[9] This may have some truth but it ignores much: it

8 *The British folklorists: a history*, vol. 1 of Richard M. Dorson (ed.), *History of British folklore* (London, 1968), pp 30, 61, 62, 63, 80. Editions of ballads, chapbooks, anthologies, and comparative studies of British folklore with other nations, encouraged perception of the figure of Robin Hood in the context of belief in elves and hobgoblins.   9 Terry Eagleton, *Myths of power: a marxist study of the Brontës* (London, 1975), pp 49, 50.

ignores the gender dimension to the novel's politics, bringing other splits in the ruling class, those between men and women; it also ignores the degree to which Brontë (boldly rather than pusillanimously) introduces into her text an array of multiple, conflicting, political responses, making its construction that of complex debate rather than monologic pronouncement. It is appropriate that on the last page the narrative voice slips back into a non-omniscient one and the unresolved antagonism between the worlds of the Hollows Bottom fairies and technological advance returns, with the ambivalence that has accompanied such oppositions throughout the novel.

The allusion to Robin Hood as a stealthy aristocratic ghost in the wood introduces a moonlit chapter that reveals Louis' hidden passion for Shirley, a feudal mistress, and the complicated power-dynamics between them. These invert, because of the woman's wealth and man's dependent position, traditional power-relations between the sexes and the chapter reveals psychological dynamics of power within his own sexual nature, his need that a powerful woman, 'a young lioness or leopardess' (596), should submit to his domination. The drowned nun foreshadows the lofty heiress' subjugation to love. The Robin Hood allusion prefaces a chapter where Louis steals some of Shirley's property. The reference to Robin as an earl parallels the impoverished Louis' contemplation of his aristocratic rival, the baronet. In a chapter concerned with cross-currents of power in sexual and economic relationships it is unsurprising that Robin's dual class identity, as earl and outlaw, is invoked. As ghosts, Robin and the phantom abbess preface a chapter where modern characters shift into the dream-like, fable-like, superhuman alternative selves that hover constantly besides their everyday personalities: in the moonlight Shirley is figured as the moon goddess and Louis as Endymion; she is Juno in her glory, lioness, leopardess, merlin, and peri.

The woods with Robin Hood connections hold a central symbolic role in the novel's exploration of the Britain of the industrial revolution in relation to its pre-industrial past. Nunnwood is the essence of a Golden Age primeval rural paradise, introduced, in an ecstatic paragraph of landscape-painting as 'Nunnwood – the sole remnant of antique British forest in a region where lowlands were once all sylvan chase, as its highlands were breast-deep heather [...]' (237). Like Robin Hood, the forest, associated at times with subversion and the demand for rights, is a British heritage. These woods represent the older world that industrialization and mechanization are injuring and revolutionizing. At the same time, these are feudal woods, and Brontë's aristocrats, Shirley and Sir Philip, are benignly constructed. The ancient woods imply, like the figure of the national outlaw-hero, that freedoms – the freedoms demanded by radicalism for workers and women – may be more ancient than oppression. That, of course, was a common contem-

The 1988 second ed. preface acknowledges the neglect of gender politics.

porary strand of thought. Just as the novel avoids a single view of factories, so it seems ready to believe the institutions of past authority can be among the forces of reform.

The language of the passage that introduces Nunnwood makes it seem also a core place of the human psyche: 'To penetrate into Nunnwood [...] is to go far back into the dim days of eld':

> '[T]hat is Nunnwood?'
> 'It is.'
> 'Were you ever there?'
> 'Many a time.'
> 'In the heart of it?'
> 'Yes.'
> 'What is it like.'
>
> 'It is like an encampment of forest sons of Anak. The trees are huge and old. When you stand at their roots, the summits seem in another region: the trunks remain still and firm as pillars, while the boughs sway to every breeze. In the deepest calm their leaves are never quite hushed, and in the high wind a flood rushes – a sea thunders above you.'
>
> 'Was this not one of Robin Hood's haunts?' [...]
>
> 'To penetrate into Nunnwood, Miss Keeldar, is to go far back to the dim days of eld [...] the very oldest of the trees, gnarled, mighty oaks, crowd about the brink of this dell: in the bottom lie the ruins of a nunnery'.   (237–8)

The intertextuality here is biblical but it stays with the theme of subversiveness. The sons of Anak, giants of Canaan who made the Israelites feel like grasshoppers below them, in the search for the Promised Land, appear in Numbers (13.33), significantly just before a political rebellion. In the following verses the people, in ancient unrest long before Luddism, murmur and threaten to rebel against their leaders, Moses and Aaron. This is a negative image of popular revolt and a positive image of wise leadership, and occurs in the context of the Old Testament narrative of search for the Promised Land – which was as central an image in contemporary radicalism as that of Albion, mentioned by Noah on page 150. In contrast, the allusion to *Coriolanus*, dominating chapter 6, casts a negative light on the attitude of the master, Robert, towards the rebels. Typifying the paradoxical tendency that rules the structures and political explorations of this novel, Brontë's mill-owner bears the name, Robert, of both the robber-earl and cruel and faithless 'Robert-a-Ree', whereas the workers' leaders (neither of them romanticized by Brontë) bear those of Noah and Moses – Old Testament leaders and saviours of their people under God.

The ancient priory woods are presented as representing both aesthetic perfection, where the two women will commune with Nature (notably in the passage beginning 'That break is a dell [...]', 238), and feminine security and sisterhood (213–4). It is this feminized Nature that Robert's industrial revolution will dominate and destroy. Appropriately, given the constellation of ideas in *Shirley*, Nunnwood, the Robin Hood wood, is also linked to the theme of the role of women in relation to masculine power, and their comradeship together. The strength of the ancient British woodland and the ancient British outlaw-subversive confirm the positive symbolism that Brontë gives to the wood belonging to the medieval nunnery, as a positive, even radical, vision of some answers to the dilemmas created by female subjugation: it is a feminine shrine and a retreat. Shirley and Caroline agree that to walk with men in this wood – the wood with the feminine name – would disturb their own communion with Nature, which is itself emphatically feminized:

> 'And then Nature forgets us; covers her vast, calm brow with a dim veil, conceals her face, and withdraws the peaceful joy with which, if we had been content to worship her only, she would have filled our hearts'.   (239)

Male presence would intrude a distracting excitement, 'More elation and more anxiety' (heterosexual attraction, like virtually everything else in *Shirley*, contains contradictions). The Edenic image of Nunnwood combines with the outlaw and Anak allusions to link the girls' companionable same-sex idyll in these primeval woods with other, radical, visions of the primeval potential of the female in the book, and especially the recurrent themes of the First Woman, a new Eve, and a paradise shared by primordial heterosexual couple. Caroline, for example, dreams, like the First Woman longing to revisit Eden, of being at Hollows Mill with Robert. The motif of angels and the Sons of God mating with ancient women recurs. Shirley invents a feminized, revisionist myth of an Eve who is also Nature, to supersede the flawed masculinist myth created by Milton (359–62).

Robert's 'Hollows Mill', a hollow where the folkloric beings of the past haunted, has an analogy with the ancient wood haunted by Robin Hood. Brontë associates these more than once with the political rebels. Shirley reminds Robert that her nurse talked of fairies at the Hollow before the first mill was built, and then these are paralleled both with the political rebels and also with the power of sex:

> 'But there are worse things than fairies to be guarded against', pursued Miss Keeldar.
> 'Things more perilous,' he subjoined.
> 'Far more so. For example, how would you like to meet Michael Hartley, that mad Calvinist and Jacobin weaver? They say he is

addicted to poaching, and often goes abroad at night with his gun',
(266)

For Shirley the danger lurking on the margins, like the fairies, is the subversive poacher, Robin Hood-like; for Robert it is sex. When, in 'A Summer Night', Shirley and Caroline watch the workers marching towards the mill, these bands too are prefigured in references to fairies and hauntings. Fairies are associated with the violence of industrial, commercial change. On the edge of the middle-class characters' ordered world, fairies (like Robin Hood's ghost, the darkness, moonlight, and ancient forest) represent the repressed rights of the workers, which Moore disregards, just as in a later chapter they represent the passions and rights of women, and the values of the heart, which he also attempts to disregard. Chapter one tells us that the revolutionary leader, Hartley, had a vision of fairies: unemployed but working as a gardener, the radical agitator sees fairy-folk. These start conventionally: fairy music, poppy-red or white tiny creatures 'like May Blossom', coming out of the wood. But they turn into something revolutionary. First they emerge from their wood and invade Sir Philip's park, and their music is military, including 'bugles, fifes, and the sound of a trumpet'; then they appear as regiment after regiment, directed by a sort of radical leader 'a man clothed in scarlet'. Marching on Briarhead, the vicarage, and to Fieldhead, the manor house, they are dispelled by a column of smoke like artillery. The radical Hartley interprets them as signifying 'bloodshed and civil conflict' (21–2). This passage is juxtaposed with the night-time bandit attack by the Luddite band against Moore's machinery.[10]

Brontë develops the ballads' motif of the Kirklees prioress and nunnery into several feminist structures and themes in the novel. Robin Hood, though significantly linked to the symbolic themes like the ancient wood, fairies, and ghosts, remains a matter of allusion. The Robin Hood of Brontë's era had been claimed by both radicals and conservatives, but particularly, as exemplified by Keats and Ritson, the early nineteenth-century Robin Hood had epitomized political dissent. The introduction of his name(s) into so political a narrative as *Shirley* could not fail to have political connotations. In his great edition of the ballads, Ritson said of Robin's death at Kirklees Priory, 'Such was the end of Robin Hood, a man who, in a barbarous age, and under a complicated tyranny, displayed a spirit of freedom and independence, which has endeared him to the common people, whose cause he maintained, (for all opposition to tyranny is the cause of the people)'.[11] As Dobson and Taylor point out, Ritson converted Robin Hood into a thoroughgoing ideological hero: these sentiments voice Ritson's support of the French Revolution.[12] It

---

10 Linda B. Figart, 'Charlotte on the Plain of Shimar', *Brontë Society Transactions*, 22 (1997) 54–70, suggests parallels with the Israelites and the Promised Land, pp 57–8.   11 Ritson, p. xi.   12 *RRH*, p. 55.

would be unsurprising if Brontë, thinking as she wrote *Shirley* of the Kirklees area, thought of Robin in his Ritsonian persona as a symbol of revolt against oppression, and his affinity with 'the common people'. Robin Hood was associated with radical protest during Brontë's lifetime more than at any other period.[13] Nottingham was also at the forefront of protests in both the Luddite and Chartist periods: and, a reminder of this link, newspapers bearing news from Nottingham and Manchester, cause concern to the two masters of businesses, during chapter two. *Shirley* is about politics: industrial politics, national and international politics, economic politics, religious politics, and gender politics. Interwoven, these create a novel of debate about the issues rather than a novel of partisan conviction. Its dialogic texture extends to the interactions, within individuals, of mixed political arenas into which their personal concerns fall: Moore's pacifism, for example, with regard to the Napoleonic War is economic in basis; Hall's sympathy with the workers has religious origins; Caroline and Shirley's love lives suffer from restraints of class and economics. Several characters are internally contradictory: Mr Helstone, Mrs Pryor, Louis, and Mr Yorke are examples. Helstone calls Moore, 'a strange, shy man, whom I never pretend to understand' (19). Louis exemplifies contradictory attitudes to power and sex. He is also a deceiving thief. Brontë's characters are often, like Robin Hood, morally ambiguous, and creatures who can cross the boundaries between the wild and the civilized. Outlawry and wilderness are at times psycho-sexual. The strange, disturbing chapter which begins with the second allusion to Robin Hood, contrasting a mundane modern evening party with more terrifying encounters – a ghostly earl, his 'shadowy ring' of merry men, a phantom abbess, and drowned nun – ushers in a narrative where the exploration of Louis' sexual feelings passes a boundary into distinctly outlawed territory. It shows Louis rifling through Shirley's possessions and recognizing that sexual fascination, for him, involves both domination and a violation of her private things. Lit by moonlight, the counterpoint to rational daylight and the symbol of the Virgin Huntress, Louis sees himself, sex-reversed, as a Semele joyously burnt up with the majesty of Shirley, a priest of the supreme goddess Juno. Robert crosses a moral boundary into banditry: an honourable man who loves Caroline, is also capable of trying to gain Shirley's hand for money: 'like a brigand who demanded my purse, rather than a lover who asked my heart' (607). This Robert of the Moor is as morally ambiguous as Robin Hood: materialistic and opportunistic yet also the romantic hero and, finally, worthy of the heroine and reader's sympathy. Shirley visualizes both Moore brothers as men who could live in the wilderness, almost as Robin Hoods in the woods:

13 On Keats see Knight, *A complete study*, pp 159–67; on Byron and Nottinghamshire poets, see Lois Potter, 'Sherwood Forest and the Byronic Robin Hood', in Hahn, pp 215–24.

'I always think you stand in the world like a solitary but watchful,
thoughtful archer in a wood; and the quiver on your shoulder holds
more arrows than one; your bow is provided with a second strong.
Such is your brother's wont. You two might go forth homeless
hunters to the loneliest western wilds; all would be well with you
[...]'   (699)

The heroines are fit wilderness mates: Caroline like a fairy maiden in the
woods when Martin meets her; Shirley, in Louis' fantasies, a wild girl, willing to live in the woods with him. Shirley's sexual fear of him is like meeting one of those elves in the wood: 'a great dark goblin meeting me in the
moonlight' (720). For Caroline, her 'bonnie Robert' is like a glamorous man
from an ancient ballad: 'black Robin-a-Ree' (117–19). Caroline, at eighteen,
is at the age when 'Elf-land lies behind us, the shores of Reality rise in front'
(109). But elf-land always surrounds and underlies the characters' adult expe-
riences in this novel whose author disavowed on page one any element from
the genre of romance would enter its text.

The plot is filled with debates – between the male characters about political allegiances, between Caroline and Shirley, and Helstone and his niece,
about gender questions (and the political and economic power conflicts underlying these), plus straightforwardly industrial and national political questions.
Even the villain and perpetrator of sabotage, riot and attempted murder, the
'Antinomian weaver [...] violent Jacobin and leveller' Hartley, is described
in the first chapter as both wishing to destroy Moore, make a political sacrifice of him, and yet also liking to *talk* with him. Just as Helstone introduces Moore to us as someone difficult to interpret, Caroline in the last chapter acknowledges that her mother is hard to understand. The 'Old Maids'
whose situation the novel explores, include the disharmonious personality –
sympathetic and unsympathetic – of Miss Mann, with her contradictory
name. The book's final lines announce gleefully, in the authorial voice, that
the reader will find it hard to determine which moral is being promulgated
by the text. It is a situation equally familiar in Robin Hood narratives. The
narrator refuses to 'offer directions'. In this highly dialectic climate, the Robin
Hood tradition's multi-facetedness is appropriate: a legend historically adopted
by political visions of both left and right, but also, in the story of his death
at Kirklees, proving capable of becoming a fertile source of images and motifs
for Brontë's own structures of feminist symbolism and myth-making.

Robin Hood and the fairies:
Alfred Noyes' *Sherwood*

LOIS POTTER

In 1908, when he first wrote *Sherwood*, Alfred Noyes (1880–1958) was still under thirty, but he had already published eight volumes of poems. As an undergraduate at Oxford, he had written critical essays for the weekly journal *Literature* (later known as the *Times Literary Supplement*). Like Tennyson, whom he admired, he never took a degree: his first book of poems was accepted for publication late in his last year, and, on learning this, his tutor agreed that the young man's literary career was 'much more important' than taking his final examinations.[1] The years that followed justified this decision. In somewhat different circumstances, he might have been poet laureate, but he was a little too young when the post became vacant in 1913. He received plenty of consolation on an American lecture tour that year, when he was awarded an honorary D.Litt. from Yale by ex-President William Howard Taft. In 1914 he talked about poetry with ex-President Theodore Roosevelt, who had written a letter praising his poems; Princeton made him Professor of Modern Literature, despite his lack of a degree, and – perhaps the highest honour of all – invited him, as a former rower, to judge the boat race between Harvard and Princeton.[2] Noyes had been passionately anti-war, but when war came he worked as a propagandist for the British government, mainly concerned to bring the United States into the war on the side of Britain. A brilliant lecturer, a fine reader of his own poems and other people's, and still only in his mid-thirties, he was regarded as the British writer best known in the U.S. and the one who had the greatest influence on young people.

Sherwood was written in the first year of Noyes' marriage and he was later (in his dedication to the revised 1926 version) to link it firmly with that event. His wife, Garnett, who greatly admired the play, was an American. Probably at her suggestion, its first publication was in the United States, where it appeared in 1911 in an attractive edition illustrated by Spencer Baird Nichols. It was first published in Britain, without the illustrations, in Noyes' two-volume *Collected Poems* in 1913. The play did not receive a professional production until 1926, but its large cast and many small parts made it attractive to schools and amateur groups, especially for outdoor settings. Like

1 Noyes, *Two worlds for memory* (Philadelphia and New York, 1953), p. 23. 2 Noyes, *Two worlds*, 102–3; Florence R. Signor, 'Biographical notes' to Noyes, *Princeton, May 1917: The call of the spring* (Danville, N.Y., 1925).

Tennyson's *The Foresters,* which it resembles in other ways, it had its greatest success in the United States.[3] In particular, it was the theme for the New
Orleans Mardi Gras procession by the 'krewe of Proteus' in March 1916,
with twenty gorgeous floats representing tableaux from the play.[4] Milner
Dorey, who prepared a shortened acting edition in 1921, called *Sherwood* a
play 'which because of its great beauty and force should live in the minds of
all who share in the enterprise as the rarest occasion in their school lives'.[4a]

Yet, by the time *Sherwood* (revised and rechristened *Robin Hood*) received
a professional production in 1926, Noyes had moved to the margins of serious literature, where he has remained ever since: the spokesman for an old
order and old poetics, his productivity stigmatized as facility and his popularity taken as lack of original thought. Noyes writes that all through the early
years of the twentieth century he was haunted by a sense of some calamity
waiting to happen. He meant, of course, World War I, but sometimes his writings give the impression that it was modern literature. Already by 1914, tastes
in England were beginning to change. As an American critic put it, recalling
that period of popularity, 'America was a little slow to realize that Noyes' reputation in England was already tarnished by the fashionable "Georgians" and
would soon be further damaged by more aggressive innovators'.[5] The worst
of this damage happened in the 1920s. Noyes disliked both Eliot's poetry and
Joyce's *Ulysses,* which he considered a filthy book. Because he was such a good
public speaker, he was frequently asked to represent the old guard in debates
about modern literature. In this polarizing situation, he soon became the man
all young writers loved to hate. When a friend of his, visiting the avant-garde
Poetry Bookshop, asked whether any of Noyes' works were on sale there, the
shop assistant looked at him coldly and replied, 'It is possible; we are broad-
minded'.[6] Noyes lived till 1958, and there are eighty-two entries under his
name in the British Library, but he is now remembered only for a few phrases:
'A highwayman came riding, riding, riding', 'Come down to Kew in lilac time;
it isn't far from London' and – among Robin Hood scholars – 'Sherwood in
the twilight, is Robin Hood awake?'. This line comes, not from the play, but
from a poem, 'Song of Sherwood', published a few years earlier.[7]

The fate of Alfred Noyes is only a small part of the triumph of modernism,
and his Robin Hood play is only a small part of that story. Nevertheless, it
seems to me worth telling, since *Sherwood* is in many ways a puzzling play.

---

3 Though in his monograph on Tennyson Noyes did not mention *The Foresters,* it is evident that he knew the play.   4 The *Times-Picayune* of New Orleans (March 7, 1916) gives
a detailed account of the twenty floats.   4a *Sherwood, or Robin Hood and the Three Kings*:
school and acting ed., with directions for production by Milnor Dorey (New Yord: Frederick
A. Stokes Co., 1911, 1921), p. 191.   5 Hoxie Neale Fairchild, *Religious trends in English
poetry,* vol. 5 (New York and London, 1962), p. 313.   6 Noyes, *Two worlds,* p. 180.   7
The poem has survived as the play has not; in an attractive setting by David Wilson, it is
part of he soundtrack for Nottingham's Robin Hood 'experience', *Tales of Robin Hood.*

Even those who admired it in 1911 were aware of its contradictory impulses. A reviewer praised its 'democratic creed of the broadest sort', its attack on feudalism, and its 'charming fancy', but concluded, 'It is a pity that Mr Noyes elected to kill his lovers. Fairy tales should not end in tragedy.'[8] The author of the only monograph on Noyes, though not necessarily agreeing with this contention, recognizes the same paradox when he calls the play 'a kind of tragic *Midsummer Night's Dream*'.[9] Tragedy and fairy tale are not totally incompatible, of course, but neither seems the most appropriate genre for the legend usually associated above all with the words 'merry' and 'adventure' – or, indeed, for the first year of what appears to have been a very happy marriage.

The play's other context, however, is the brief period when Noyes was very much involved with the theatre. In 1909 Herbert Beerbohm Tree urged him to dramatize *The Forest of Wild Thyme*, a narrative poem 'for children from nine to ninety' published in 1905. In *The Flower of Old Japan* (1903), Noyes' previous narrative poem, several young children travel to a fantasy Old Japan (Noyes makes no pretence that it is like the real thing) and finally realize that home is just as exotic and wonderful a place. In the sequel, the same children set out to seek their lost younger brother. The characters include, beside the children and their parents, a wicked spider, The King of fairy-land, and the fairies Peaseblossom and Mustardseed, who explain that they came to this forest because they were banished from their former home in Sherwood. The fairies guide the children through the ivory gates of the City of Sleep, but have to leave them at the end because 'we fairies have no souls'.[10] The reminiscence of Dante and Virgil is intentional, since the children go on to see their lost brother in a dazzlingly bright vision like the mystic rose that Dante sees at the end of *Paradiso*; they then awake to find they have been sleeping beside his grave. When they tell their story, it effects a reconciliation between their parents, who have previously been divided in their grief over the child's death, with their father accusing his wife of equating heaven with fairyland. To a large extent, the poem seems to endorse the wife's view. Like other early works by Noyes, it has been accused of 'amorphous religiosity',[11] but the vagueness of the religious references is partly justified by the fact that it is the children themselves who are supposed to be telling the story, as they put it, 'In words we scarce can understand'.[12] The narrative is interspersed with songs, many of them versions of nursery rhymes, and there are magic horn-calls: the bugle of fairyland and, more surprisingly, the horn that Little Boy Blue is asked to blow. The delinquent shepherd of the nursery rhyme here becomes capable, through his innocence, of bringing redemption to a sick world:

8 *Nation* 94 (4 Jan. 1912), p. 17.   9 Walter Copeland Jerrold, *Alfred Noyes* (London, 1930), p. 156.   10 *The Forest of Wild Thyme: a tale for children under ninety* (Edinburgh and London, 1905), p. 86.   11 Fairchild, *Religious trends*, p. 215.   12 Noyes, *The Forest of Wild Thyme*, p. 12.

Little Boy Blue, if the child-heart knows
  Sound but a note as a little one may;
And the thorns of the desert shall bloom with the rose,
  And the healer shall wipe all tears away;
Little Boy Blue, we are all astray,
  The sheep's in the meadow, the cow's in the corn;
Ah, set the world right, as a little one may;
  Little Boy Blue, come blow up your horn!"[13]

Tree wanted to direct this fantasy, presumably as a Christmas pantomime, where he could have made much of its world of giant plants and animals and fairies; he also wanted to play the spider who is the villain of the play. For a while, Noyes became fascinated by the stage and the theatre world, and realized, as he said later, 'that one might waste many years in the attempt to write poetic drama'.[14] Tree's production never materialized: first he was busy with other projects, then came the war, and Noyes finally decided that he would prefer to write for 'the theatre inside my own head.' (74) He says, however, that Garnett had always wanted to see *Sherwood* acted; I suspect that he had the same wish, and waited until 1913 to publish it in England because he was still hoping that it might be performed. *Sherwood* is the same imaginative conflation of the Shakespearian fairyland and the historical Sherwood that Noyes had already drawn on in his works for children. Although *Sherwood* seems intended for adults, its success as a school production suggests that Noyes was not altogether sure of his intended audience.

The plot, for the most part, uses familiar material. The opening scene depicts the misery of the country under Prince John's regency and the longing of ordinary people for Richard's return from the Crusades. (Blondel also appears from time to time, singing of his search for 'the king'). Though Robin does not appear, his spirit is embodied in Little John and the jester Shadow-of-a-Leaf, who lead in a donkey with a large sack of food for the poor on its back. In the next scene Noyes follows Peacock and Tennyson, with the outlawing of the Earl of Huntingdon just as he is about to celebrate his betrothal to Marian. Huntingdon is already known as Robin Hood and famous for his help to the poor. But he is a Norman rather than a Saxon, and when he talks of oppression, he condemns himself as well as the other Normans:

              We came,
We saw, we conquered, with the Conqueror.
We gave ourselves broad lands; and when our king
Desired a wider hunting ground we set
Hundreds of Saxon homes a-blaze and tossed

13 Ibid., p. 37.   14 Noyes, *Two worlds*, p. 75.

> Women and children back to the fire
> If they but wrung their hands against our will.
> And so we made our forest, and its leaves
> Were pitiful, more pitiful than man.
> They gave our homeless victims the same refuge
> And happy hiding place they give the birds
> And foxes.[15]

His sense of guilt is unusual, less suggestive of the cheerful ballad figure than of the shell-shocked veterans of the imminent war. He is no match for Prince John, a sophisticated and sardonic villain who cried out to be played by Basil Rathbone, or for Queen Elinor, John's mother, who claims to be trying to save the lovers from John but is really working against them both. Act II returns to the forest, where Robin and his men are joined by most of the rest of the cast, including Marian, who reveals that Queen Elinor had tried first to make her jealous of Robin and then to kill her. It turns out that Elinor is in love with Robin herself and has been ever since he was her page. Elinor eavesdrops on this account, as well as on their plan for rescuing Will Scarlet, which will involve leaving the women behind in the forest. She tells Prince John (between the acts) that this would be a good opportunity to abduct Marian. Act III, unlike the earlier ones, has plenty of action. Robin's feats of archery and the rescue of Will Scarlet lead to a fight with the sheriff's men, after which the hero gallops back to the forest just in time to stop John and the sheriff from carrying off Marian and her maid Jenny. In both fights, he has the help of a mysterious (but, to anyone familiar with the legend, easily recognizable) knight. Predictably, John is forgiven, they settle down to a feast, and King Richard reveals himself. He briskly sorts things out, telling Robin and Marian that they need postpone their marriage no longer and must join him back at the court. The happy ending? Oh, no; this is a five-act play and we are only at the end of Act III.

From this point on, Noyes differs greatly from his predecessors. Although everyone in the first half of the play has reiterated, 'O that the king would come from the Crusades!', it becomes clear that his return has made very little difference. At the beginning of Act IV John is regent again: Richard, bored with his own country, has gone overseas again immediately after Robin's marriage. That marriage has turned the queen's love to hate and she no longer opposes John, who ambushes Robin and walls him up in a room at the top of a tower, intending to starve him to death. Fortunately the jester learns what has happened and shoots an arrow through the window, with a rope attached, then climbs in with equipment to file away the bars. He also warns Robin that Richard is dead and that he and Marian should flee the court.[16] Robin

---

15 *Sherwood, or Robin Hood and the Three Kings* (New York, 1911). All quotations from the first version of the play are taken from this edition.   16 While *Sherwood* was sup-

escapes but is seriously wounded. In search of Marian, he attends a decadent masked ball at John's court; one of the signs of its decadence is that some fashionable masqueraders are speculating on whether Robin and Marian really did remain chaste in the forest. Robin has a curious little scene with Prince Arthur, whose child's-eye-view of Richard's already mythologized return he wearily ratifies, but in tones that show his disillusion with the myth. To gain time for Marian to escape, he confronts John and his guests with the news that 'the Great King lives'. Assuming that he means Richard, they freeze in terror as the eerie sound of Blondel's song is heard offstage. When Blondel arrives, all he does is confirm the news of Richard's death, but meanwhile both Robin and Marian have escaped to the greenwood.

At the beginning of Act V, Robin, though delirious from the effects of his wound, insists on conducting a trial of the latest group of prisoners. Among them is one of his own followers, whom he expels for 'wronging a woman'; at the end of the trial scene this man, accidentally discovering that the wounded chief is to go secretly to Kirklees Priory, steals away to inform on him. The final scene is in Kirklees, where the Prioress is easily tricked into letting a visitor look after Robin in her place. It is, of course, the terrible Elinor, disguised as a nun. She lets Robin bleed almost to death in an alcove and, when Marian arrives, kills her. Robin and Marian can exchange only a few words before she dies, then he shoots his arrow, his men come running and the familiar death scene follows.

Most of these episodes have recognizable sources. The rivalry between Prince John and Robin for the love of Marian and between Marian and Queen Elinor for Robin can be found in Munday's Huntington plays. Robin's past as Elinor's page, to which she refers several times, seems to derive from *Look about You*, a prequel to *King John*. Noyes must have discovered how ludicrously unhistorical this part of the plot was (for a start, Elinor of Aquitaine would have been seventy at the period in which the play is supposedly set), because when he revised it in 1926 he made the villainess Prince John's sister instead of his mother. Marian's escape to the greenwood is ballad material, possibly based on Munday's play; Much's love for Jenny, Marian's maid, is also from Munday, while the rescue of Will Scarlet, the return of Richard from the crusades, and Robin's bleeding to death in Kirklees Priory

posed to have been one of the sources consulted in the writing of the script for the Douglas Fairbanks film of 1922, it is hard to find any resemblances. However, Noyes may have inspired the highly cinematic use of Nottingham Castle for elaborate climbing feats. He may also have had something to do with the film's gruesome depictions of cruelty under Prince John and with the long tradition of suave villains, whether in the form of Prince John, the Sheriff, or Guy of Gisborne. Moreover, Fairbanks' Robin was not a Saxon. See Katharine M. Morsberger and Robert E. Morsberger, 'Robin Hood on film: can we ever again "make them like they used to?"' in Potter, ed., *Playing Robin Hood*, pp 211–12.

are to be found in virtually every version of the legend after the *Gest of Robyn Hode*. Noyes, however, was always strongly sympathetic to the Catholic Church, which he later praised for reconciling Saxon and Norman by providing them with a common language.[17] Thus, he carefully clears it of any responsibility for the deaths of the hero and heroine: it is not a real nun, but the disguised Elinor, who kills them.

This account has so far omitted the most important and distinctive aspect of the play. Robin Hood and his men share the forest with, though they do not see, its other inhabitants, the fairies. Noyes presumably knew of the 'fairy rings' that are still pointed out by forest rangers in today's Sherwood. The idea of bringing Oberon and Titania into the Robin Hood story can be traced to Tennyson, following a suggestion made by Henry Irving, who at one point planned to produce and act in the play. Tennyson had them appear to Robin Hood in a dream, where they recognize that they are about to be banished from their forest by cruel mortals; Noyes develops the idea in *The Forest of Wild Thyme*. In the 1911 version of *Sherwood*, the fairy rulers, Oberon and Titania, act as a frame for the entire play. At the end of the opening scene, which has emphasized the sufferings of the poor, Oberon and Titania preside over the ivory gates of fairyland, which is also the City of Sleep from *The Forest of Wild Thyme*; it is only in dreams, they explain, that the poor can have happiness in their lives. At the end of the play, they open the gates again and Robin and Marian themselves pass through them.

Shadow-of-a-Leaf, the fool who is said to have 'fairy blood', is really the most important character in the play, as well as the most deeply personal. As a child, Noyes had had an imaginary friend to whom he gave this name, and, as he wrote later, 'the strange thing was that he never altogether left me'.[18] This friend, he believed, had prophetic power, frequently gave him the topics for poems, and suggested some of his more daring metrical experiments. As depicted in the play, the character obviously derives from the Shakespearean fool, a topic on which Noyes gave one of his best public lectures.[19] Being mad, Shadow has the right to move between the fairy world and the real world but, like all prophets, is unable to make himself understood when he tries to use his superhuman knowledge to help mortals; moreover, the penalty for doing so is banishment from fairyland, the thing he dreads most. He sometimes appears with Blondel, who sings of his search for Richard and for love. It is from the fairies that Shadow learns, in Act IV,

17 See 'The young friar', in *Collected Poems*, vol. 4 (London, 1927), p. 199.   18 Noyes, *Two worlds*, p. 184.   19 Much of what he says there anticipates later criticism: he notes, for instance, that the fool can disappear from *King Lear* because Lear himself becomes the fool, and that Hamlet takes on the same characteristics that Jacques wishes for when he asks to wear motley. One of Noyes' poetic collections is called *Songs of Shadow-of-a-Leaf*; Noyes later saw it as an unconscious anticipation of his conversion to Catholicism (*Two worlds*, pp 185–7).

that Richard is dead and Robin is in prison. Though he knows he will suffer
the penalty for revealing knowledge learned in the fairy world, he enables
Robin and Marian to escape the court. At the end, as the couple join the
others entering into fairyland, Shadow-of-a-Leaf is shut out, sobbing. But
then Blondel reappears, still singing of his quest. 'The king is dead!' cries
Shadow, but Blondel replies, 'The great king lives! Will you not come and
look for him with me?' (V.ii.225).

If we had not already realized it, we would certainly know at this point
that we were in a religious drama. The full title of the play, as published in
1911 was *Sherwood, or Robin Hood and the Three Kings*. Noyes dropped the
subtitle, with its religious associations, when the play was reprinted in his
1913 collection, but it is retained in the acting edition. In any case, it is clear
to any reader that the kings Richard, John, and Oberon are only shadows of
'another king beyond the world' (II.ii, 133). There are hints of a religious
message from the start: when Shadow-of-Leaf leads in his donkey, he remembers a time when palms had been thrown before it. Robin himself has some
of the qualities of a Christ figure: in the first act he tells his men to 'put up
your swords' rather than fight to defend him, and he is betrayed by one of
his own men, as happens in no other version of the story. But his attempts
at goodness are always limited because his knowledge is so imperfect compared to the fool's. Oberon's account makes clear that even when Robin rescued a fairy from the spider, he thought it only a may-fly. The ivory gates
of fairyland, which he enables Oberon and Titania to open for the poor, are
the gates through which false dreams come. Ultimately, his story is tran-
scended by one that the play only hints at.

But there is a side of Robin and his men that is more permanent than
their attempts at establishing social justice on earth. Throughout the play the
men in Lincoln green are associated, especially in Shadow's speeches, with
something that wants to reclaim the world from human attempts to control
it. As Noyes said in his essay on 'The Spirit of Touchstone', the Fool-plough
traditionally broke up the garden and the court fool was 'a kind of fool-plough
breaking up the gardens of ceremony and telling the truth to the lords of the
earth'.[20] When Robin describes his plan for rescuing Will Scarlet he uses the
same terms:

> We shall join the crowd
> Around the gallows; then, when the bugle rings,
> The Sheriff will find that, somehow, Sherwood Forest
> Is thrusting its branches up between his feet [...]
> Oh we break up like nature through the laws
> Of that dark world.   (II.i, 46)

---

20 'The spirit of Touchstone', in *Some aspects of modern poetry* (New York, 1924), p. 178.

Shadow uses this language when he climbs the tower to rescue Robin, throwing a rose and a sprig of fern through the bars, 'So that the princes of this world may know / The forest let you out' (IV.iii, p 166–67). When Robin and Marian are dying, it is heard again:

> Awake, Robin, awake!
> The forest waits to help you! All the leaves
> Are listening for your bugle! Ah, where is it?
> Let but one echo sound and the wild flowers
> Will break thro' these grey walls and the green sprays
> Drag down these deadly towers. (V.i., 213)

It is the same language that had called for Little Boy Blue to sound his horn in *The Forest of Wild Thyme*. As the first act had ended with a song prophesying, 'The forest will conquer', the play ends with Shadow singing, 'The forest has conquered', perhaps the most eloquent moment in the play:

> My nightingales chant in their chapels,
> My lilies have bridged their moats! (220)

The fool's sacrifice, in shutting himself out of fairyland, has made possible a whole rebirth in which Robin and Marian take part. But, since the two lovers pass through the ivory gates, which the fairies says 'may close / for ever now' (224), Noyes is apparently consigning them to the world of happy and consoling dreams.

A further sense of rebirth is implicit in Shadow's other role, also derived from that of Noyes' imaginary friend, that of a muse, or spirit of poetry. Characteristically, in Act II he tells one outlaw that he ought to talk in rhyme, and a moment later, as if by accident, another outlaw speaks a line that rhymes with the first one (86). For Noyes, literary tradition was as organic as the natural world. As he insisted in one of his lectures, 'There is neither new or old poetry. There is only poetry'.[21] In *Sherwood*, characters sometimes quote from earlier works by way of stressing Noyes' place in this continuum. Friar Tuck arrives in Sherwood with a brief passage reminiscent of the Friar in Munday's play, who because he is supposedly played by John Skelton breaks out from time to time in Skeltonics; here, the Skeltonics fight against the blank verse rhythms in which they are embedded: 'The heads I have cracked, the ribs I have thwacked, the bones / I have bashed with my good quarter-staff' (II,ii, 74). Munday also had Robin Hood tell Marian that 'What we lose in halls we find in bowers' and Noyes' Robin echoes the phrase, though with different lineation (85). Of course, there is a great deal

---

21 Noyes, *Some aspects of modern poetry* (New York, 1924), p. 44.

of direct quotation from Shakespeare. Shadow-of-a-Leaf greets Robin Hood's men with the same poetic phrases that Falstaff uses for his fellow-thieves: 'minions of the moon', 'Dian's foresters' (I.ii, 21–22). Oberon and Titania appear at the end of each act, and a mischievous Puck appears and speaks a line from *A Midsummer Night's Dream*, breaking off to apologize (IV.ii, 150). Oberon's address to the fairies as 'Elves, pixies, nixies, gnomes and leprechauns' (II.i, 92) recalls Prospero's 'Ye elves [...]' At one point Noyes harks back to Tennyson, who was himself quoting Peacock; when Fitzwalter says that unless Marian promises not to meet Robin again he'll lock her up in the castle, she replies, 'Then I'll swim / The moat!' (I.ii, 25). Noyes believed strongly in the relation of tradition and the individual talent, though not exactly in the way that Eliot used those terms.

When he prepared the play for performance in 1926, under the more obviously attractive title of *Robin Hood*, Noyes revised it extensively. One reason must have been the need to make it more easily stageable by Lena Ashwell's touring company (which starred Esmé Percy as Shadow-of-a-Leaf and Godfrey Kenton as Robin Hood). Many of his cuts are the same as those made in Dorey's 1921 acting edition; if anything, he was more cautious than Dorey, who had, for instance, assured the nervous director that 'with practice' the donkey of Act I 'may be enticed across the stage'.[22] Noyes must have realized that asking an actor to walk across the stage with a live donkey was probably asking for trouble, and he cut the episode.

The 1926 revision was also affected by real world events. 1926 was the year of the General Strike, and the miners were still out at the time the play arrived in London. Probably for this reason, Noyes drastically reduced the speeches that called for political or social reform: Robin's long speech about Norman oppression of the Saxons (see above), 42 lines long in 1911, was reduced to 13 in 1926.The scene in which Friar Tuck reads the forest laws, adapted from Munday's play, could be seen in the 1911 version as advocating a kind of Christian socialism:

> Fifth, you shall never do the poor man wrong,
> Nor spare the priest or usurper. You shall take
> The waste wealth of the rich to help the poor,
> The baron's gold to stock the widow's cupboard,
> The naked ye shall clothe, the hungry feed,
> And lastly shall defend with all your power
> All that are trampled under by the world,
> The old, the sick, and all men in distress.   (84)

In 1926 these lines became simply:

22 Dorey, p. 185.

> Fifthly, ye shall defend
> All that are trampled under by the world,
> And spread the forest arms of Sherwood round them. (47)

Noyes also cut a strange passage where Oberon recalls a vision of Merlin's wealth which seems to prophesy capitalism and industrialization:

> While, all night long, fed with the souls of men,
> And bodies too, great forges blast and burn
> Till the great ogre's cauldrons brim with gold. (II.i, 95)

Other cuts removed some of the play's disturbingly vivid evocations of pain and torture, like Robin's vision of Friar Tuck attacking corrupt clergy, 'Those big brown hands of thine / Grape-gathering at their throttles' (II.i, 77) – though it is possible that the author's chief motive here, as elsewhere, was respect for the Catholic Church.

Finally, Noyes removed Oberon and Titania, replacing them with the less obviously derivative Thorn-Whisper and Fern-Whisper, with their brownie-servant Bramble-Scratch. These fairies now belonged to the 'Shining Glen', a location with fewer associations than fairyland, and with fewer analogies to Christianity.[23]

It is evident to any reader of *Sherwood* that it belongs to an earlier age than the works that were being written at the same time, such as the first version of what would become Eliot's 'Love Song of J. Alfred Prufrock'. Yet in many ways the difference between Noyes and Eliot lies in their perceptions of themselves – Noyes as defender of the past, Eliot as a writer in the present. Noyes shares with Eliot a strong sense of the contrast between the imagination's longing for beauty and the ugliness it finds in the world as it exists. Eliot's first essay on Dante, published in *The Sacred Wood* (1920), states that 'the contemplation of the horrid or sordid or disgusting, by an artist, is the necessary and negative aspect of the impulse toward the pursuit of beauty'.[24] In his own collection of essays, *Some Aspects of Modern Poetry* (1934), Noyes defended the famous song in Browning's *Pippa Passes*, that concludes 'God's in his heaven, / All's right with the world':

> A great deal of scorn has been poured upon the last two lines of this poem and the intellect of its author by those who have forgotten or never known that it had any context, and that it occurs immediately

---

23 It should be noted that fairies had recently been in the news, with Sir Arthur Conan Doyle's *The coming of the fairies* (London, 1923), an account of the supposed sighting by two young girls, with photographic evidence. This was later found to be a hoax. 24 'Dante,' in T.S. Eliot, *The sacred wood: essays on poetry and criticism* (1920; London, 1960), p. 169.

after one of the most vivid murder scenes in poetry. Browning deliberately paints the world in its blackest and most evil disorder before
he gives you that exquisite moment in which he reintegrates it and
shows you once more 'the glory of the sum of things'.[25]

Sherwood, among the other works of Noyes, attempts to achieve this kind of
'reintegration'. The designer of floats in the New Orleans Mardi Gras procession of 1916 seems to have understood this very well. Produced in the
middle of World War I (the front page of the *Times-Picayune* juxtaposes its
account with a story about Zeppelin raids on eight counties of England), the
procession included a title float that showed an effigy of Robin Hood bearing the title 'Sherwood'; in the background 'Butterflies and fairies were seen
sporting about a great web, in which lurked an ugly black spider' (Noyes'
symbol of evil in his early works). Another float actually depicted Merlin's
prophecy, with an image of the world as he had envisaged it: 'a red ball representing the earth, in smoke and flames; woods hewn down and a lurid sun
begrimed and greasy'.[26] The combination of visual beauty with a tragic story
must have seemed as modern then as it seems outdated now. If it now seems
an anachronism, it is partly because Noyes' love of tradition led him to follow
familiar – too-familiar – models and partly because the highly coloured language in which he evokes suffering is so poetic as to suggest that he is enjoying it (Wilfred Owen is sometimes liable to the same objection). Moreover,
the alternative to this suffering is deliberately kept vague. No-one is able to
speak directly for the author: even Shadow can express his knowledge only
obliquely. The world of the play encompasses the 'falling towers' and 'unreal
city' of Eliot's *The Wasteland,* but its most intensely poetic visions evoke an
inevitable process that makes all human activity meaningless, as nature invades
and replaces the stone walls and paved streets of civilized society.

   Noyes and Eliot – the Englishman with an American wife and the
American with an English wife – were both influenced by something that they
kept as private as possible: their marital situation.[26a] Eliot, who is now known
to have written *The Wasteland* in the context of his unhappy marriage, insisted
that 'the emotion of art is impersonal' ('Tradition and the Individual Talent').
Noyes, with equal restraint, dedicated the revised text of his play to his first
wife, in words that only those close to him would understand:

> You believed in this play when it was first written, eighteen years
> ago, and you always hoped to see it one day. It is dedicated to you
> now, a little too late for that, on the eve of its first performance in

25 'Some characteristics of modern literature', in *Some aspects of modern poetry,* pp 276–7.
26 *Times-Picayune,* 7 March 1915, p. 5.   26a Another connection: Eliot's long-time con-
fidante, Emily Hale, directed *Sherwood* in Milwaukee in 1926, with a cast of 125; Lyndall
Gordon, *T.S. Eliot: an imperfect life* (London, 1998), p. 234.

England, because – for all its author's faults – the sunlight of those youthful hopes and memories always hovers over it, and that sunlight always belonged to you.[27]

It was 'a little too late' for Garnett to see the London production because she had died suddenly in the previous year. As he puts it in one extraordinarily restrained sentence in his autobiography, 'She knew the end was near, but she had kept this knowledge from me, and it was not until some months later that I discovered she had known'.[28] Even as he wrote the dedication, Noyes must have known that this chapter in his life had closed. He remarried in the same year, with a daughter of an old English Catholic family, and was received into the Catholic church in 1926, the year before T.S. Eliot became a member of the Church of England. The marriage resulted in three children; his marriage to Garnett had been childless.

In the context of Garnett's death, the play, written in the first year of their marriage, must have become a still more personal work in 1926 than it had been in 1911. Perhaps Noyes' revision of the final scene reflects this fact. In 1911, Robin is awakened by Shadow-of-a-Leaf just in time to exchange a few last words with Marian before she dies; in 1926 she is already dead when he finds her. But it is his revision to 'The Song of Sherwood' that is perhaps the truest homage to his late wife. He had used its opening lines as the epigraph to the 1911 edition of *Sherwood,* but dropped them when the play was published in his *Collected Works* of 1913. In 1926, he seems to have conceived the poem as a sort of prologue, since one of his alterations brings in a reference to the play's new character of Bramble-Scratch. Taken on its own, 'Song of Sherwood' can be criticized, as Stephen Knight criticizes it, for its facile nostalgia and for other 'Georgian' qualities: 'The worm of nationalism is firmly in the bud of greenwood beauty'.[29] Noyes himself may have come to a similar view himself, since in 1926 he altered one line – 'Merry, merry England hath kissed the lips of June' – that Knight singles out for special criticism. There is much that is vague about the poem: Robin Hood is urged to wake and sound his horn, yet, when his 'bugle note' is finally heard, it is 'faint and far away'. Is this really a return to 'Merry, merry England' – Little Boy Blue's horn call setting the world aright – or the cry of someone near death? In two poems written about this time, Noyes mentions that Garnett's death had occurred shortly after they visited Roncesvalles. She apparently knelt to pray in the chapel there, and the fact remained in his mind, perhaps because he knew that Roncesvalles was famous as the setting of Roland's last battle, when he blew his horn, despite the urgings of

---

27 Noyes, *Robin Hood: a play in five acts* (Edinburgh and London, 1926). 28 *Two worlds,* p. 198. Perhaps this restraint was due to the fact that Noyes, blind with Glaucoma since 1942, had to dictate this book. 29 Knight, *A complete study,* p. 280.

his friends, too late to save his life. Seen as a prologue to the play, the poem is not so much a study in nostalgia as a reminder that not only Shadow-of-a-Leaf but all the characters are shadows. 'The dead are coming back again, the years are rolled away', but only because we have longed for this to happen, and only for the duration of the play. Robin Hood is only the object of dreams: 'a shadowy man who winds a shadowy horn'.[30]

30 I should like to thank Paige Harrison, Michael Clody, Gail Stanislow of the Brandywine Conservancy, and Wayne Everard of the New Orleans Public Library, for help with the research for this essay.

Robin Hood in the landscape:
place-name evidence and mythology

MICHAEL R. EVANS

Much of the investigative literature about Robin Hood produced in the last
two centuries has been devoted to argument over his historicity. Many works,
especially of 'popular' history, have attempted to identify him with one of a
number of people in the historical record. However, there is an alternative
possibility that Robin Hood's origins may lie in mythology rather than history. This idea has tended to be discounted of late by both 'serious' and 'popular' historians, but may be worth renewed consideration.

The idea of a mythical Robin was first suggested over 150 years ago. In
1846 Thomas Wright argued that Robin Hood should be viewed 'among the
personages of the early mythology of the Teutonic peoples'.[1] This statement
ran counter to the efforts of Joseph Ritson, whose collection of Robin Hood
ballads, published in 1795, attempted to work the ballad tradition into an historical framework, and Wright's contemporary Joseph Hunter, who was the
first to seek Robin in the historical record, identifying him with a Wakefield
man of the reign of Edward II.[2] Ritson's full title was *Robin Hood, A Collection
of All the Ancient Poems, Songs and Ballads Now Extant Relative to the
Celebrated Outlaw (To Which are prefixed Historical Anecdotes of His Life).*

In 1891, Sidney Lee devoted an entry to Robin in the *Dictionary of
National Biography* that argued for his subject's non-existence. He followed
Wright in seeing Robin as a wood-sprite:

> There can be little doubt ... that, as in the similar case of Rory o'
> the Hills in Ireland, the name originally belonged to a mythical
> forest-elf, who filled a large space in English, and apparently in

1 Thomas Wright, 'On the popular cycle of the Robin Hood ballads,' *Essays on Subjects
Connected with the Literature, Popular Superstitions and History of England in the Middle
Ages,* 2 vols (London, 1846), vol. 2, pp 164–211. Wright suggests Robin Hood has common
origins with the German spirit Hudekin. He proposes, 207–211, 'Robin of the Wood' as
an origin for the name and cites place-name evidence (whose generally rather recent date
he did not, of course, realize) to support the argument that Robin originated in belief in
a supernatural being connected in popular folklore with wells and, like dwarves, ancient
tumuli. 'The legends of the peasantry are the shadows of a very real antiquity . . . they
enable us to place out Robin Hood with tolerable certainty among the personages of the
early mythology of the Teutonic people. See Holt, pp 54–5. 2 Joseph Hunter, 'The great
hero of the ancient minstrelsy of England: Robin Hood, the period, real character, etc.,
investigated,' *Critical and Historical Tracts* (1852), vol. 4, pp 28–38.

Scottish, folk-lore, and that it was afterwards applied by English
ballad-writers [...] to any robber-leader who made his home in
forests or moors.[3]

The decline in interest among Robin Hood scholars in the last fifty years or
so in exploring possible relationships with folklore reflects, on the one hand,
changing critical perspectives, more concerned with the interpretation of individual extant texts, in their contexts, than speculation about whether ancient
rituals or belief might lie behind them, and also, on the other hand, a scepticism about the concept of folklore, with an awareness that many songs, ballads and rituals show the influence and inventiveness of later antiquarians,
collectors and performers.

There are, however, undoubtedly elements of the Robin Hood legend
that suggest, at least superficially, an affinity with wood-sprites or similar
mythological figures. The name Robin recalls Robin Goodfellow, Robin a-
Tiptoe, and similar figures.[4] Robin and his men dwell in the forest, outside
everyday human society. There are a few elements in the ballads that have
been felt by some critics to belong to some ancient substratum of supersti-
tion, magic or ritual. The most obvious case is *Robin Hood and Guy of
Gisborne*: Guy is clad in the skin of a horse with the horse's head, tail and
mane still attached to it. Knight and Ohlgren say this 'seems more like a
ritual costume than a disguise'.[5] *Robyn and Gandelyn*, usually regarded as a
Robin Hood poem, takes the device of ellipsis characteristic of the ballad
form so far that its tragic and violent events seem mysterious.[6] The 'pagan'
interpretation of Robin has proved particularly appealing to New Age thinking, as shown notably in the 1980s television series *Robin of Sherwood*. Even
the name Hood (which has still not been satisfactorily explained) may be
derived from 'Robin of the Wood', reinforcing the idea of Robin as a wood-
sprite.[7] More recently, some writers have proposed a pagan Robin Hood
based on the Green Man, with varying degrees of romanticist imagination.[8]

---

3 *Dictionary of national biography*, 22 vols (Oxford, 1885–1901), vol. 9, p. 1152.   4 These
were sometimes imagined as helpful household spirits, sometimes as outdoor elves and
goblins.   5 *RHOOT*, 169.   6 Observing that Douglas Gray calls it 'mysterious and eerie',
Knight and Ohlgren, *RHOOT*, pp 227–8, point out that it can either be read in terms of
mystery, magic and taboo or as a purely human drama that concerns central themes of
the Robin Hood tradition like the honest outlaw and the loyalty of Robin and his comrades to each other. They also discuss whether it is a Robin Hood ballad at all.   7 First
suggested by Wright. It might have been an English equivalent to a name used elsewhere
in medieval outlaw tradition. The thirteenth-century outlaw Fouke Fitz Waryn adopted
the pseudonym 'Amis de Bois', according to the Anglo-Norman romance about him; see
Two medieval outlaws, trans. Glyn Burgess (Cambridge, 1997), pp 165-6.   8 For example, John Matthews, *Robin Hood: green lord of the wildwood* (Glastonbury, 1993). For
opposing arguments on the Green Man see Kathleen Basford, *The Green Man* (1978; rpt.
Cambridge, 1996); Lorraine K. Stock, 'Lords of the wildwood: the Wild Man, the Green

One possible objection to the mythological interpretation of Robin is the nature of the ballads, which present him as a human hero with only human strength and powers, rather than a superhuman figure. The most substantial early version of the Robin Hood story in the *Gest of Robyn Hode* presents Robin and his men in a realistic setting, identifiable with real places in Nottinghamshire and the West Riding of Yorkshire, engaged in conflict with realistic enemies, the Sheriff and corrupt clerics. Robin (not yet ennobled as Earl of Huntingdon) is a 'good yeoman'. The other early ballads are similar. As the legend developed through the ballads of the sixteenth or seventeenth centuries, Robin acquired additional adventures and followers, but his deeds remained those of a human. His fighting and archery skills may have been superlative (reminiscent of figures such as William Tell) but they were not supernatural or superhuman. A favourite motif in Robin Hood ballads is that of 'Robin meets his match' where – far from having a superhuman invincibility – Robin is beaten by a plucky opponent in a fight and, full of respect, invites the man to join his band. Robin, though ready to oppose clerics, is also depicted as a man of strong, conventional, medieval Christian piety: what supernatural help he gets comes from Mary and Christ, not from magic power, wizards, or anything suggesting pagan survivals.

If we contrast this with that other great figure of British legend, King Arthur, a rather different picture emerges. The high medieval Arthur had his deeds historicized by Geoffrey of Monmouth, and resembles Robin Hood (albeit at a socially exalted level) in that his deeds are superlative but not superhuman. Magic and enchanters do, however, come into Arthurian narratives. Moreover, in Welsh tales rooted in traditions dating to before Geoffrey, there are elements of a very different figure of Arthur, one who dwells in a realm where the supernatural can occur. In *Culhwch and Olwen*, Arthur leads the hunt of the boar Trwyth, a king who has been magically transformed as a punishment for his sins.[9] *Culhwch and Olwen* is a tale full of

Man, and Robin Hood,' in Hahn, pp 239–49; and Bella Millett, 'How green is the Green Man?' *Nottingham Medieval Studies* 38 (1994), 138–41, which argues that the concept of the Green Man as a fertility spirit developed in the twentieth century, whereas the Wild Man was an authentic medieval figure. There are, however, early occurrences of 'Green Man': it appears 1784 as pub name, equivalent to an earlier pub name 'The Wild Man', and Pepys a century earlier, visited a Green Man tavern: Barrie Cox, *English inn and tavern names* (Nottingham, 1994), pp 18, 24–25, 101. For a suggestion that Robin and Marion replaced the Lord and Lady of May in the early modern period, see William E. Simeone, 'The May Game and the Robin Hood legend', *Journal of American Folklore*, 64 (1951), 265–74, p. 271. Malcolm A. Nelson argues Robin's role as Lord of May developed in the sixteenth century. He cites a seventeenth-century jestbook showing Robin Hood among an eclectic troop of legendary characters including Merlin, the Nine Worthies and Robin Goodfellow, as evidence for Early Modern popular traditions of rural revels involving pageants, rather than direct survivals of paganism: *The Robin Hood tradition in the English Renaissance*, Elizabethan and Renaissance Studies, Salzburg Studies in English Literature (Salzburg, 1973), pp 191–205. **9** *The Mabinogion*, ed. and trans. G. Jones and

heroes with incredible powers, of giants and witches. Arthur is not portrayed as a demigod (the tale was, after all, written down in the fourteenth century in a thoroughly Christian milieu), but he inhabits a semi-magical landscape. The supernatural setting for Arthur is even preserved by Geoffrey, in his collection of *Marvels*, and his highly influential *Prophecies of Merlin*. Merlin is advisor to Uther and Arthur in Geoffrey's *Historia regum Britonum*, and he and other enchanters, male and female, together with other magical motifs, feature in many Arthurian romances from the twelfth century onwards.

Arthurian place-names suggest a mythical rather than historical Arthur. In the words of Oliver Padel:

> wonderful animals, supernatural events, and remarkable features in the landscape need to be explained by reference to Arthur and his attendant legends. The process can alternatively be seen as the use of natural features in the landscape to give local credence to Arthur and his legends.[10]

Place-names of this type suggest a superhuman Arthur; the naming of mountains, for example, as 'Arthur's Seat' or 'Arthur's Table' suggests a giant or a god more than a man. There is a tendency to attribute impressive and unexplained elements of the landscape to supernatural figures. Earthworks were often attributed to the god Woden (also known as Grim), such as Grim's Ditch and Wansdyke in southern England, or to the devil, as in Devil's Ditch in Cambridgeshire.

Robin Hood names in the landscape do at times fit this pattern of giant features attributed to a mythological figure.[11] Hills or rock formations bear the name Robin Hood's chair (in Cumberland and Derbyshire), table (Derbyshire) and bed (a range of hills in Lancashire).[12] Where place-names are linked specifically to Robin's feats, they suggest not merely a highly skilled archer, but a superhuman one. For example, Robin Hood's Stoop at Hathersage in Derbyshire is said to be the site from which he fired an arrow into Hathersage churchyard, 2,000 yards away, while two large stones in Northamptonshire, named Robin Hood and Little John, are said to be two great arrows fired by the heroes, which have turned into stone.[13] Robin's name is also frequently associated with prehistoric remains, in much the same way as earthworks were attributed to the pagan gods. Robin Hood's Arbour, in Berkshire, is a prehistoric earthwork, while Robin Hood's Ball in Wiltshire

T. Jones, rev. ed. (London, 1989), pp 131–4. **10** Oliver J. Padel, 'The nature of Arthur', *Cambrian Medieval Celtic Studies*, 27 (1994), 4. **11** See M.R. Evans, '*Robynhill* or Robin Hood's hills? Place-names and the evolution of the Robin Hood legends', *EPNS Journal*, 30 (1998), 43–52. **12** *RRH*, pp 295, 297–8, 302. **13** *RRH*, 297; *The place-names of Northamptonshire*, ed. J.E.B. Glover, A. Mawer, F.M. Stenton, EPNS (Cambridge, 1933), p. 233.

is a Neolithic tumulus. The latter name again recalls feats of superhuman strength, in this case throwing, similar to those associated with Arthur in the name 'Arthur's Quoits', a collection of megaliths said to have been thrown by Arthur. In Westmorland, a cairn is named Robin Hood's Grave.[14] Robin Hood names in the topography of Derbyshire occur in areas rich in prehistoric remains: Robin Hood's Stoop near Hathersage is a stone – perhaps the remains of a medieval cross – on a hill that also contains a tumulus and cairn, while Robin Hood's Stride near Bakewell is close to a stone circle and the Castle Ring hill fort, and only a little over a mile form the Nine Stones circle and a series of cairns on Stanton Moor.[15]

Place-name evidence, therefore, gives a very strong picture of a mythical Robin in the landscape, who shares more in common with pagan gods and superhuman heroes than with the Robin of the ballads. There is, however, a problem of chronology that must lead us to be cautious about relying too strongly on place-name evidence for Robin's origins. If Robin began as a mythological figure, and was later humanized by the ballad-makers (as suggested by Lee), then we would expect those place-names that suggest a supernatural Robin to be of greater antiquity than the ballads. The truth, however, seems to be the opposite. The earliest extant ballad texts are from the fifteenth century, and we know of the earlier existence of 'rymes of Robyn Hode' from Langland's allusion in a version of *Piers Plowman* of *c*.1377.[16] There is an early reference in the cartulary of Monkbretton, Yorkshire, to a Robin Hood's Stone in the Barnsdale area. The reference is probably about 1422.[17] (Henry VIII passed this *en route* from York: it seems to have been shown to visitors travelling in the Barnsdale area.) However, Robin Hood place-names appear generally to be of early-modern or modern provenance. An early 'Robin Hood's Well' appears in the Barnsdale area from 1622.[18] It is the eighteenth century when many make their first appearance in the written record. In Sherwood Forest, the area most closely associated with Robin, no features are recorded bearing his name before 1700. In the High Peak in Derbyshire, another area with a concentration of Robin Hood names and associations, no Robin Hood place names are recorded earlier than 1800. One of these is the name of an inn; the popularity of Robin Hood as a pub name in the nineteenth century is another complicating influence on place-names.[19] Some places-names were

---

14 *The place-names of Westmoreland*, ed. A.H. Smith, EPNS (Cambridge, 1967), p. 160. **15** *The place-names of Derbyshire*, ed. Kenneth Cameron, 3 vols (Cambridge, 1959), vol. I, p. 6. Ordnance Survey maps OL 1 and OL 24. **16** William Langland, *Piers Plowman*, ed. George Kane and E. Talbot Donaldson (London, 1975), p. 395. **17**. *The place-names of the West Riding of Yorkshire*, ed. A.H. Smith, 8 vols, EPNS (Cambridge, 1961), vol. 2, p. 36. **18** Evans 'Robynhill', p. 43; *RRH*, p. 296; see also *Place-names of Derbyshire*, p. 118. **19** Cox sees the arrival of 'Robin Hood' pub names as part of a fashion for literary names such as 'The Shakespeare', beginning in the early nineteenth century, *Inn and tavern names*, p. 35.

adapted to become Robin Hood names, such as Robin Hood's Hills in Nottinghamshire, and Robin Hood's Cross near Hathersage, Early Modern names for features known in medieval times as *Robynhill* and *Robin Crosse* respectively. Both names occur in areas with strong Robin Hood associations (Hathersage churchyard possesses the alleged grave of Little John), and popular etymology seems to have changed the names to fit local legend at a rather late stage in the development of the Robin Hood tradition.

It seems, then, to be the case that the place-names follow the ballads, not vice-versa, contradicting Lee's interpretation of the process. J.C. Holt argued that

> the Robin Hood place-names illustrate the spread of the legend, not
> the doings of the outlaw [...] those who told or listened to the sto-
> ries tried to add to their realism by transferring the hero's name to
> familiar places in the immediate locality.[20]

The authors of the *Place-Names of the North Riding* concur, viewing the place-name Robin Hood's Bay (one of the earlier Robin Hood toponyms, being first recorded in 1532) as arising from 'popular ballads', as it is not found in medieval times.[21] The chronology of the spread of Robin Hood place-names would seem to confirm Holt's theory that they reflect the popularity of the ballads, but, given the apparently mythological nature of many such names, they do not all suggest a desire to 'add to their realism'.

But why should a hero who is never presented as a giant or a hero with supernatural powers in the textual tradition have become associated in the eighteenth and nineteenth centuries with the type of place-name that suggests a giant or god? One explanation might be that by the eighteenth and nineteenth centuries when most of this nomenclature seems to have been invented, Robin Hood had become very clearly a national popular hero, known through tales encountered in childhood, through carnival, and later pantomime. He belongs to the same world of fantasy as Tom Thumb, Jack the Giant-Killer, as well as reflecting the fanciful tendency to envisage mountains, cairns, or stone circles as the relics of the play of giants and heroes, turned to stone in the landscape.

When at this period ordinary features of the landscape, not necessitating belief in supernatural size or powers, are linked to his name, in the form of wells, fields, caves, or crosses, this may be because he is associated with what is both local and English, ancient and benevolent. In a Catholic society perhaps a saint's name would have been an obvious equivalent. In some cases perhaps Robin's name replaced a saint's name or a name that was orig-

---

20 Holt, p. 106.   21 *The place-names of the North Riding of Yorkshire*, ed. A.H. Smith, EPNS (Cambridge, 1928), p. 118.

inally one denoting a god, hobgoblin or other spirit. There are plenty of place-names that go back to early medieval records and contain elements (such as 'thyrs', 'grendel', 'shuck', going back to Anglo-Saxon) that meant some kind of supernatural being, and Lud, Gog and Magog are among ancient national legendary figures, who were probably believed to be super-human, still recalled by place-names. It is possible that Robin Hood names may sometimes have replaced such names, or, of course, they may alternatively represent a survival in oral memory of a mythological substratum preserved in the figure of Robin Hood the outlaw. It could also be, however, that the impulse behind names had somewhat shifted by the eighteenth century: the patterns of place-name creation that had once attributed certain massive or allegedly numinous landscape features to gods, bogeys, and spirits, perhaps softened or degenerated into a consciously fantastical or antiquarian pleasure in linking them to the nation's most popular legendary hero.

If the place-names evidence does not support the existence of a pagan wood-sprite Robin Hood, then neither does it support an historical outlaw, as in either case there is no evidence of an early origin for most of the place-names, or for any of them pre-dating the earliest references to a literary tradition. The reality may well be more complex and reflect multiple cultural influences. We know that the Robin Hood legend was capable of absorbing elements from other traditions, as when Maid Marion was brrowed from the morris dance's 'marriam' or Marian, or perhaps influenced by the French pastoral *Robin et Marion* tradition. We also know that Robin's legend is adaptable and has been open to different interpretations by different social groups and in different historical periods. It is surely not impossible, therefore, that the Robin of the ballads could have merged with other Robins and Hobs who inhabited the wild places of the early-modern countryside in popular imagination. Robin Hood may not actually be a 'personage of Teutonic mythology', but, once established as a popular figure by the success of the ballads, he could easily have become conflated with figures of that nature, especially given the similarity of name and woodland abode to one of them, Robin Goodfellow. This latter character, it has been suggested, may be the source for the place-name *robynilpit* recorded in Rutland c. 1275, which 'may be an early reference to Robin-a-Tiptoe alias Robin Goodfellow, the drudging goblin, who threshes corn and does domestic work whilst the farmer and his household are asleep'.[22] The place-names suggesting a supernatural Robin Hood may reflect this process. It is true that a Robin who fires great arrows or throws huge stones is a rather grander figure than the 'drudging goblin', but the two may share a place in a fantastical mythological world.

---

22 *The place-names of Rutland,* ed. Barrie Cox, EPNS (Nottingham, 1994), p. 238.

Appendix:
Written epitaphs of Robin Hood

DAVID HEPWORTH

ACTUAK EPITAPH AT KIRKLEES
Created in 1773

Hear Underneath dis laitl Stean
Laz robert earl of Huntingtun
Ne'er arcir ver az hie sa geu
An pipl kauld im robin heud
Sick utlawz az hi an iz men
Vil England nivr si agen
Obiit 24 kal: Dekembris 1247[1]

CAPTAIN A. SMITH EPITAPH
*Compleat History of the Lives of the
Most noted highwaymen, footpads, shop-
lifts, and cheats* [...], (1713–14), p. 31;
ed. A.L. Hayward (London, 1926), p.
408[2]

Here, underneath this Marble Stone,
Thro' Death's Assault now lieth one,
Known by the Name of Robin Hood,
Who was a Thief, and Archer good:
Full twenty Years, and somewhat
  more,
He robbed the Rich to feed the Poor,
Therefore his Grave bedew with
  Tears,
And offer for his Soul your Pray'rs. 3

MARTIN PARKER,
A True Tale of Robin Hood (1631)

Robert Earle of Huntinton
Lies under this little stone.
No archer was like him so good:
His wildnesse named him Robbin Hood.
Full thirteene yeares, and something
  more,
These northerne parts he vexed sore.
Such out-lawes as he and his men
May England never know agen.
Decembris quarto die, 1198: anno regni
Richardii Primi 9[3]

J. JONES EPITAPH
(1727)

Here underneath, this little stone,
Thro Death's assaults, now lieth one,
Known by the name of Robin Hood.
Who was a thief and archer good
Full thirteen years, and something
  more
He robbed the rich to feed the poor:
Therefore his grave bedew with Tears
And offer for his soul your prayers.
1195

1 Thomas Gale, Dean of York (1697–1702), copied this text in his papers, reporting it could be seen on the grave. It was published in Ralph Thoresby, *Ducatus Leodiensis Sepulchrorum Inscriptiones* (London, 1715), p. 576. Essentially the same text (with variants on the fake Middle English spelling) appears in Roger Dodsley, *The travels of Tom Thumb* (London, 1746); Richard Griffiths, *Kirk-Leas: a descriptive poem* (1760, published 1802); and Ely Hargrove, *Anecdotes of Archery* ... (York, 1792). Without giving any date it appears in Daniel Defoe, *A tour through the whole* [...] (London, 1769), III. letter 111, and Percy's *Reliques of ancient English poetry* (London, 1765) 4th edition, 1794, III. 81–95.   2 Also found in Charles Johnson, *A general history of the Lives* [...] (London, 1734) and Anon., *The whole life and merry exploits* (London, 1772).   3 Essentially the same text appears in a garland

MORETON PAPERS EPITAPH
18th century, BL Add. MS 33938,
vol I, f i

Hear undirneeth dis laitl stean
Lay Robert earl of Huntingtun
Ne'er arcir ver ay hi sa geud
An pipl kauld im robin heud
Sick utlawz az hi an uz men
Vil England niver vi agen
Obit 24 kel Dekembies 1237

FRANCIS PECK EPITAPH
18th century BL Add. MS 28638,
ff.18–19

Here underneath this little Stone
Lies [famous] Robert Earl of
  Huntington/

No archers were or [he &] his so good:
The [common] people call'd him
  Robin Whood.
Such outlaws as he and his [merry] men
Will England [hardly] every see again
Famous Robin Whood, Famous
  Robin Whood.

RITSON QUOTING 'MODERN'
TOM THUMB
Robin Hood (1795), vol. 1, xlix

Here, under this memorial stone,
Lies Robert earl of Huntindon;
As he, no archer e'er was good,
And people call'd him Robin Hood
Such outlaws as his men and he
Again may England never see.

Nathaniel Johnston's drawing of the grave of Robin Hude and others, 1669

collection Robin Hood ballads, Thomas Gent's *The English archer* (London, 1762) and in
Anon., *The adventures of Robert Earl of Huntington* (London, 1777), p. 83.

Index

Adam Bell, 18, 29, 32, 38, 40, 44, 145–6, 148, 149, 152
Aers, D., 16, 29, 49
Alayn, T., 111, 112
Allen, T., 100
Andrew of Wyntoun, 35, 113
Aquinas, St Thomas, 72
Aristotle, 73
Armytage family, 92, 98–100, 105–11
Armytage, A. (Adam dell Hermitage), 100
Armytage, F., 107
Armytage, G., 102, 108
Armytage, G.II, 108
Armytage, G.III, 108
Armytage, G.J., 108
Armytage, J. I, 106
Armytage, J. II, 106, 107
Armytage, J. III, 96, 107
Armytage, J. IV, 97, 107, 108
Armytage, J. V, 94, 108
Armytage, J. VI, 118
Armytage, R., 110
Armytage, S., 98, 100, 108
Armytage, T., 109, 100
Armytage, W., 110
Arthur, king of England, 32, 39, 42, 89, 183, 184
Ashwell, L., 176
Astley, P., 145
Austria, 21
Avis, P., 118
Ayres, P., 123

Babes in the Wood, 12
Bacon, F., 118
Bacon, H., 76
Bakewell, 185
Bakhtin, M., 18
Ball, J., 48
Balshaw, W., *A Mirror for Magistrates*, 119
Barker, J.R.V., 155

Barnsdale, 17, 24, 26, 94, 185
Barnsdale (Rutland), 24
Barthes, R., 128
Barton, A., 130–1, 132, 137, 139, 143
Basford, K., 182
Bawcutt, P., 33
Beasley, J., 152
Bedier, J., 80
Bellamy, J.G., 12, 59, 90, 110
Belvoir Castle, 130
Belvoir, Vale of, 130, 132, 144
Benecke, I., 79
Beowulf, 44
Berkshire, 25–6, 184
Béroul, 80, 81, 83, 85
Bertin, G.A., 87
Bessinger, J.B., 12, 24
Bevington, D., 116, 117
Bichill, 110, 111
Billy the Kid, 21–2
Blake, W., 153
Blakeslee, M.R., 80, 81
Blanch, R.J., 80
Blind Harry, 79
Bodin, J., 118
Bower, W., 35, 93, 94, 113
Bracton, H., 82
Brazil, 14
Briggs, A., 155
Bromyard, J., 54
Brontë, C., 13, 19, 154–61
   Jane Eyre, 155
   The Professor, 155
   Shirley, 18, 19, 154–61
Bronte, M., 158
Browning, R., 177
Bunyan, J., *Pilgrim's Progress*, 151
Burgess, G., 182

Caesarius of Hiesterbad, 57
Call, A., 76
Call, R., 76
Camden, W., 96, 101, 102, 113, 118

Carpenter, K., 19
Cave, R., 136, 137
Caxton, W., 15
Chadwick, S.J., 101
Chandler, J., 94
Chettle, H., 113
'The Cheylde and her Stepdame', 77
Child, F.J., 24, 26, 43, 51, 76,
'The Chronicle of Dale Abbey', 17,
    57–8
Clare, J., 122
Clawson, W.H., 23
Clifton on Calder, 107
Colman, G., 146
The Complaint of Scotland, 28
Coss, P., 16
Cox, B., 183, 185
Cooper, H., 143
Crook, D., 12, 24–5, 26, 28
Crossley, E.W., 97
Croscombe, 28, 29
Culhwch and Olwen, 183–4
Cumberland, 184

Daniel, S., *Fair Rosamund*, 117
Dante, 169, 172
    Paradiso, 169
Davenport, R, 124, 126
de Bourbon, E., 56
de Certeau, M., 114
de Lange, J., 79
de Staynton, E., 93, 98, 101, 105, 111,
    112
de Troyes, Chrétien, 70
de Vitry, J., 56, 60–1, 68
Deane, P., 72
Defoe, D., 188
Derbyshire, 184, 185
Derrida, J., 124
Dobson, R.B., 13, 22, 23, 25, 26, 42,
    48, 72, 92, 96, 164
Dodsworth, R., 96, 107
Dodsley, R., 188
Doel, I., 20
Dorey, M., 168, 176
Dorson, R.M., 160
Douglas, G., *The Palice of Honour*, 35
Doyle, A.C., 177
Drayton, M., 117, 132–5, 142

Matilda, the faire & chaste daughter of
    Lord R. Fitzwater, 117, 127
Poly-Olbion, 94, 96, 132, 141
Dronke, P., 34
D'Urfey, T., 150
Dunbar, W., 27, 29, 33, 36–7
    'Sir Thomas Nornay', 33

Edward the Confessor, king of England,
    79
Edward I, king of England, 113
Edward II, king of England, 181
Edwards, P., 120
Eagleton, T., 160
Eilhart von Obingen, 80, 81, 83, 85, 89
Eisner, S., 80
Ekelund, R.B., 72
El Cid, 37
Eliot, T.S. 177, 179
    The Sacred Wood, 177
    The Waste Land 178
Ellis, R., 124
Elmkirk, E.M., 76
Estoire de Seint Aedward le Roi, 89
Eustache li Moin, 78, 79
Evans, M., 10, 11, 109, 181–7

Fairbanks, D., 172
Fairchild, H.N., 168
Fellowes, E.H., 148
Ferrante, J., 89
Ferrett, M., 155
Figart, L.B., 164
Fisher, J.H., 81
Fleming, T., 110
Fletcher, J., 143
    The Faithful Shepherdess, 132, 139
The Forresters Manuscript, 9, 26
Forrester, J., 111
Fouke FitzWaryn, 11, 13, 60, 79, 80,
    82, 89, 90, 182
    Fouke li fitz Waryn, 79
Frank, R., 101, 108
Frappier, J., 80–1
Friar Tuck, 121, 122, 124, 127, 133,
    139, 175, 176, 177
Fries, M., 80
Froissart, J., 18
Fowler, D., 33

Gaimar, G., *Lestoire des Engles*, 89
Gale, T., 92, 97, 100, 103, 188
Gamelyn, 80
Gaskell, E., 34
Gent, T., 97, 189
Geoffrey of Monmouth, 183, 184
George a Green, 110, 133-4
The Gest of Robin Hood, 15, 16, 17, 23,
   31-3, 38, 40, 43, 44-5, 51, 59, 67-8,
   70, 82, 89, 115, 116, 139-42, 143,
   156, 157, 173, 183
Gesta Herewardi, 79, 83, 87, 89
Girart de Roussillon, 84
Godwin, Earl, 79, 80, 82, 83, 89, 90
Godwin, W., 153
Gottfried von Strassburg, 80, 80
Gough, R., 101, 104-5, 113
Grafton R., 94, 95, 102, 113, 114, 115,
   135
Gray, D., 9, 10, 12, 13, 15, 16, 17, 19,
   21-41, 42, 182
Green, B., 111
Green, R.F., 15, 17, 24, 37, 40, 93
Greene, R.L., 35, 134
Greer, D., 148
Grettir Asmundarson, 86
Griffiths, R., 108, 158, 187
Gutch, J., 106
Guy of Gisborne, 29

Hadcock, R.N., 94
Hahn, T., 11, 13, 95, 106
Haider, J., 21, 41
Hanawalt, B., 13, 37, 40
Hargrave, E., 188
Hartshead, 155, 156
Harty, K., 13
Harvard University, 167
Hathersage, 96, 155, 184, 185, 186
Hazlitt, W., 145, 146, 147, 153
Hearne, T., 98, 101, 105, 108, 113
Heath, A.R., 26
Hebert, R., 72
Helgerson, R., 114
Henry III, king of England, 113
Henry VIII, king of England, 19, 29,
   95, 115, 118, 119, 185
Henryson, R., 17, 30
Henslowe, P., 113, 116

Hepworth, D., 10, 15, 17, 58, 91-112,
   188-9
Hereward, 11, 13, 78, 80, 87, 89, 90
Herford, C.H., 130, 131, 132, 134, 136,
   138
'The Hermit and the Outlaw', 17, 52-9
Hill, C., 13, 21
Hilton, R., 12, 23, 42,
Hobsbawm, E., 13, 21, 51-2, 58
Hoffman, D., 85
Hogan, C.B., 146
Holcroft, T., *The Noble Peasant*, 18,
   145-53
Holderness, G., 118, 119
Holinshed, R., 113, 114
Holt, J.C., 12, 16, 22, 23, 39,42, 58, 96,
   109, 111, 112, 181, 186
Hood, J. (of Wakefield), 109
Hood, M. (of Wakefield), 92, 109, 111
Hood R. (Raghnild, of Wakefield), 109
Hood, R. (Robert, of Wakefield), 92,
   109, 111, 112
Hook, A., 155
Hook, J., 155
Hopkins, A., 90
Huddersfield, 157, 158
Hunter, J., 10, 11, 15, 96, 108, 109,
   111, 181

Ikegami, M., 91, 93
Ilkeston, 17
International Association for Robin
   Hood Studies, 9, 18, 21
Irving, H., 173
Ismay, J., 96, 100, 101, 102, 105, 108
Isolde, 81, 82, 83, 84, 85, 86, 87, 88,
   89, 100, 107

James I, king of England, 118
James IV, king of Scotland, 29
Jefferes, A.N., 155
Jerrold, W.C., 169
Jesus Christ, 44, 50, 174, 183
Jewell, H.M., 109
John, king of England (*see also* under
   Prince John), 43, 49, 90, 113, 126,
   135, 174
John of Fordun, 93
Johnson, C., 188

Johnston, N., 92, 97, 101, 102, 103, 104, 105, 107, 111
'The Jolly Pinder of Wakefield', 136
Jones, J., 18
Jones, T.S., 13, 15, 79–90
Jonson, B., 16, 19, 129–44
  'The May Lord', 129–30, 143
  The Sad Shepherd, 16, 18, 129–44
  The Tale of a Tub, 131

Kaluza, M., 52
Keatman, M., 111
Keats, J., 155
Keen, M., 12, 79, 80, 81, 82, 90, 91, 92
Kelly, G., 152
Kelly, Ned, 37–8
Kenton, G., 174
Ker, W.P., 24, 31, 34
Kiesman, R., 23
King Melodyas, 86
'The King and the Barker', 76
Kirklees, 15, 39, 55, 59, 91–122, 135, 154, 155, 156, 157, 158, 159, 164, 165, 166, 172, 188
Kittredge, G.L., 52
Klapp, D., 39
Knight (in *Gest*), 60, 64–8
Knight, S., 13,15, 16, 18, 19, 20, 24, 26, 27, 41, 42, 45, 49, 69, 72, 93, 104, 113, 115, 116, 117, 119, 124, 126, 127, 128, 149, 155, 165, 179, 182
Knowles, D., 94

Lancashire, 184
Langford, P., 149
Langland, W., 17, 185
Lancelot, 89
Latimer, 9, 10
Lee, S., 180, 181, 185,
Leicestershire, 133
Leland, J., 9, 94, 95, 101
Levy, F., 118
Lewis, B., 111
Liber de Hyde, 89
Lindahl, G., 150
Little John, 11, 13, 27, 28, 35, 38, 39, 40, 41–50, 64, 65, 66, 69, 73, 84, 119, 124, 133, 141, 155, 156, 180
Look About You, 172

London, 124
London, Ontario, 21
Loomis, R.S., 80
Lloyd, A.L., 40
Lucian, 132
Lukis, W.C., 104, 105

Machiavelli, N., 118
Maddicott, J.R., 23
Macgeach, H.F., 106
Maitland, F., 82
Major, John, 29, 35–6, 38, 113
Malory, T., 14, 15, 28, 73. 80, 82, 85, 90
Manchester, 165
Map, W., 82
Marian (see also Matilda), 26, 27, 117, 125, 126, 127, 128, 135, 136, 142, 146, 170, 171, 172, 173, 174, 175, 179, 187
Mark, king of Cornwall, 82, 83, 85, 86, 87, 88, 89, 90
'The Maner of the Crying of a Play', 27
Marshall, J., 13, 18, 27, 28, 29, 35, 38, 144
Marsk Stig, 31, 37
Martin, J.D., 103
Matthews, J., 182
Matilda (see also Marian), 125,127, 128
Marx, K., 78
Merlin, 178
May games, 14, 18, 27, 127, 144
Meagher, J.C., 120
Mere, F., 123
Mill, A.J., 28
Millett, B., 183
Milton, J., 163
Minot, L. 33
Mirfield, 100
Morsberger, K.M., 172
Morsberger, R.E., 172
Much (the Miller's son), 44, 46, 65, 100, 133
Munday, A., 14, 95, 96, 107, 113–18, 131, 135–9, 175, 176
  A Brief Chronicle, 118
  The Death of Robert, Earl of Huntington, 95, 113, 114, 115, 118, 120, 123, 124, 125–6, 127, 128, 135

The Downfall of Robert, Earl of Huntington, 11, 14, 113, 114, 115, 116, 117, 118, 119, 120, 121, 123, 124, 125, 127, 128, 135, 135, 137, 138, 139
Metropolis Coronata, 124
Palmerin of England 124
Palladine of England, 124
Gerileon of England, 126
The Triumphs of Ancient Drapery, 124
Muskham, T., 58

Nelson, M.A., 113, 115, 116, 117, 127, 183
Nerlich, M., 70–1
New Orleans, 168, 178
Newgate Calendar, 13
Newton, 110
Newstead, H., 80
Nichols, S.B., 167
Norfolk, Duchess of, 76
Nottingham, 10, 44, 58, 69, 71, 133, 168, 183, 186
Noyes, A., 19
   The Flower of Old Japan, 169
   The Forest of Wild Thyme, 169, 173, 175
   Princeton, May 1917, 167
   Sherwood (Robin Hood), 167–80
   Some Aspects of Modern Poetry, 174, 177
Noyes, G., 167, 170, 179

Oakley-Brown, L., 11, 14, 15, 113–28
Ohlgren, T., 9, 15, 16, 18, 24, 29, 32, 69–78, 79, 93, 117, 119, 182
Orwell, G., 38
Owen, W., 178
Owst, G.R., 54
Oxford English Dictionary, 134, 139

Padel, O., 184
Papplewick, 141, 142
Parker, M., 100, 107
   The True Tale of Robin Hood, 94, 96, 97, 143, 180
Past and Present, 11, 13, 26
Paston family, 9, 70
Paston, J., 29

Paston, J.III, 75–7
Paston, M., 76
'Le pauvre mercier', 63–4, 66
Peacock, T.L., 170, 176
Pearsall, D., 13, 14, 15, 19, 42–50
Pearcy, R., 15, 16, 60–8
Peasants' Revolt, 40, 48
Peck, F., 58, 189
Peele, G., *The Famous Chronicle of Edward I*, 114
Pelbart of Temesvar, 57
Percy, E., 176
Percy Folio, 30, 52, 93, 140
Percy, T., *Reliques of Ancient Poetry*, 146, 188
Phillips, G., 111
Phillips, G.S., 157
Phillips, H., 18, 24, 31, 32, 39, 154–66
Piggott, S., 103, 104, 105
'The Pinder of Wakefield', *see* 'The Jolly Pinder of Wakefield'
Pinder of Wakefield, 133
Playford, J., 150
A Pleasant Pastoral Commedie of Robin Hood and Little John, 114
Pollack, F., 82
Pontefract, 91, 97, 104
Potter, L., 18–19, 24, 114, 167–80
Prince John (*see also* King John), 116, 117, 119, 124, 127, 170, 171, 172
Princeton University, 167
Prose Tristan, 82
Public Record Office, 11
Pylkyngton, A., 106
Pylkington, R., 106

Queen Elizabeth, 86

Ranulf, Earl of Chester, 39
Rastell, J., *The Interlude of the Four Elements*, 35
Rathbone, B., 171
Ravenscroft, T., 148
Red Riding Hood, 12
Reichel, K., 33
Richard I, king of England 23, 43, 49, 114, 118, 119, 171, 172, 174
Richards, J., 13
Richardson, F., 107

Richardson, R., 108
Riggs, D., 131
Richmond, C., 14, 26, 40, 41
Ritson, J., 22, 37, 41, 77, 140, 147, 155,
    164, 181, 183
Robert of Jumièges, 83
Robehod, W., 25
Robin a Tiptoe, 182, 187
Robin Goodfellow, 9, 182, 183
Robin of Sherwood, 182
'Robin Hood and the Butcher', 65, 140
'Robin Hood and the Curtal Friar', 15
'Robin Hood and the Friar' (play), 126
'Robin and Gandelyn', 15, 182
'Robin Hood and Guy of Gisborne', 15,
    30, 140, 182
'Robin Hood and the Monk', 13, 15,
    19, 30–1, 42–50, 113, 140
'Robin Hood and the Potter', 9, 15, 18,
    31, 65, 69–78, 140
'Robin Hood and the Tanner', 28
'Robin Hood's Death', 15, 17, 26, 30,
    52, 55, 93, 156
Robbins, R.H., 39–40
Le Roman d'Eustache, 60
Le Roman de Tristan, 80
Rome, 123
Roosevelt, T., 167
Ross, T.W., 74
Rous, J., 26
Rowland, S., 150
Rudolph, C., 41
Rutland, 133
Ryder, P., 101

Sanders, E.R., 125
Sanders, J., 134
Saunders, C., 39
Savage, H.L., 39
Saville, J., 96, 100, 107, 111
Saville, M., 112
Scattergood, J., 20, 37
Schoepperle, G., 81, 85
Scotland, 11, 17, 19, 27, 35–6
Scott, W., *Ivanhoe*, 129, 155
Seal, G., 13
Selden, J., 118
Sermones Vulgares, 62
Shakespeare, W.

As You Like It, 129, 132
Coriolanus, 154, 162
Hamlet, 173
King John, 117, 172
King Lear, 173
A Midsummer Night's Dream, 169, 176
A Winter's Tale, 132
Sheriff of Nottingham, 14, 45, 48, 50,
    70, 74, 77, 78, 82, 116, 124, 183
Sherwood Forest, 17, 58, 94, 95, 132,
    134, 141, 142, 144, 185
Shield, W., 145, 147, 148
Sidney, P., 118
Signor, F.R., 167
Simeone, W.F., 183
Simpson, E. and P., 130, 131, 132, 134,
    136, 138
Singman, J.L., 95, 113, 114, 115, 116,
    119, 121, 125, 127, 128, 144
Sir Gawain and the Green Knight, 39
Sir Tristrem, 82, 84
Skaife, R., 107
Skelton, J., 14, 15, 35, 37, 115, 119,
    120, 121, 122, 123, 125, 126, 127,
    128, 139
    Why Come Ye not to Court ?, 37
Sloane 'Life of Robin Hood', 95, 106,
    114
Smith, A., 188
Smith, A.H., 109
Society of Antiquaries, 118
Sondergard, S., 152–3
South Crosland, 110
Speak, H., 111
Spenser, E., 132
    The Faerie Queene, 136, 138
    The Shepheardes Calendar, 132, 144
Spisak, J.W., 80
St John, H.F., 103
St Mary, 62, 66, 67, 105, 183
Stead, J.J., 155
Stock, L.K., 182
Stow, J., 9, 113, 118
Sternfeld, F.W., 148
Stubbes, P., 10, 27
Stukeley, W., 100, 102, 103, 104, 105,
    112
Sturgess, A.H.C., 106
Summerson, H., 25

Taft, W.H., 167
Tardif, R., 29
Taylor, J., 13, 22, 23, 42, 77, 92, 96, 164
Taylor, N., 111
Tennyson, A.,167, 170, 173, 170
  The Foresters, 168
Theocritus, 132
Thomas d'Angleterre, 80, 81, 85, 89
Thomas, W.J., 106
Thoresby, R., 97, 100, 102, 108, 188
Thornhill, 102
Tiddy, R.J.E., 28
Topclifffe, R., 123
Towneley Plays, 36
Tree, H.B., 169, 170
Tristan, 79, 83, 84, 85, 86, 87, 88, 89, 90
Troost, L., 10, 16, 145–53
Turner, C., 114, 117, 123, 124,
Turner, H., 92
Turner, V., 14, 38

Venn, J. and J.A., 106
Villa, P., 39
Virgil, 132, 169
Vita Aedwardi Regis, 83, 89

Wakefield, 9, 10, 15, 92, 95, 109, 110, 111, 112
Walker, J.W., 10, 15, 92, 100, 101, 110

Waldron, F. (with Ben Jonson), *The Sad Shepherd, or A Tale of Robin Hood*, 143
Wallace, W., 78, 79
Walsingham, T., 48
Warner, W., *Albions England*, 115, 135, 142–3
Wasserman, J., 20
Watson, J., 98, 100, 112
Weimann, R., 39
Westmorland, 188
Whitehead, F., 80, 84
Wiles, D., 23, 27, 119
Will Scarlett, 135, 171, 172
  as Scarlock, 133
  as Scathlock, 135
William of Goldesborough, 112
William Tell, 183
Wilson, D., 168
Wilson, R., 36, 40, 41, 129
Wirral, 39
Wollstonecraft, M., 153
Wolsey, T., 123
Wright, T., 11, 181, 182

Yale University, 167
Yorkshire, 10, 17, 43, 48,112, 135, 183

Zapata, E., 39